OCT 1 8 2017

P9-CAB-741

FIFTY YEARS

of

60 MINUTES

The Inside Story of Television's Most
Influential News Broadcast

JEFF FAGER

SIMON & SCHUSTER

NEW YORK LONDON TORONTO SYDNEY NEW DELHI

Simon & Schuster
1230 Avenue of the Americas
New York, NY 10020

Copyright © 2017 by CBS Worldwide Inc.

All rights reserved, including the right to reproduce this book or portions
thereof in any form whatsoever. For information, address
Simon & Schuster Subsidiary Rights Department,
1230 Avenue of the Americas, New York, NY 10020.

First Simon & Schuster hardcover edition October 2017

SIMON & SCHUSTER and colophon are registered trademarks of Simon & Schuster, Inc.

For information about special discounts for bulk purchases,
please contact Simon & Schuster Special Sales at 1-866-506-1949
or business@simonandschuster.com.

The Simon & Schuster Speakers Bureau can bring authors to your live event.
For more information or to book an event. contact the
Simon & Schuster Speakers Bureau at 1-866-248-3049
or visit our website at www.simonspeakers.com.

Interior design by Ruth Lee-Mui

Manufactured in the United States of America

1   3   5   7   9   10   8   6   4   2

Library of Congress Cataloging-in-Publication Data is available.

ISBN 978-1-5011-3580-4
ISBN 978-1-5011-3582-8 (ebook)

CONTENTS

THE BEGINNING

Fifty years is an eternity in the television world. The average show lasts around just over two years. But in 2017–18, *60 Minutes* celebrates its fiftieth season on television.

How many programs have lasted that long in prime time? Just the one. And *60 Minutes* is still going strong. It's the longest-running prime-time broadcast ever and still one of the most-watched programs in America. This would be remarkable for any TV show, but it's an astonishing feat for one that asks its viewers not to escape on a Sunday night but to focus on stories about the world around them.

What is it about our broadcast that has sustained it all these years? There are many factors, and a lot of them can be traced all the way back to our conception. It's an unlikely story because there never would have been a *60 Minutes* if Don Hewitt hadn't been fired in 1965. Yes, we owe our creation,

Don Hewitt, founder of *60 Minutes*, at his desk in 1986.

our standards, our values, and our longevity to a most humiliating set of circumstances that our creator confronted when he was only thirty-six years old.

When Don Hewitt joined CBS in 1948, he was in awe of the people around him, particularly the Murrow Boys—the gentlemen correspondents who filed World War II dispatches under the watchful eye of Edward R. Murrow, the man who became the dean of broadcast news and the paragon of journalistic integrity. The Murrow Boys were elegant and battle-tested, and knew how to write a story and deliver it on the radio.

Don wasn't one of them and he knew it. He was a feisty kid from New Rochelle, New York, who never got a college degree. Growing up, he had always wanted to be in show business. His two childhood heroes were fictional characters from Broadway: Julian Marsh, the theater director in the show *42nd Street*, and Hildy Johnson, the star reporter in a lesser-known play called *The Front Page*. Don later said his problem was that he couldn't decide which one he wanted to be, but as it turned out, he didn't have to.

Don joined CBS with some journalism cred: he had written for *Stars and Stripes,* the daily paper of the US military, during the war. But it wasn't reporting that got him most excited: it was lights and action. CBS was primarily a radio network in those days, with television just getting started. Don liked to tell the story that someone said to him, "You should think about getting in television," and he said, "Whatavision?" But television grabbed him, and he never looked back. It was news with the flair of showbiz: that was Don Hewitt in a nutshell.

But this vision wasn't shared by the people he went to work for, people such as Murrow and Fred Friendly, pioneers of broadcast journalism who built CBS News. They were not excited by the lights. Radio was king, and they looked down on the new invention.

So TV became Don's domain. He quickly became a pioneer in his own right, among the first to figure out how to do things as simple as putting writing on the screen (what became known as chyrons and supers) to identify a person or place. He was in a diner when he saw a blackboard with

Don Hewitt in 1960, with John F. Kennedy and Richard Nixon, on the set of the first televised presidential debate, which he directed.

little white letters spelling out the specials of the day. He paid for the board along with his breakfast and took it back to the studio, where he worked with technicians to figure out a way to superimpose the white letters on a camera image.

Over the next fifteen years, Don became a significant figure at CBS News. His most influential role came as director of the first presidential debate between Vice President Richard M. Nixon and Massachusetts senator John F. Kennedy in 1960. He offered makeup to Nixon, grim-faced and cursed with a perpetual five o'clock shadow. But the Republican candidate, looking tired and sweaty, declined and lost the debate to the tanned, vigorous-looking young Democrat. It was a transformational moment. Polls indicated those who heard the debate on radio thought Nixon had won. Television's power in forming public opinion had never been fully appreciated before. On Election Day, Kennedy edged Nixon by less than 0.17 percent of the vote. Don often said that if Nixon had listened to him, he probably would have been president. Within a few years, Don was named executive producer of the *CBS Evening News with Walter Cronkite*. He was riding high. But he should have known he was in trouble the moment Fred Friendly was made president of CBS News in 1964. They didn't like each other one bit, though Hewitt always credited Friendly with teaching him more about journalism and storytelling than anybody else. "Don't talk down to viewers," Don would quote Fred as saying, "but don't assume they know as much as you do."

Friendly, on the other hand, considered Hewitt a flashy showman. Don didn't fit his image of the leader of the news division's flagship broadcast. In 1965 Friendly called Don into his office and told him that the Cronkite news program wasn't big enough for him. He was going to create a special unit just for Don—his own empire. Don was ecstatic. In one account of what happened next, he called his then wife Frankie with the good news. In another, it was his friend Bill Leonard, vice president of

Don Hewitt was executive producer of the *CBS Evening News with Walter Cronkite* before starting *60 Minutes*.

CBS News. Either way, the reaction was the same: You weren't promoted, Don. You were just fired. The golden boy who had directed the first Nixon-Kennedy debate, who was in the catbird seat at the *Evening News*, was out of favor.

Don would spend the rest of his life proving that he understood good television journalism. For the thirty-five years he ran *60 Minutes*, Don Hewitt hammered into us everything he had learned from Fred Friendly and Ed Murrow, and then added his own significant touch: including pizzazz. He had learned a lot during his exile with his "special unit," where he produced documentaries—"hourlong snoozers" he called them—that he said later nobody was

4

watching. He was bored, and he didn't understand why television should ever be boring. Why couldn't news be entertaining and compelling?

By 1967, it was pretty well understood around CBS News that if Don Hewitt was coming toward your office at a breakneck pace, arms flailing, the best thing to do was hide, because he was probably about to ambush you with his latest notion about how to reinvent television news. Many of his ideas were not very good, but one of them, a new concept for an hour-long newsmagazine, is what we now know as *60 Minutes*.

It wasn't an easy sell. He wanted to create *Life* magazine on television with the same mix of serious and light stories: an interview with Marilyn Monroe on the same broadcast as one with the president of the United States or a migrant worker. It would be like Edward R. Murrow's two 1950s broadcasts—the serious documentary program *See It Now* and the softer celebrity interview program *Person to Person*, which Don called "High Murrow" and "Low Murrow"—rolled into one compelling hour of television. The stories would be much shorter than traditional documentaries. Don had a short attention span and thought most people did as well.

Fred Friendly hated the idea. But in 1967, when Dick Salant replaced Friendly as president of CBS News, Don tried again. Salant was reluctant at first, but with encouragement from Don's pal Bill Leonard, Salant decided to give it the go-ahead.

Don envisioned a one-anchor program, and wanted steady veteran broadcaster Harry Reasoner. But he was talked into adding Mike Wallace. At the time, it seemed like a simple change, but it turned out that putting Hewitt with Wallace was like introducing Lennon to McCartney.

60 Minutes started to take on its own identity, much of which was a mix of these two larger-than-life personalities. Don pushed his ideas for what stories to cover and then worked intensely on how to tell each one. Mike would pin down people with tough questions, a talent he had perfected in the 1950s while hosting the New York City program *Night-Beat*, bringing

a hard edge to the new broadcast. A few years later, Morley Safer joined the program and brought his storytelling finesse, taking us on an adventure with his beautiful prose. Unique and accomplished reporters continued to join the ensemble over the years: Rather, Rooney, Bradley, Sawyer, Kroft, Stahl, Simon, Pelley, Rose, Cooper, and Whitaker. They

Mike Wallace and Don Hewitt in 1975, the two larger-than-life figures on the broadcast.

were complemented by the best news producers, their names not well known, but who were just as crucial as our on-air correspondents.

60 Minutes took a while to catch on, but Don's invention changed television news for good. Together he and his team built a broadcast that succeeded beyond anyone's expectations, including his own, and eventually earned him the respect he sought from the now elderly Murrow Boys. *60 Minutes* soared into the 1990s, becoming the most-watched program of the year for the third, fourth, and fifth time. Nobody imagined that so many people would watch a news program or that news could be so profitable. We set out to do good, Don would say, and we ended up doing well. Very well.

When I started at *60 Minutes* in 1989 as a young producer working with the youngest correspondent, Steve Kroft, the broadcast still very much resembled Don and Mike in character: tough, direct, lively—and loud. It wasn't unusual to hear arguing in the hallways, and every so often Don would screen a piece and declare it "the worst" he had ever seen. This happened to me once, not long after I began. Steve and I showed Don a piece we thought was pretty good, but when the lights came up in the screening room, he asked me, "Where do you want it, kid? Right between the eyes?" It was never mean-spirited, though. It was all in the interest of making stories better, and there were few that Don couldn't fix.

But by the end of the last century, the kid from New Rochelle was

Mike Wallace and Harry Reasoner in a 1968 promotional photo for *60 Minutes*, which premiered in September of that year.

Don Hewitt handed over the reins to Jeff Fager in 2004.

showing his age. So was the broadcast. Tensions had boiled over in 1995 during the hard-fought battle over Mike Wallace's interview with tobacco whistle-blower Jeffrey Wigand, which for legal reasons the CBS Corporation wouldn't allow *60 Minutes* to air. The showdown went on for months, fraying relationships and leaving everyone feeling raw and probably tired.

In the years after that, something was different at *60 Minutes*. Some of the magic had gone away. The broadcast lost about five million viewers over the next eight seasons. A lot of that could be attributed to the loss of NFL football as a lead-in during the nineties. Even so, it started to seem like it might be time for change at the top, even with Don insisting that he planned to die at his desk.

It's probably some kind of natural law that you don't want to be the guy to replace the legend. But I did in 2004. As I look back almost fifteen years later, it was a difficult transition at first. But I had enormous support from most of the people on the broadcast, whom I had worked with for many years. Don wasn't very helpful in the beginning—he wasn't comfortable, and who could blame him? It took him almost two years to get used to the idea of someone else being at the helm. But once he started liking the broadcasts, he was his old self again: supportive and fun and clever. And he was kind and respectful to me.

I knew that we could keep the magic alive as long as we maintained our standards and values. But that didn't mean the broadcast would just keep doing the same things. *60 Minutes* had constantly evolved over the previous thirty-five years. We would continue this evolution.

60 Minutes had been doing too many stories not tied to any particular current event; stories that could air anytime during the year. I wanted our broadcast to be much more current. The program had always been known for getting big interviews. Our goal became to do them more often and to stay on top of the big stories of the moment—conflicts, tsunamis, and economic calamities—while continuing to take the time for and commit significant resources to serious investigative reporting more often geared toward subjects in the news.

That being said, I'm not sure if any of our regular viewers have really been able to tell how the broadcast changed—and that's a good thing. One of the first rules of running a broadcast or publication—or a business venture of any kind, for that matter—is never alienate your core audience. Our audience has stuck with us through the years.

We've heard people give all kinds of reasons for *60 Minutes*'s continued success, beginning with the time slot: Sunday at seven in the evening, when most people are at home; the sizable lead-in audience afforded us by Sunday afternoon NFL football games; the pull of tradition for American families. All of those things are probably true, but there's a lot more to it—and not necessarily things you'd expect.

By almost every measure of conventional wisdom, *60 Minutes* should not be successful. In a time when audience research is the driving force behind coverage decisions in newsrooms across America, we don't do audience research. Ever. And here's why that matters: rather than depend on research to tell us what stories our audience might like better than others—a process I believe is fundamentally flawed—we decide which stories to cover based on how important or how interesting we believe they are. The onus is on us to make each story so damn interesting that you get sucked in. Since we don't rely on knowing which stories the audience wants, we must rely on other ways to keep viewers engaged. That starts with how we tell the stories.

It may surprise you to hear that we don't cover issues: we tell stories that often illuminate issues. But mostly we tell stories. And we've told virtually every kind of story there is to tell. Harry Reasoner got to wax poetic about *Casablanca*, the greatest movie ever made. Morley Safer took a ride on the Orient Express. Bob Simon found joy in the Congo and peace in the secluded monasteries of Mount Athos in Greece, one of the most sacred spots in the Christian world.

We pride ourselves on original, knowledgeable, and experienced reporting. We tell stories nobody else is telling—and stories everyone is covering. We find a narrow lane to shine light where it hasn't been shed to give our viewers a better understanding of the big picture. In Baghdad, Iraq, when Saddam Hussein was captured in 2003, we found the only eyewitnesses to have seen the fallen dictator in jail. In Kurdistan, in 2014, we saw the black flag of the Islamic State of Iraq and Syria, or ISIS, flying right on the other side of the Al Rashad Bridge, showing how much Iraqi territory had been taken. After Hurricane Katrina in 2005, we discovered that the bridge to Gretna, Louisiana, offered safe passage out of New Orleans but had been blocked by police. After the deadly Indian Ocean tsunami of 2004, we came across the sea gypsies off the coast of Myanmar, a nomadic tribe called the Moken that had escaped the storm before it hit because they were able to read the patterns of the sea.

Over the last fifty years, we've been to the ballet and to the opera and to the White House, where we've interviewed almost every US president since Richard Nixon. Our largest audience in the last two decades watched

---

1 Morley Safer took a ride on the Orient Express in 1977.

2 Bob Simon interviewing a monk on Mt. Athos for a report that aired Easter Sunday 2011.

3 Scott Pelley at the edge of the Al Rashad Bridge in Kurdistan in 2014 for a report about the rise of ISIS.

4 Bob Simon interviewing a Moken leader off the coast of Myanmar in 2005.

5 Steve Kroft conducted the first interview with Barack and Michelle Obama after the historic election of 2008.

6 Mike Wallace and Luciano Pavarotti in Barbados in 2002.

7 Lesley Stahl conducted the first interview with President-elect Trump after his victory in 2016.

8 Steve Kroft had a laugh with Beyoncé in 2010.

9 Charlie Rose interviewing Russia's president Vladimir Putin in 2015 at his state residence outside Moscow.

10 Lesley Stahl got a shoulder massage from U2 front man Bono after interviewing him in 2010 about his role as composer and lyricist for the Broadway musical *Spider-Man: Turn Off the Dark*.

11 Scott Pelley aboard Air Force One with President George W. Bush en route to Fort Benning, GA, in 2007.

12 Mike Wallace interviewed China's president Jiang Zemin in 2000 at the presidential compound in the seaside resort of Beidaihe.

13 Anderson Cooper and Lady Gaga were followed by paparazzi when they took a walk along the Thames River in London.

14 Anderson Cooper with Eminem in his Detroit studio in 2010.

15 Steve Kroft went to Tehran in 2015 and sat down with Iran's president Hassan Rouhani.

the first interview we conducted with President-elect Obama and Mrs. Obama ten days after the historic election of 2008. Another huge audience tuned in for Donald Trump's first interview as president-elect. We've met generals on the battlefield and leaders from nearly every corner of the world. The Ayatollah Khomeini of Iran. Fidel Castro of Cuba and Hugo Chavez of Venezuela. Two Chinese leaders: Deng Xiaoping and Jiang Zemin. And two Russians as well: Vladimir Putin and Boris Yeltsin, the latter of whom answered a few questions on his tennis court in between points. France's Nicolas Sarkozy answered four questions in his presidential palace before walking out on Lesley Stahl, who at that moment asked the whereabouts of his estranged wife.

There have been revealing portraits of Lena Horne and Lady Gaga. Bob Dylan and Eminem. Bono and Beyoncé. Clint Eastwood and Sean Connery. Katharine Hepburn and Angelina Jolie. There was Michael Jackson, Michael Jordan, Miles Davis, and Derek Jeter. Dolly Parton. Woody Allen. Arthur Miller. Jerry Seinfeld. Chris Rock. We met Mark Zuckerberg and Sergey Brin, Clarence Thomas and Antonin Scalia, Queen Latifah and Prince Charles . . .

We tell stories about space and about scientific breakthroughs such

---

16 Steve Kroft with Sean Connery in 1999.

17 Steve Kroft with Clint Eastwood in 1997.

18 Lara Logan flying over Afghanistan with General John Campbell, commander of US forces there.

19 Ed Bradley interviewed Yankees captain Derek Jeter at Yankee Stadium in 2005.

20 Bob Simon with Angelina Jolie in Budapest, where she was filming her directorial debut, *In the Land of Blood and Honey.*

21 Harry Reasoner profiled Miles Davis in 1989.

22 Morley Safer interviewed Dolly Parton in Tennessee in 2009.

23 Anderson Cooper got in the pool with Olympic gold medalist Michael Phelps in 2008.

24 Ed Bradley with Muhammad Ali in Havana, Cuba, in 1996.

25 Steve Kroft sat down with Prince Charles in 2005.

26 Katie Couric with tennis champion Andre Agassi in 2009 at Arthur Ashe Stadium in New York.

27 Lesley Stahl with Mark Zuckerberg in 2008 at Facebook Headquarters.

28 Bob Simon interviewed snowboarder Shaun White at his private practice facility in Silverton, Colorado, in 2010.

29 Steve Kroft with New England Patriots quarterback Tom Brady at Gillette Stadium in 2005.

30 Lesley Stahl with Supreme Court Justice Antonin Scalia in 2008.

as the polio virus being used to kill brain tumors. We report hard-hitting exposés: why BP's Deepwater Horizon oil drilling rig blew up in the Gulf of Mexico in 2010; the myth of Lance Armstrong; the false rape charges against three Duke University lacrosse players who were all but convicted in the court of public opinion. We've been courtside, ringside, in the pool, on the slopes, and on the sidelines with some of the greatest athletes in the world, including the Greatest, Muhammad Ali.

Many of our stories take only a few days to complete; we'll finish them Sunday afternoon just before airtime. Most of them take much longer than that. Producer Graham Messick spent nine months unraveling the CIA practice known as rendition, in which agents snatched terrorism suspects from foreign countries, bundled them onto private planes, and flew them to overseas prisons, many of them known for their use of torture. The title of another story, "Curve Ball," came from the code name for the Iraqi engineer whose false claims that Saddam Hussein possessed biological weapons of mass destruction served as a justification for the 2003 invasion of Iraq. His story took three years for veteran producer Draggan Mihailovich to report. Producer Howard Rosenberg and Steve Kroft spent over a year reporting on twenty-eight pages of 9/11 investigation documents kept secret because of what they revealed about a network of Saudi involvement with the 9/11 hijackers before the attack was launched. After we broadcast the story President Obama ordered those pages be made public.

I believe we succeed in drawing huge audiences Sunday after Sunday because we offer something fulfilling, important, informative, interesting and sometimes just fun. Many of these stories news executives would deem "not good for TV," but we pride ourselves on tackling stories that you might not ordinarily see on television. The war in Afghanistan is a good example. We covered America's longest war regularly—even though high-level news executives at major networks, including our own, were calling it a "turnoff."

It's true that if you ask members of a focus group whether they would rather watch a story about the war in Afghanistan or a story about prices at the gas pump, the answer would be pretty obvious. But we did not tell stories about "the war." We told stories about what happened during the war, stories about soldiers and battles and friendly fire and collateral damage. We did stories about the generals in charge and about strategy, about brothers fighting side by side, and about the enemy. If you tested an audience after showing one of those stories and compared their interest to a story about gas prices, I believe they would prefer the story involving the war.

What about Steve Kroft's story on how credit default swaps brought our economy crashing down? That's not going to work on TV! But it sure did, because he and producer Frank Devine told the story so well. As a viewer, you learned about a difficult subject and walked away with a much better understanding of how complicated and crazy Wall Street trades had become. Believe me, there was plenty of blood on the floor after that one. Tempers can flare when taking on that kind of difficult story because it can be so complicated and frustrating to tell. But it was worth every bit of it, because we defied conventional wisdom by attracting one of our biggest audiences of that entire fall television season.

One secret to our success is the system we've set in place for producing stories. There are about seventy-five reporters here, with six or seven who just happen to be on the air. And all seventy-five of them compete against one another to outwrite and outinvestigate their colleagues. Producer Harry Radliffe once described the place as a bunch of teams set up as terrorist cells, "ruthlessly and secretly operating in complete isolation." But actually *60 Minutes* is a pretty collegial and collaborative place. We know that we are at our best when a team works together on a story.

We try hard to avoid a formula; we do not ever want to be predictable, but we also have a few unwritten rules. We write for the ear, and make sure every sentence is easy to follow so that the viewer never gets lost.

We do our best to avoid cliché—especially words and phrases used incessantly by news people. There's a board of forbidden words in my office. The first ones are the words "clear" and "clearly" because they represent "newspeak"—the language of reporters used in almost every news story. Listen for it the next time you watch the news. The irony is that, in our world, almost nothing is clear—everything is a little fuzzy. You also won't hear the word "exclusive" on *60 Minutes,* even though we have more exclusive reports than any other television news outlet. But the word has been so overused in broadcast news that it no longer carries any meaning. We don't pander to any segment of the audience. We want our stories to appeal to everyone in the audience, not one demographic or another.

We never underestimate the viewer's intelligence, though we understand we know more about our stories than they do. We never overstate, we always understate. We look for simple details for description in our stories, and avoid hyperbole. We work hard on keeping the stories compelling. We can never afford to be boring or dull, but we try hard to keep our copy spare, without unnecessary adjectives or adverbs.

Our constant goal is to report the truth, which often is a reflection of what we have learned from our sources and what we have witnessed for ourselves. We never set out to recite the facts. But it is also important for us to tell our viewers what we don't know, what we were not able to confirm or witness. We strive for fairness in everything we touch. One of our primary rules is to make sure we are fair to everyone in our story, including those who declined to help us or participate in our reporting. We avoid tabloid-style sensationalism. Every story is G-rated in language and visuals because we appreciate that families gather to watch *60 Minutes.*

I know this will sound a bit dramatic but most of the people at *60 Minutes*—whether in front of the camera or behind it—consider what they do a calling. But they don't kid themselves. *60 Minutes* is no television monastery: we all know we're part of a commercial operation. So although we don't do audience research about what stories to cover, we watch our ratings closely.

We want the biggest audience we can possibly get because we understand that if we do well, we can continue to do what we want to do and cover what we want to cover. My favorite Nielsen measurement is the cumulative number, the number of viewers who tune in at least once during an entire television season not counting sports—original viewers per year. For the past ten years, *60 Minutes* has finished number one in this category with as many as 120 million Americans tuning in each year. In recent years, NBC's *The Voice* has been in second place, almost 20 million viewers behind. We are number one in this measure with the younger demographics as well.

CBS News, like a lot of old institutions, has had its good times and its bad. So has *60 Minutes*. But there have been some constant characteristics that have kept us ticking for all these years, and so many memorable individuals who contributed along the way. When you last as long as we have, you also live through a lot of loss. Our broadcast has spanned generations, and so many of our colleagues (it sometimes feels more appropriate to call them family members) came from the greatest generation: Don and Mike, Andy Rooney and Harry Reasoner. The deaths of Ed Bradley and Bob Simon were shocking. Our good pal Artie Bloom, the first director of *60 Minutes*, died at sixty-three. Producers George Crile, Harry Radliffe, Michael Rosenbaum, Trevor Nelson, and Clem Taylor were among many others who left us at a young age. All of them loved being a part of this great broadcast. They dedicated their professional lives to it and understood what made it so special. All of them will come back to life in these pages.

There is an irony to our enduring success: it is owed to both Don Hewitt, the guy who got fired back in 1965, and Fred Friendly, the guy who fired him. The two of them, in different ways, represent the best values and standards of CBS News, passed down through them over seventy-five years. But if there are any words that all of us recognize, words that define us, they should be the four words we always heard from Don Hewitt: tell me a story. They're words that every kid in the world knows.

That's what we will do in this book: tell the story of fifty years of *60 Minutes*, with the help of many fine people who have made this great broadcast succeed.

DECADE

3

1988 to 1998

SEASONS

21-22

1988 to 1990

In the beginning, at least, in our beginning, when we began to put shape to a new kind of television broadcast with the unlikely title of *60 Minutes*, no one— least of all us—dared hope that someday we'd be celebrating our twentieth anniversary.

—Mike Wallace, *60 Minutes* Twentieth Anniversary Special, October 10, 1988

M ike Wallace was speaking for just about everybody who worked at *60 Minutes* from its beginning. They had no reason to believe their invention would last twenty years, let alone fifty, or that it would be considered one of the most successful broadcasts in television history.

In its first year, 1968, the broadcast came in 75th out of the 81 programs airing that season. It took six years and several moves to different time slots until *60 Minutes* landed in its permanent spot on the schedule, Sundays at 7 p.m. Only then did it start to get traction.

Being around the old guard—Morley, Harry, Ed, and Mike—was a thrill and an honor, but they were nervous about us newcomers.

By the time my generation came along, twenty years later, it had become a hit.

We will get to the very early days of the broadcast in the following chapter but this book begins at the twenty-year mark in our history because that prime decade encapsulates in many ways the reasons *60 Minutes* did achieve enduring success, both through its original genius and its ability to constantly reinvent itself.

Like a lot of young producers who first arrive for work at *60 Minutes*, I wasn't quite sure what to expect. But Don Hewitt settled that within a few hours on the job. "We don't have meetings, and there are no memos to the staff," he told me. "Just bring us good stories and everything will be all right."

There was a journalistic spirit at *60 Minutes* that I felt from that first day on the job in 1989, during the twenty-first season. It was a sense that the story came first, and that the rituals and obsessions of most every other television news organization, including our own CBS News organization, did not matter so much.

I was hired as a producer to work with Steve Kroft, the first young male correspondent since Ed Bradley had joined in 1981. There was a lot of pressure on him and on me. Could we do the kind of work expected of

Steve Kroft and Jeff Fager, photographed in 2011, started working together at *60 Minutes* in 1989.

us? I remember Mike Wallace taunting me in the hall: "We'll see if you can handle it soon enough; see if you're good enough to be here." There was a twinkle in his eye, but I couldn't tell if he was kidding or not, which was a fundamental part of his appeal. He was a rascal—a very likeable rascal—with a big heart and a manic personality.

60 Minutes executive editor Phil Scheffler, at his desk.

Being around Don and Mike and Morley Safer and Ed Bradley was a real thrill and an honor, but they were nervous about us newcomers. Nobody wanted the "kids" to screw up what they had worked so hard to build. Still, we were pretty much left to fend for ourselves.

It was an adult place to work, with little supervision and high expectations, a refreshing place to be for Steve and me. We had grown up in the hard news part of CBS News, covering conflicts, summits, plagues, and floods out of the London bureau. Steve had already earned a reputation as one of the finest storytelling correspondents in an organization that included the very best. He was confident he could do the work well.

Still, we both had to earn the right to be there. I found that out early in a conversation with Don's number two, Phil Scheffler, the executive editor of the broadcast. Phil was crucial, always trying to make sure the journalism was solid and accurate. We liked to joke that his sour and gruff exterior camouflaged his prickly interior.

A month or so after starting on the job, I took a deep breath, entered his office, and said, "Phil, I have worked at CBS News since 1982. I have covered the world and every kind of story, and I always thought that coming here would be a promotion. So, I've been looking for a raise."

He looked up with a scowl and said, "Then why don't you start looking for another job." He looked back down at his papers, and I slowly, one step at a time, backed out of his office.

At the time they were handing out new computer terminals to replace the old typewriters. I didn't get one of those, either.

. . .

The first story Steve and I did was about the chief of orthopedics at San Francisco General Hospital, Dr. Lorraine Day, who was angry that not enough was being done, in her opinion, to protect physicians against the occupational risk of infection with HIV. Producing the story was a first lesson in life at *60 Minutes*.

In 1989 the AIDS epidemic was raging, and San Francisco, with its huge gay population. was at the epicenter. Not since polio had there been such a fear of a virus, and Dr. Day wanted doctors to understand their risk of infection. The story promised to be provocative and controversial, and Dr. Day did not disappoint. We had heard that she wore what amounted to a space suit in the operating room to protect her from the potentially infected blood of her patients. She agreed to let us film her in the suit.

Lorraine Day was a perfect *60 Minutes* subject because she wasn't at all shy about her position. She was outspoken and passionate, though we wondered if there wasn't some homophobia behind her complaints. Her position did not include much, if any, compassion for the predominantly gay population suffering horribly from the disease, but she was unequivocal: treating AIDS patients could be life-threatening. She backed her opinions up with a statistic that accidental injury from a contaminated needle was estimated at one in two hundred by the US Centers for Disease Control.

"If you came to work every day and flipped the light switch on in your office, and only one out of two hundred times you would get electrocuted, would you consider that low risk?" she asked on camera.

Dr. Day had created a stir at the hospital, and she had significant opposition, articulated well in our story by Dr. John Luce:

LUCE: I think that having fears about HIV infection and AIDS is very appropriate and I think any physician that doesn't have fears about getting infected is crazy. At the same time I think carrying the fear to the point that Dr. Day does, and to try to instill [fear], and I believe she has instilled fear in other people, is wrong. I think that Dr. Day is an alarmist.

We reported and filmed the story during our first summer and got ready to show it to Don in August so that it could run in the new television season starting in mid-September. By the time we sat down to interview Dr. Day, she had promised to reveal on *60 Minutes* that she had decided to quit over the issue. Now we had some news to go with our first story.

After about six weeks of shooting and writing and rewriting and reorganizing, we thought we were ready to show the story to Don. Screenings at *60 Minutes* are infamous. In CBS News mythology, they're usually associated with strong language and shouting matches. A team made up of a producer, a correspondent, and a videotape editor had worked for months to get the story into good shape, but it was well known that Don could hate the result. This was a frightening possibility even for the veterans; for a newcomer, the experience was like being a rookie up at bat for the first time in Yankee Stadium. And there was an added twist at our first

Steve Kroft's first studio introduction for *60 Minutes*, for "Dr. Day Is Quitting."

screening: Mike Wallace decided to attend to see if the new guys were any good. We knew that if the screening did not go well, Mike would make sure that everybody on the Eastern Seaboard knew about it.

To our relief, we got a round of applause when the lights came on. And Don made the story better by making it more about Dr. Day. He had us drop a scientist, calling him "Marvin the expert." You don't need Marvin the expert, he argued, when you know as much about this story as he does.

. . .

One of the rules you learn early at *60 Minutes* is that you are only as good as your next story, and so you had better get going on it. Most producers have several stories going at once to make sure there's a steady flow in case one falls through. We were required to produce four to five stories per year, with each correspondent expected to finish as many as twenty, adding up to just under a hundred new stories per television season.

The challenge was finding original stories. Taking a story from the newspaper, a common crutch in television news, was not acceptable. You needed to either advance a running story significantly or come up with something unique and important. "I didn't know that!" was one of the most desired reactions.

The pursuit of stories was very competitive. Occasionally in reporting, you might run across a producer from ABC working on the same story, or somebody in the office next door. That kind of competition was encouraged. Don thought he would always get the best out of everyone if we were driven to do a little better than our *60 Minutes* colleagues.

Mike Wallace was the most competitive of all: he stole at least one story from his own son, Chris, and he stole more stories from Morley Safer than Morley cared to count. Mike always wanted to get on the air more than anyone, and a few months before I arrived, he landed a big one: the exit interview with President and Mrs. Reagan in January 1989, just as George H. W. Bush was entering the White House.

Mike had an unusual relationship with the Reagans, mostly because of his friendship with Nancy, which dated back to her days as a student at Smith College. That may be part of why the January exit interview was criticized, on our floor and in a few newspapers, for being too soft. It was a kind of criticism that Mike—the tough guy of all tough guys—didn't ever hear. For the most part, he had asked the right questions. An exit interview is different from an interview with a sitting president: it shouldn't be entirely about pinning him down on policy positions, because his time in power is over. It's traditionally meant to be more about what it was like in the job, where his administration might have done better, what concerns he might have about the future of the country, and what advice he has for his successor. Even so, was Mike as tough as he might have been otherwise if he didn't so admire the president and didn't harbor a soft spot for the First Lady? Probably not.

The interview included this classic exchange:

WALLACE: Why hasn't this job weighed as heavily on you as it has on some other occupants of this Oval Office?

PRESIDENT REAGAN: Well, Mike, I don't know what the answer to that would be. Well, maybe none of them had a Nancy.

Mike Wallace and Nancy Reagan had a long-standing friendship.

The president went on to define, in just a few sentences, his view of his legacy:

"I came here with the belief that this country, the people, were kind of hungering for a sort of spiritual revival. The whole thing of the sixties, the rioting and so forth and the disillusionment with Vietnam, it seemed that people had kind of lost faith in the destiny of this country and all. And I came here with, as I say, plans, and set out to implement them. No, we didn't get everything we asked for, but you don't fall back in defeat."

Mike Wallace went over interview questions for President Ronald Reagan with Don Hewitt and producer Rich Bonin in 1989. *60 Minutes* cameraman Gregory Andracke is in the background.

It was *60 Minutes* doing what the broadcast had become known for doing: capturing a moment in history. And if Mike had gone a little easy in that January interview, Rich Bonin, who produced the story, doesn't believe it was because of his friendship with Nancy. Bonin remembers that the aura of the Oval Office got to Mike. He didn't go soft on Mrs. Reagan the following fall when he interviewed her alone upon the publication of her memoir of her time in the White House.

He cut right to the chase and asked about a controversy that had subjected her to ridicule when she was First Lady: her use of an astrologer. Mrs. Reagan acknowledged, for the first time, that her astrologer had set the dates for the president's news conferences as well as for some of his trips.

WALLACE: I'm told by somebody senior in the White House that the president's news conference was never scheduled without her input saying—

MRS. REAGAN: She would pick out dates that were good or bad.

WALLACE: For?

MRS. REAGAN: For trips. If he were going, say, to Chicago, and I would say to her, "Gee, is it better if he leaves in the morning or in the afternoon or maybe the night before?" And she'd tell me. I didn't see anything wrong with that.

WALLACE: And the same was true with news conferences?

MRS. REAGAN: Same thing, yeah . . .

WALLACE: Did the president know?

MRS. REAGAN: Not in the beginning.

WALLACE: Why not?

MRS. REAGAN: Well, I guess I chose not to tell him.

Mike Wallace interviewed Ronald Reagan at the White House in January 1989.

WALLACE: Secrets from your husband? Did you think this was maybe a little bit nutty, and that he might not understand?

MRS. REAGAN: And that I probably did. But then he did find out, and he did say, "Nancy, I think, you know, this might be a little bit embarrassing."

Mrs. Reagan's admissions made news everywhere. It was widely known that she had played a strong role as First Lady, but the revelations that she also relied as heavily as she did on astrology were stunning.

Mike also pushed Mrs. Reagan on the influence she had wielded as First Lady. He referred to a section in her memoir regarding White House Chief of Staff Don Regan, whom she and members of the president's Cabinet thought should be fired or resign. She wrote that Vice President George Bush told her he agreed that Regan should go. But the First Lady was unhappy that Bush had come to her instead of going directly to the president. In the interview, Mrs. Reagan told Mike she challenged the VP to go to the president.

MRS. REAGAN: I said, "George, won't you please tell my husband that? Everybody is calling me instead of going to my husband." And he said, "Well, no, that's not my role," and I thought it was.

WALLACE: And you felt that George Bush lacked political courage in failing to tell your husband?

MRS. REAGAN: Well, for whatever reason.

WALLACE: What do you mean "whatever"? That's what you felt.

MRS. REAGAN: You're putting words in my mouth, Mike Wallace.

WALLACE: You can take them out right now.

MRS. REAGAN: He didn't do it . . . so.

The implication was that Mike was on to something.

Mike also tried to pin her down on fees the Reagans were accepting for a trip to Japan, probably the beginning of what has become common practice for ex-presidents.

WALLACE: You're going to be in Japan, and I am told it is a two-million-dollar two weeks.

MRS. REAGAN: They're getting two of us. They're working us like crazy. We're taking the wives of servicemen over there so that they can see their husbands.

WALLACE: But it's going to be a well-recompensed two weeks.

MRS. REAGAN: It is for everybody who goes there, which you probably know. Now, you really didn't need that question.

Shortly after the interview, Mike heard that Nancy felt she had been sand-bagged and that she would no longer be speaking to him. In the end, their falling out lasted only a few months. She publicly made up with him on CNN's *Larry King Live*.

That kind of spat was expected at *60 Minutes*. It was not unusual for one of the correspondents, usually Mike, to offend somebody with his or her questions. What was less expected was the controversy that erupted a few months later when Andy Rooney crossed a line in a commentary. It was the first full-on crisis I witnessed at *60 Minutes*—and it was a wild one.

By the third decade of *60 Minutes*, Andy had become a fixture at the end of the broadcast. He succeeded in that spot because he was direct, original, and provocative. People always asked me, "What's he like?" The short answer is "Just like what you see on TV: not a phony bone in his body." I remember being with him years later at a Super Bowl cocktail party. He was sipping his usual Maker's Mark on the rocks when a friend of mine, Bruce Taub, approached. I said, "Andy, you should meet this man. He's the CFO of CBS. He's the one who signs your paycheck every week. He's responsible for all of that money at CBS."

Andy, without missing a beat, said, "Well . . . nobody's perfect," took a sip of his bourbon, and walked away.

Andy was thoughtful, quick, smart, and funny. His genius was as an absurdist, commenting on the things in daily life that make no sense at all. Most of his comments were benign or simply amusing—about silly trends or consumers getting ripped off.

This was a typical Andy piece from that period:

"Here's a regular box of fake strawberry Jell-O that costs $1.05. And here's a smaller box of Jell-O without sugar that costs $1.19. Now, you could say that whatever they put in instead of sugar costs more than the sugar in Jell-O, but what about these cans of Hunt's tomato sauce? Both the same size, but this one costs ten cents more than this one, because they didn't put any salt in this one."

But soon after that, in his twelfth year on the air as a weekly commentator, Andy got into the worst trouble of his professional life. In a special broadcast near the end of the year, entitled "A Year with Andy Rooney," he said this:

"There was some recognition in 1989 of the fact that many of the ills which kill us are self-induced: too much alcohol, too much food, drugs, homosexual unions, cigarettes. They're all known quite often to lead to premature death."

The gay and lesbian community was furious. Andy then made the

Jeff Fager and Andy Rooney at the Super Bowl, 2010.

situation worse by repeating his view in a letter about a month later, at the end of January 1990, to a national gay newspaper, the *Advocate*. In that piece, he wrote that what gays did was "repugnant" and that homosexuality itself was "abnormal." As if things could not get any worse, he went on to give an interview to the same publication, in which he was quoted as making not only homophobic remarks but racist ones too, allegedly saying: "I've believed all along that most people are born with equal intelligence, but blacks have watered down their genes because the less intelligent ones are the ones that have the most children. They drop out of school early, do drugs, get pregnant." Andy immediately denied making those remarks, and the reporter had not recorded them. But that didn't matter. For the first time, at age seventy, the guy who could say anything he wanted was in trouble for something he said.

Don Hewitt, who created Andy's role on *60 Minutes,* had been ambivalent about a lot of Andy's work. He worried all of this would hurt the broadcast. The president of CBS News, David Burke, wanted to suspend Andy. But Don wanted him fired, according to Burke's number two, Joe Peyronnin, who was VP in charge of prime-time news broadcasts, including *60 Minutes.*

Burke wasn't willing to go that far and instead issued a statement saying that CBS News could "not tolerate such remarks or anything that approximates such comments, since they in no way reflect the views of the organization." Andy Rooney was suspended for three months without pay, his future at CBS News in doubt.

But thirty years ago, views about sexual orientation had yet to mature into the general tolerance of today, and regular viewers of *60 Minutes* were not inclined to turn on Rooney for his transgression. It quickly became apparent—especially to Don Hewitt—that the program's ratings were slipping each week that Andy didn't appear. By February 25, the third week of his suspension, the broadcast had fallen from fifth place to eighteenth for the week—a 20 percent drop in viewership. For the first time in nearly twelve years, *60 Minutes* was losing to an entertainment show, *America's Funniest Home Videos* on ABC.

Never one to lose a ratings battle, Don—who had been ready to get rid of Andy just a few weeks earlier—now wanted to bring Andy back before he had served out his suspension and launched a campaign to do that. As it turned out, Don had a lot of help from the viewers. The network received more than 5,200 phone calls while Andy was gone—and only 76 praised the suspension. More than 4,000 letters were written in support of him.

Andy was reinstated just three weeks into his three-month suspension. On March 4, 1990, he appeared in his regular spot at the end of the broadcast. He didn't apologize that night. But he came as close as he could:

There was never a writer who didn't hope that in some small way he was doing good with the words he put down on paper. And while I know it's presumptuous, I've always had in the back of my mind that I was doing a little bit of good. Now I was to be known for having done not good, but bad. I'd be known for the rest of my life as a racist bigot, and as someone who had made life a little more difficult for homosexuals. I felt terrible about that, and I've learned a lot. What do I say to defend myself? Do I say I'm not a racist? Sounds like I'm saying "I'm not a crook." How do I apologize to homosexuals for hurting them with a remark that I didn't realize would hurt them. It's demeaning to have to sit here and demean myself . . . What do I do to justify the action David Burke, the president of CBS News, has taken in putting me back on the air? What do I do about the kind words heaped on me by friends and strangers? It's overwhelming. How do I live up to such praise? Let's face it, even on the nights when I'm good, I'm not that good. Do I have opinions that might irritate some people? You're damned right I do. That's what I'm here for.

The Rooney episode is a powerful example of how much our culture has changed in the past three decades. It's hard to imagine, if it were to happen today, that Andy's suspension would be shortened—or that he would even get his job back at all. But Andy showed us all that he would try his best to understand when he went wrong.

•   •   •

Significant change was taking place in the world. The Berlin Wall had come down that fall, a professionally frustrating moment for those of us who had previously covered hard news. *60 Minutes* rarely covered the big story of the day, and so nothing was done about the fall of the wall—not then, anyway. We looked for stories that could be developed after the big story.

Steve Kroft's report from Chernobyl, Ukraine, nearly four years after the 1986 nuclear disaster there, is one of the all-time best examples of an original approach to a huge news story. It was the worst meltdown of a nuclear power plant since the rise of nuclear power, and yet there was almost no way to find out what had happened in the vicinity of the disaster because, with Ukraine being part of the old Soviet Union, reporters were restricted from the area and not allowed to cover it properly.

Steve was the first American television reporter to visit the decommissioned Chernobyl plant, traveling there with producer Bill McClure (one of the original *60 Minutes* producers) and cameraman Mike Edwards. Here, early on in his *60 Minutes* career, Steve put his tremendous writing abilities on display:

Few words translate as quickly and with as much impact as the word *Chernobyl*. In English, it means "wormwood," the biblical name of the great star that fell from the heavens in the book of Revelation, poisoned a third of the Earth's waters, and signaled the Day of Judgment. But for the Soviet Union, it's more than an apocalyptic vision. It's reality . . . The traffic through the Ukrainian countryside starts to thin out long before you get to Chernobyl. Out the window, villages that have survived Turks, Tartars, and Nazis stand undisturbed. Then slowly it begins to hit you: what's wrong with the picture. People. For mile after miles, there are no people . . . Entire villages have been bulldozed, hosed down, and buried, except for Pripyat. It was one of the largest Soviet cities built in the twentieth century, with luxurious ultramodern accommodations by Soviet standards . . . Today Pripyat

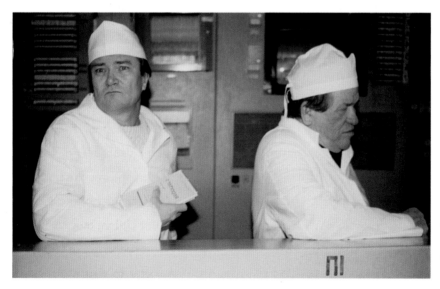

Steve Kroft and producer Bill McClure in the control room of the last working reactor at Chernobyl.

is a ghost town. The only sign of life is the music, piped in continuously to keep the decontamination crews that have to be here from going crazy . . . You can't see the contamination, and you can't feel it. All you can do is hear it on a Geiger counter. In some hot spots, we found radiation levels one hundred times normal.

The Chernobyl story had it all: it was newsworthy, it was original, it was incredibly well told, and it was an adventure. I learned early on at *60 Minutes* that adventure was a valued genre of storytelling. We take people places they can't visit otherwise, including to the edges of hell. But we also take people on adventures to territories that are sometimes not at all far flung. On that very same broadcast, Morley Safer reported one of my favorite kinds of adventure: the kind you find right under your nose.

Morley took a memorable journey through Grand Central Station to reveal a subterranean world filled with caverns and tunnels providing shelter to as many as four hundred to five hundred homeless people living as far as ten stories down in "nooks and crannies . . . and fifty-six miles of steam tunnels." The producers were Paul and Holly Fine, a husband-and-wife team who spent more time on their stories than most producers. With Paul doing a lot of the filming himself, their stories often ended up looking like beautifully filmed short documentaries. Morley could turn anything into poetry, and this worked particularly well with Paul's pictures:

The terminal once was called the greatest enclosed space in the country. An architectural masterpiece. In its prime, it greeted presidents and world statesmen, an international grande dame. Its name, Grand Central, and its trains like the 20th Century Limited, captured the romance and elegance of an age. At dawn, with the terminal still closed, that age is still alive, at least in your mind. It's easy to imagine a scene of bustling Pullman porters and matched leather luggage and passengers bound for distant California. But now, from its early-morning opening, to its late-night closing, squalor overwhelms the old terminal. At five thirty in the morning, grimness waits at the gate. The first arrivals are not travelers but shuffling legions of New York's homeless.

An important lesson learned eventually by most everybody who works at *60 Minutes* is to choose your stories well, because you will be living with them for a long time, and it can be very painful if they don't work out well. Soon after the fall of the Berlin Wall, the Soviet Union's future was the biggest story—and Steve and I wanted to get in on it. We looked at the Eastern Bloc states, which were winning their freedom one by one. I started working on a story about Poland attempting to start up a free market system, and came upon the Harvard University economist Jeffrey Sachs, who was working to help the country pull it off.

We sent the story idea to Don and Phil Scheffler in the form of a blue sheet: the traditional term for a story idea because the paper on which a producer used to pitch a story was blue. Don told me within a few days that he didn't like the idea, but that we could do it if we thought he might be wrong. Don always wanted us to work on stories we wanted to work on. He was the boss, but even if he didn't like your idea, he would give you the green light if you were passionate about it.

We decided to go ahead, against Don's instincts, and shot the story in Poland. By midwinter, we were ready to show it to him. The *60 Minutes* screening room is a comfortable place, with theater seating and a big monitor in the front of the room. In those days, the correspondent sat out in the theater seats with senior producer Merri Lieberthal, while Don and Phil sat behind a small desk. The producer sat in an elevated area toward the back of the room, next to the senior editor, Esther Kartiganer, who timed the story with a clock. The lights dimmed, the tape rolled, and everybody watched. In this setting, a story always looks different, even to those who have been editing it for weeks. Sure enough, as I watched it with the group for the first time, our story seemed . . . kind of boring.

Ed Bradley interviewed comedian George Burns for a profile that aired in November 1988. Also pictured are producer Ruth Streeter on the left and associate producer Roz Karson.

When the lights came on, Don swiveled his chair around in my direction and looked up at me sitting on the elevated platform. That's when he asked me, "Where do you want it, kid? Right between the eyes?"

Don hated the story, and at that point, so did I. So did Steve. A bad screening was one thing, but "right between the eyes" seemed worse. I remember going home to my wife and kids in a bit of a daze. Then the phone rang. It was Don. He said he had an idea for how to fix the story and asked that we meet him the next day in the edit room. The story became much more about the brilliant young economist Jeff Sachs—called in to save the new independent Polish government—and much less about turning an Eastern European economy toward capitalism. Within a week, we were back in the screening room. Don gave us all the credit for turning around the story, even though the suggested improvements came from him.

Several years later, when I was offered the job of executive producer of the *CBS Evening News*, I asked Don what he thought I should do. He told me to take it because there is no better feeling than helping someone make his or her story better. I remember thinking back on that damn Poland story and knowing he was right.

SEASON

23

1990 to 1991

Nowhere in all of journalism are news people as well paid and as loudly applauded as you are. Come on, for Christ's sake, start turning out stories.

—Don Hewitt in a note to the staff

In 1990, as our television season was about to begin, President George H. W. Bush spoke before a joint session of Congress and first used the phrase "new world order." It applied to the post–Cold War international landscape but was used at this moment in the context of Iraq's recent invasion of Kuwait. The date was September 11. The president was mustering support for his military buildup under way in Saudi Arabia, preparing to push the Iraqi army out of Kuwait. He was assembling the largest coalition of international allied forces since World War II.

These are his words: "We stand today at a unique and extraordinary moment. The crisis in the Persian Gulf, as grave as it is, also offers a rare opportunity to move toward an historic period of cooperation. Out of these troubled times, our fifth objective, a new world order, can emerge: a new era, freer from the threat of terror, stronger in the pursuit of justice, and more secure in the quest for peace."

The president's words take on a new meaning as we look back on them almost three decades later. One could make the case that the presence of so many Western troops gathered in Saudi territory for a fight against an Arab neighbor was the beginning of what provoked the great jihad against America and a new world order nobody in the West could imagine. This was practically predicted on *60 Minutes* just a few days after Iraq invaded Kuwait.

The invasion took place on August 2, 1990. Three days later, on August 5, Mike Wallace started the broadcast by introducing Dan Rather in Jordan, where he and producer George Crile had interviewed King Hussein of Jordan. The king's concerns in trying to prevent a U.S. intervention had no impact on the events yet to unfold, but looking back, they were prescient.

> KING HUSSEIN: If there is a threat of external pressure or intervention in a military sense, I believe that all this could go out of control. My feeling is that we, as Arabs, ought to have a chance to try our best to resolve this problem. And please believe me, all that intimidation doesn't work, that it could be counterproductive and we could be in a far worse situation than we are facing at the moment.
>
> RATHER: Could you honor us by being frank of what personal emotions that you've undergone while trying to work out some compromise here?
>
> KING HUSSEIN: Sorrow and regret and concern and particularly over the fact that, as has happened so many times in my life, sir, nobody listens, and then suddenly you are in the middle of a crisis. In many, many different parts of the Arab world, if, let us say, there is military intervention, it is going to be regarded by the Arabs, including myself, as an attempt to destroy the Arab nation

once and for all. And this is going to be resented, and this is going to be thought [by] . . . the man in the street and by everybody.

Was he warning of the birth of Al Qaeda? Did he know some of the extreme elements of Saudi culture would never get over the presence of so many Western troops so close to the holiest of Islamic places? Looking back, it sure seems that he did.

That interview took place almost two months before the new season of *60 Minutes* was set to start. But there was already an energy around our floor and, for the first time in years, a real commitment to break stories of great importance. And there were many stories to report. That August of the invasion, there were real fears that Saddam Hussein would use chemical weapons against American and allied forces. Frank Devine, a young associate producer on the Kroft team, had seen a story in *Newsweek* that said the American military chemical suits, tested in Holland, were considered among the least effective in protecting against an attack. As soon as we told Don, he shouted, "Great! Go!" But the next day, we got the head of the Dutch labs on the phone. He said *Newsweek* had it wrong. The American suits were actually good.

I went to tell Don that the American suits were actually pretty good, and he shouted the exact same thing: "Great! Go!" There was still a story. It didn't matter that it wasn't the one *Newsweek* had reported. This one was even better.

We had three days to get the story. We started rolling on our first interview in Holland at five o'clock on Friday afternoon. The story had evolved still further: the lab director thought the suits were good but could be compromised by the heat of the Saudi desert. As soon as we finished filming, we headed to the Amsterdam airport for a flight to Leeds, England, where the best expert on the subject of protection against chemicals, Professor Alastair Hay, taught at the University of Leeds.

Unfortunately, the camera crew arrived at the airport first and checked everything through—all the gear, all the tapes—rather than carrying it on board. This is a cardinal sin among those who work on short deadlines overseas. When we got to England, our stuff was nowhere to be found, lost somewhere between the check-in counter in Amsterdam and Leeds. We ended up interviewing the professor that evening without lighting or batteries; we used the available lamps and stopped tape after every question to save power. When we had enough—four or five questions and answers—we drove to London, where we were expected to edit our story in time for that Sunday's broadcast. I remember praying that some act of God would help us recover the missing tapes. Lucky for us, the tapes were found Saturday afternoon. They were delivered to the London bureau, and we worked through the night to get the story finished in time.

That same August 26 broadcast included more about the Middle East conflict. Dan Rather interviewed Egyptian president Hosni Mubarak, with Morley Safer reporting from the Soviet Union about how the end of the Cold War was changing Moscow's foreign policy and diminishing its status as a world superpower. It was the most aggressive *60 Minutes* had been about covering a big breaking story in all of its history, and it made Don Hewitt very nervous. Was covering breaking news getting in the way of producing the program's traditional magazine stories?

On September 6, just eleven days after our story about the chemical suits, there came a note from Don on official CBS memorandum paper. I realized it must be important because it went against his opening remarks to me: that there are no memos at *60 Minutes*. But there it was, on my desk, hand delivered to every producer on the floor.

It's all well and good to take bows and curtsies for being number one. But unless you get off your backsides and start working harder, we are going to be lucky to end up number fifty-one. I got enough blue sheets [story ideas] to paper the Great Wall of China, but blue sheets are not what we put on the air. Among other things, your stories stay in editing twice as long as they should.

It was not unreasonable for me to expect that each producer would have two stories ready to go by the time the new season started. After all, we went into repeats eighteen weeks ago. It's difficult for me to figure out what you (with one or two notable exceptions) have been doing since you turned in your last story.

Nowhere in all of journalism are there news people as well paid and as loudly applauded as you are. Come on, for Christ's sake, start turning out stories.

The note shook up the place, though there was also some quiet laughter because of the way he had written it. It was pure Don Hewitt. After the dust settled a bit, I strolled down to Don's corner and asked his secretary, Bev Morgan, if I could have the original. She gave it to me, and I've had it framed in my office ever since.

His note obviously gave everybody a real jolt, because what followed was an excellent season. It included one of my favorites, a story called "Cream Puff" about how used-car wholesalers in Houston were rolling back odometers—or "busting miles"—before re-selling their cars to dealers at higher costs. It's funny that it became such a classic because Steve Kroft didn't really think it was much of a story at first (rolling back odometers was not his idea of groundbreaking original reporting), at least not until he and producer Bob Anderson met the so-called granddaddy of the Houston mile busters, a large fellow named Bill Whitlow. He came right out of central casting. He made $50,000 a month tax free rolling back odometers, a practice that Steve and Bob knew they could capture only by using a hidden camera. So they concealed one behind a wall. Steve put on a pair of sunglasses,

Steve Kroft confronted Bill Whitlow, a Houston "mile buster," for a story that aired December 9, 1990.

posed as a potential investor in the illegal rollback operation, and listened as Whitlow admitted to the scheme. When he was done, Steve walked Whitlow over to the wall where the camera was hidden and had him look right into the lens. What followed was one of the best punch lines in *60 Minutes* history:

> KROFT: I want to show you one thing.
>
> WHITLOW: All right.
>
> KROFT: You know what's back there?
>
> WHITLOW: No.
>
> KROFT: It's a TV camera back there.
>
> WHITLOW: Oh, is it?
>
> KROFT: Yeah. Yeah, we've been taping this whole thing.
>
> WHITLOW: Well, all right.
>
> KROFT: The good news is we're not cops.
>
> WHITLOW: Well, I didn't think so.
>
> KROFT: The bad news is we're *60 Minutes*.

Steve has said he had a ball delivering that line, and, to this day, it still gets a laugh. But not from Bill Whitlow. He was sentenced to six years in prison and blamed Steve. "I think you could scrape the bottom of hell with a fine-tooth comb," he said later, "and never come up with a man like Steve Kroft."

· · ·

But as lively and successful as the season was, Don Hewitt was also facing new challenges. One of the worst moments of Don's career—something he never expected to be so debilitating—came when he was chastised for a Mike Wallace report about the Temple Mount killings in Israel. It kept him up at night that his own company, CBS, which had helped give birth to the best kind of broadcast journalism, was now against him for a story he knew *60 Minutes* got right.

The Temple Mount, located on a hill in East Jerusalem, is one of the holiest sites in the world for both Jews and Muslims—and one of the most contested. On October 8, 1990, three years into the Palestinian uprising, or intifada, in the occupied territories, the Temple Mount was the site of a violent clash between Israeli police and Palestinian demonstrators. When it was over, seventeen Palestinians had been killed, and about three hundred more had been injured. The Israeli government defended the police, saying they had no choice but to use deadly force, and that was how the story was generally reported, including on the *CBS Evening News*. But that was not how Mike Wallace and producer Barry Lando reported the story on *60 Minutes*, which didn't go over well with the American Jewish community—or with CBS's big boss and owner, Laurence "Larry" Tisch.

Mike Wallace presented Palestinian eyewitness accounts and video that portrayed the Israeli army as aggressors using brutal force against un-armed Palestinians.

The response to the story was swift and severe. The Anti-Defamation League accused *60 Minutes* of demonstrating "clearly a bias and prejudicial attitude towards the incident." There was a barrage of letters from viewers, some of which Morley Safer read the week after the story aired:

"Too bad you couldn't find your swastika arm band to wear during that report."

"It was vicious propaganda aimed at the heart of Israel."

Don Hewitt had to defend himself to friends. He walked out of a Manhattan dinner party after Barbara Walters and Mort Zuckerman, the owner of *U.S. News & World Report*, had criticized the story for being biased against Israel. Don told the

Larry Tisch and Don Hewitt may have been all smiles at this reception but there was no love lost between the two men.

Los Angeles Times: "They zeroed in on me, giving me a lecture, and I began to feel like I'd just painted a swastika on the door. Why can I question the Bush administration without being called a self-hating American, and not question the Shamir administration [in Israel] without being called a self-hating Jew?" Yitzhak Shamir was then the Israeli prime minister.

But nothing got to Don as much as the reaction he got from Larry Tisch, who was an ardent supporter of Israel and very influential in the American Jewish community. Don had worried when Tisch took over CBS in 1986 that covering Israel under him would be tough. He was right. After the Temple Mount story aired, Tisch summoned Don and Mike to a breakfast meeting and asked them to defend the story—which they did. But their answers didn't appear to satisfy him.

Don saw Tisch at a cocktail party not long after the piece aired. He told the story of walking up to him and saying, "Hi, boss." According to Don, "Don't you 'Hi, boss' me" was what he got in return. Tisch then walked away.

That attitude continued even after an Israeli judge, Ezra Kama, began uncovering evidence that contradicted much of the Israeli government's version of events and showed that things had played out largely the way *60 Minutes* reported. Don felt vindicated and said as much in a letter he wrote to Abraham Foxman, then national director of the Anti-Defamation League:

> *The vilification Mike and I suffered at the hands of our fellow Jews was touched off by the reaction of Jewish leaders to what* 60 Minutes *said about the 'Temple Mount Incident.' Now that a Jerusalem judge has said ostensibly the same thing, is it unreasonable to think that some of those Jewish leaders will so inform their congregations and that maybe, just maybe, some of those who wrote such vile, nasty letters might want to take this opportunity to say they were wrong?*

Three months later, the Israeli judge issued his final report. Abe Foxman sent a letter of apology to Don:

The facts are now in regarding the Temple Mount incident. Judge Kama rejects some of the claims the Israeli officials made and came closer to some of the conclusions reached by 60 Minutes. *On that basis, while I still have some problems with the methodology* 60 Minutes *used, I want to publicly apologize to you, Mike, and the staff of* 60 Minutes. *I hope we can put this long and difficult situation behind us.*

Abe Foxman copied three people on that letter: Mike Wallace, Eric Ober (president of CBS News), and Laurence Tisch. Mike hung a framed copy of the letter in his office. As for Tisch, he never acknowledged, at least not to Don, that *60 Minutes* had gotten the Temple Mount story right.

Don said later that Tisch's anger at him and Mike for reporting that story "truthfully and objectively" was the low point of his more than fifty years at CBS.

His staff problems that year seemed small in comparison, but they were more significant than he realized at the time. It involved the new correspondent Meredith Vieira, who had joined *60 Minutes* a few months after Steve and I did in 1989. For those of us in the new generation, Meredith was an exciting addition. She was a great storyteller joining us from CBS's hipper newsmagazine show, *West 57th.* From the moment that program went on the air in August 1985, a rivalry began.

Don disliked *West 57th* because it went against everything he stood for: he thought it pandered to a young audience and tried to be "cool." He believed stories should appeal to every generation. The tension between the two broadcasts exploded when somebody taped an offensive message near the elevator shared by the two staffs. I cannot remember the sign, but I remember people talking about it, and different versions of what it said. One was this: "Eighth floor, video-fluent people get off here." The other was: "Ninth floor, yesterday's people get off here." Either way, they were "fightin' words" and implied that the people on the ninth floor—the *60 Minutes* floor—were old and done.

By season 23, two new correspondents had been added to the ranks: Steve Kroft and Meredith Vieira.

Don, never one to shy away from a skirmish, told the *New York Times* that he doubted the new show, led by executive producer Andy Lack, would pose a threat to *60 Minutes*. "We play major league baseball," he said. "That doesn't mean there isn't room for the minor league."

As much as Don disliked the new program and what it represented, he appreciated some of the fine work being done there, especially by Steve Kroft and Meredith Vieira. So both of them were brought on. It was time for *60 Minutes* to get a fresh batch of young reporters on and off air.

Meredith and Steve were both half-time correspondents, which meant they had to deliver ten stories per season for their first two years, about half of the load of the other correspondents. By the time Meredith's first story was broadcast, there was already tension between her and Don. He didn't like that she wanted to put her baby before his baby, *60 Minutes*.

For Meredith, being offered the opportunity to be a correspondent at *60 Minutes* was a dream. But the offer came a week before she gave birth to her first child. She was always among the most grounded people I had ever met who ended up on the air—so many of them are egomaniacs to begin with. So for her the fact that she was now a mother added a new dimension to her life she would not just put aside for her career aspirations. She took the baby to her first meeting with Don and Phil Scheffler. She didn't remember it as trying to send any kind of message, but it was a fact that the baby was going to have an impact on how much she could do, and they needed to know that.

Not long after Meredith's first story aired in January 1990, she did an interview with Verne Gay of *Newsday*, who described her as "a puzzling mix of elation and unhappiness—even anger—over her newfound status."

Meredith was very open about her predicament. She admitted that she found herself thinking about her new baby as much as her next story. To this day, as she thinks back on it, the anger in that description might have been how she felt toward Don because he was so negative about her situation.

Despite the tension, Meredith's second season got off to a good start: she had an excellent story about the convicted felon-turned-actor Charles Dutton that aired on the season premiere in September. She followed that with a story about the influence of the Japanese lobby in Washington. And a month later she had perhaps her most memorable story, a powerful report called "Ward 5A," about dying patients on the AIDS ward at San Francisco General Hospital and the nurses who treated them. The story won an Emmy Award.

In November, Harry Reasoner announced he would retire at the end of the season. Meredith knew she would have to carry a full load of stories after Harry's departure, which wouldn't be easy: she had just learned she was pregnant again and her doctors had advised her not to get on a plane for three months. She kept the news from Don—until he called her with

Meredith Vieira interviewed an AIDS patient at San Francisco General Hospital for "Ward 5A," a report that aired October 21, 1990.

what he said was a great story. He told her to get on the Concorde to Paris. She broke the news to him that she couldn't fly because she was pregnant. He assigned the story to Morley instead.

It was as good (or as bad) a time as any to have a difficult conversation. Meredith told Don that, with her baby due in August, she'd be out on maternity leave until well into the next season and unable to do the number of pieces required of her. She asked to work one more season part-time, but Don had no interest in a part-time correspondent, and started looking for a replacement.

In March 1991, CBS News announced that Meredith Vieira's tenure at *60 Minutes* was over. Don's decision launched a national dispute about the feasibility of balancing motherhood and careers that played out in newspapers across the country.

Meredith told the *Washington Post* that she was sorry to lose the job. "I wish they could have shown some flexibility, but I understand," she said. "I felt like I was a trailblazer; there are a lot of women coming up through the ranks and if you're working toward the top jobs, it's almost as if you can't raise a family too . . . I'm 37 now, and I was looking forward to a long career with *60 Minutes*."

Don was attacked for being sexist and behind the times. He insisted that his decision to let Meredith go was not due to her pregnancy but about making his broadcast work. "I need five full-time reporters," he said to the *New York Times*. "I don't care if they are men or women. I need someone who can pull his or her own weight . . . A baseball team operates on 9 players, not 10. You need the same correspondents showing up over and over again to get that familiarity."

I remember he shared his strong belief that correspondents needed to put all of their attention into *60 Minutes* when, years later, I wanted to hire Charlie Rose for the spin-off broadcast *60 Minutes II,* even though Charlie did not want to give up his nightly PBS program. Don thought it was a mistake for me to hire him without his full attention. I hired him anyway because I thought he would add so much to the program. And in retrospect, I think Don made a mistake not allowing Meredith Vieira more flexibility.

But he was also a creature of his generation. Don had many strong women around him, especially in the producer ranks. But there wasn't much accommodation for women who wanted to have children and keep their jobs, until a new generation took command. Perhaps because of the difficulties Meredith Vieira experienced, *60 Minutes* became over time a place where women could choose to raise a family while continuing to work by sharing jobs with other women in similar situations, even before this became the norm.

•   •   •

The allied effort to liberate Kuwait took place in January and February 1991, and *60 Minutes* moved quickly to report from inside the invasion. On January 20 Morley Safer reported on a man who claimed to be one of Saddam Hussein's bodyguards and who was believed to be part of the Iraqi attempt to build nuclear weapons. That same evening, Steve Kroft and producer Lowell Bergman reported on "the man who armed Iraq," the largest private arms dealer in the world, who gave us insights into what American soldiers could expect when they took on Saddam's army in Kuwait.

Nobody really knew what to expect from the Saudi army, the United States's ally, so in early February Ed Bradley and George Crile went to the Saudi capital of Riyadh to find out if they had the right stuff. The conventional wisdom at the time was that American and British troops were fighting the Saudis' war for them. But as Ed reported, that didn't seem to be the case. He interviewed Saudi prince Khalid bin Sultan, commander of the joint Arab Forces, about his relationship with the American general in charge, Norman Schwarzkopf.

BRADLEY: How do you and General Schwarzkopf get along?

PRINCE SULTAN: Many people had doubts before, and as—in the first few months. But I think what happened until now prove that we are not only working together, but we are working and making decisions as—as one person.

Later that month, Steve Kroft and I reported from a Sheraton Hotel in the Saudi Arabian town of Taif, where the Kuwaiti government in exile had set up shop. Multiple generations of the al Sabah ruling family and their servants were all jammed into several cramped hotels. The entire Cabinet worked out of a conference room: monitoring the war, supervising branch offices, and managing the country's $100 billion portfolio by fax machine. The state-owned Kuwait Petroleum Corporation was in room 301. We found them because they had typed out a sign and hung it above the door.

On one early March broadcast, Morley Safer, working with Rich Bonin, compared Syria's president, Hafez al-Assad, to Saddam Hussein and found him just as bad as the Iraqi dictator, if not worse—as we discovered years

Producer George Crile and Ed Bradley with Saudi prince Khalid bin Sultan in the coastal city of Khafji, site of one of the first major offensives of the Gulf War.

later held equally true for his son, Bashar. Here's how Amnesty International's executive director, Jack Healey, described the elder Assad to Morley back in 1991: "He's been the low-key player in the Middle East. He's been clever, but essentially his determination to kill his own people, torture his own people, has been every bit as tenacious, as tough, as mean as Saddam Hussein."

CBS News correspondent Bob Simon after his release from Iraqi captivity in March 1991.

• • •

The war officially ended after just six weeks on February 28, but there was still huge unfinished business for CBS News. Bob Simon and his team had disappeared in the Saudi Arabian desert more than a month earlier, their car found abandoned at a customs post near the Kuwaiti border. They had been checking out the so-called no-man's-land between the two countries when out of nowhere some Iraqi soldiers drove up in a jeep and took them away. CBS launched a campaign to find the men, not knowing, for much of the time, where they were or if they were dead or alive. Diplomats, government leaders, journalists, and private citizens appealed to Saddam Hussein for their release—and on March 2, two days after the end of the war, he complied. They had been missing for forty days.

Getting Bob and his team back was a huge relief to all of us. The next day, at a London hospital, Bob, Peter Bluff, Roberto Alvarez, and Juan Caldera told Ed Bradley about their ordeal for that Sunday's edition of *60 Minutes*. Bob described being held in solitary confinement for twenty-four days, while he and his colleagues were blindfolded, interrogated, starved, and beaten with sticks and canes.

SIMON: If you had asked me at any time during these twenty-four days—and this will be a horrible admission—"What do you want more than anything else, apart from being free? If you could have anything now, would you want to see your wife? Would you want

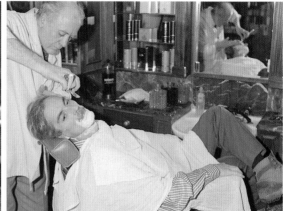

CBS News cameraman Roberto Alvarez, correspondent Bob Simon, soundman Juan Caldera, and producer Peter Bluff appeared on *60 Minutes* on March 3, 1991, just a day after they were released from Iraqi captivity.

Bob Simon got a shave in London in March 1991 after being released from captivity in Iraq.

to see your daughter?" I'd say no. I want food. At one point, I heard somebody being brought up onto—onto the floor, and I heard him being kicked. Four times he was being kicked. But I was so deep at that moment, so deep—I was walking down Broadway with a chocolate ice cream cone in one hand and some popcorn in the other—that I couldn't pay attention to the kicking. You develop defense mechanisms you don't know you're capable of.

BRADLEY: Has it changed you?

SIMON: Yeah.

BRADLEY: How?

SIMON: I don't know. It's too early to tell.

BRADLEY: You've covered virtually every war, skirmish that there has been. Is this it?

SIMON: Don't know. I think I'll cover wars again, but it will never be the same, because what permitted me to cover wars the way I did, what permitted Peter [Bluff] to cover wars the way he did—and we've done many together—is, I think, a certain childlike sense of invincibility, but that's gone. And I'll never get it back.

Bob's capture and recovery—and his typical elegance in getting across what had happened to him—made Don certain he wanted him at *60 Minutes*.

SEASON

24

1991 to 1992

Watch *60 Minutes*. I've said all I'm going to say, and I'm not going to say any more.

—Bill Clinton

Television news correspondents are different from average humans in many ways. Time in front of the camera is oxygen to them. They need it to function. But sometimes being on TV too much goes to their heads. Edward R. Murrow called the experience "heady wine." Dan Rather called it "rocket fuel for the ego."

There are other attributes that set them apart. They say "me" a lot more than the rest of us and tend to smile when they watch themselves on television. They often don't get along with one another because they're too competitive. They're the ones who came up with that famous term to describe themselves: the talent.

I once introduced Ed Bradley at an awards ceremony with lines like that. It was in a big Washington ballroom in front of about a thousand

Ed Bradley and Jeff Fager hit it off from day one.

people—all of them television people, so they were enjoying it. Ed looked a little nervous, though, until I said, "Hiding among the aliens is a real human being, Ed Bradley."

It was a joke and it got a laugh, but it really didn't apply to most *60 Minutes* correspondents, who have almost all been real human beings, even if very intense ones.

Ed was the perfect correspondent for *60 Minutes*. He was blessed with many good qualities, including this: he could be spontaneous. No matter how the subject responded, Ed could come up with just the right next question. That turned out to be an especially valuable skill when he met with Bob Dylan for one of my all-time favorite interviews. Ed knew that all the notes in the world probably wouldn't do him much good sitting across from someone as elusive and mercurial as Dylan. The best interviewers go into it understanding that it isn't about them, it is about what they can get out of their subject that is somehow illuminating or revealing. With Ed it was never about him, and always about the story.

The Dylan interview got off to a rocky start. It was conducted in an old hotel in Northampton, Massachusetts, and the electrical system couldn't handle all the lights and cables the camera crews had plugged in. Just a few questions in, a fuse blew. The room went pitch black. There was silence until a familiar singsongy voice pierced the darkness: "Whoa, the lights went out." It broke the tension.

When the lights came back on, Ed got Dylan to reminisce about his early songwriting.

> BRADLEY: I've read somewhere that you wrote "Blowin' in the Wind"
> in ten minutes. Is that right?
> DYLAN: Probably.
> BRADLEY: Just like that?
> DYLAN: Yeah.

Ed Bradley interviewed Bob Dylan for a profile that aired December 5, 2004.

BRADLEY: Where'd it come from?

DYLAN: It just came. It came from like right out of that wellspring of creativity, I would think, you know?

BRADLEY [*narration*]: That wellspring of creativity has sustained Bob Dylan for more than four decades and produced five hundred songs and more than forty albums.

BRADLEY: Do you ever look at music that you've written and look back at it and say, "Oh, that surprised me"?

DYLAN: I used to. I-I don't do that anymore. I don't know how I got to write those songs.

BRADLEY: What do you mean you don't know how?

DYLAN: Well, those early songs were like almost magically written. "Darkness at the break of noon, shadows even the silver spoon, handmade blade, a child's balloon."

DYLAN: Well, try to sit down and write something like that. Th-there's a magic to that, and it's not Siegfried and Roy kind of magic, you know, it's—it's a different kind of a penetrating magic. And, you know, I did it—I did it at one time.

BRADLEY: You don't think you can do it today?

DYLAN: Mmm-mmm.

BRADLEY: Does that disappoint you?

DYLAN: Well, you can't do something forever, and I did it once, and I
can do other things now, but I can't do that.

When the interview was over, Ed told his producers, Michael Radutzky
and Tanya Simon (correspondent Bob Simon's daughter), that he thought
it had gone pretty well, though he likened the experience to having his
teeth pulled without anesthesia. But his pain didn't come across on the air.
I always thought he was the closest anyone ever came to Walter Cronkite;
it all seemed to come easily to him, and he oozed credibility.

All of the *60 Minutes* correspondents over the years have been good
interviewers. They have to be. They're good listeners and respond spontaneously to what's being said. But each has also brought other unique qualities to *60 Minutes*. Mike practically invented the confrontational interview.
Morley presented his stories with elegant prose and a sometimes biting wit.
Steve Kroft was a true reporter who could tackle difficult subjects and then
write about them well, making them easier for the viewer to understand.

With Meredith gone, and before her Diane Sawyer, who left for ABC
after five years on *60 Minutes*, the correspondents were now all men. The
next hire had to be a woman, and the obvious choice was Lesley Stahl. She
was the host of CBS's *Face the Nation* at the time and had proven week
after week that she could think on her feet and be tough in interviews.
Lesley was also a real pioneer, as one of the first women to be hired as a
reporter in our Washington bureau. Just three weeks into the job, she was
assigned what was then considered a relatively mundane story: a burglary
at the Watergate office complex. She pursued the story aggressively—*TV
Guide* once described her as "a watch dog with perhaps a streak of pit
bull somewhere in her ancestry"—and was eventually promoted to White
House correspondent.

•   •   •

In the spring of '91, when Harry Reasoner retired, Don went to each correspondent—the council, he liked to say—and proposed Lesley for the job. One of them voted no. Lesley always assumed it was Morley. But Ed told her years later that it was him. He was afraid she was too much of a Washington reporter

Lesley Stahl was the moderator of *Face the Nation* before joining *60 Minutes*.

who wouldn't have the necessary range, even though, at that moment, Lesley already had more reporting experience than most correspondents joining *60 Minutes* in our history, having covered the White House over three administrations and having moderated *Face the Nation* for years. She answered Ed's concerns about her range soon after joining the broadcast.

Lesley appeared on the 1991–92 season premiere with a story about one of the best brain surgeons in the world: Thoralf Sundt at the Mayo Clinic, who operated on patients that other surgeons deemed inoperable. But that wasn't the story. At the time Lesley profiled him, Dr. Sundt was dying of multiple myeloma, a cancer of the blood cells and bones. His bones were so brittle that he could break a rib just by coughing and had to wear a brace on his body when he operated, which he still did three times a week.

This was unchartered territory for Lesley: a human interest feature story, not the sort of thing that typically interested her. She had been trained, during her time covering Washington, to be objective and to never let on to what she was thinking. But Lesley had grown genuinely fond of Dr. Sundt during the course of profiling him. When she returned from the shoot, she told Don she was worried he wouldn't run her story because her feelings came through. He laughed and explained, "There are stories we do at *60 Minutes* where you're allowed to like." Lesley says she felt liberated.

The press initially cast Lesley as the opposite of Meredith Vieira in her priorities, even though she too was a mother. Lesley said this portrayal made her "extremely uncomfortable," because she thought it implied she was an inattentive mother. She wanted to be considered a complete partner on the broadcast. "It wasn't gonna be the man's club that tried to marginalize me," she said. "It was going to be, 'She's welcome in this club.'" It didn't take her long to become a member of the club and a pillar of our broadcast for the next quarter of a century.

·   ·   ·

Mike Wallace had a way of turning just about anything—even a celebrity interview—into a confrontation, and he did that with Barbra Streisand in one of the most memorable *60 Minutes* profiles ever. Barbra had been a guest of Mike's thirty years earlier on a syndicated nighttime show he'd hosted briefly called *PM East*. But that November on *60 Minutes*, he received a lot of criticism for making her cry.

This was one of their tenser exchanges:

WALLACE: You know something? I really didn't like you back thirty years ago.

STREISAND: How come?

WALLACE: And I don't think you liked me.

STREISAND: I thought you were mean. I thought you were very mean.

WALLACE: I didn't think that you paid that much attention to me because you were totally self-absorbed back thirty years ago.

STREISAND: Wait, wait, wait. I resent this. How do you dare call me self-involved?

WALLACE: Self-involved is one thing. Self-absorbed is—you know something? Twenty or thirty years of psychoanalysis, I say to myself, "What is it she's trying to find out that takes twenty to thirty years?"

STREISAND: I'm a slow learner.

Mike's interviews were almost always good television. It didn't matter who he was interviewing; the viewer always wondered what he might ask next. But the interview of the year was conducted by Steve Kroft with Democratic presidential candidate Governor Bill Clinton of Arkansas and his wife, Hillary, on Super Bowl Sunday, January 26, 1992. It was the culmination of a chaotic week for the Clintons, one that would affect both of their careers in politics.

It began with a *Time* magazine cover story anointing Clinton as the front-runner for the nomination and was quickly followed by allega-

Mike Wallace with Barbra Streisand for a profile that aired November 24, 1991.

tions in a supermarket tabloid that he had engaged in an affair with a woman named Gennifer Flowers, a former television reporter in Little Rock.

The story was immediately picked up by the mainstream media, and Clinton found himself besieged by reporters at every stop on the campaign trail in advance of the New Hampshire primary. It quickly became obvious that the issue would have to be addressed, and soon.

Steve had been in touch with Anne Reingold, a former political producer at CBS who was then working for the Democratic National Committee. She told Steve that Clinton was scheduled to appear on *Nightline* Thursday night, but for some reason the interview didn't happen. When Anne and Steve spoke the following morning, she suggested he do the interview for *60 Minutes* on Sunday, and put him in touch with Harold Ickes at the Clinton campaign, who seemed very interested.

There was one big problem. *60 Minutes* wasn't on that Sunday because CBS was carrying the Super Bowl.

Steve managed to track down Don Hewitt at San Francisco International Airport, where he was about to catch a plane back to New York. Don was all for the idea and began working on CBS to carve out about ten minutes of airtime after the Super Bowl for a special, abbreviated edition of *60 Minutes*. The network was also interested.

So Steve delivered the message to Clinton's young press attaché, George Stephanopoulos, explaining that *60 Minutes* did not have a regular

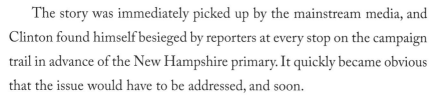

show on Sunday but that it might be possible to get about ten minutes after the game.

George, obviously preoccupied with the campaign, sheepishly asked, "What game?" When Steve told him "the Super Bowl," George went silent for about five seconds before asking, "You mean this would be on after the Super Bowl?"

The interview was on.

The campaign requested that Hillary be allowed to join the interview. Much had been written about her and how impressive she was, but no one had ever really seen her. This would be her political debut.

The Clinton team told us they planned to do only one interview on the alleged affair, then close the book and move on with their campaign. That meant that Steve and producer Frank Devine had no choice but to try and get to the bottom of it all in a limited amount of time, leaving no questions unasked. It would be messy, but the Clintons had decided to roll the dice.

When Don arrived at the Ritz-Carlton hotel in Boston, the place chosen to meet for the interview, Stephanopoulos wanted to make sure there would be some questions about policy; what Bill Clinton would do as president. Don told him that would depend on how forthcoming the Clintons were about topic A. But Clinton was so evasive that there wasn't any time left to talk about anything other than their marriage and the question of his infidelity. Here's how Don described the interview: "Kroft came at them every which way but Sunday, but they weaved, bobbed, and ducked and left the ring, I thought, unbloodied."

KROFT: You've said that your marriage has had problems, that you've had difficulties. What do you mean by that? What does that mean? Is that some kind of—help us break the code. I mean, does that mean you were separated? Does that mean you had communication problems? Does that mean you contemplated divorce? Does it mean adultery?

Steve Kroft interviewing Bill and Hillary Clinton about the Gennifer Flowers allegations.

BILL CLINTON: I think the American people, at least people that have been married for a long time, know what it means and know the whole range of things it can mean.

KROFT: You've been saying all week that you've got to put this issue behind you. Are you prepared tonight to say that you've never had an extramarital affair?

BILL CLINTON: I'm not prepared tonight to say that any married couple should ever discuss that with anyone but themselves. I'm not prepared to say that about anybody.

KROFT: Governor, that's what—excuse me. That's what you've been saying, essentially, for the last—

BILL CLINTON: But that's what I believe.

KROFT: —couple of months.

BILL CLINTON: Look, Steve, you go back and listen to what I've said. You know, I have acknowledged wrongdoing. I have acknowledged causing pain in my marriage. I have said things to you tonight and to the American people from the beginning that no American politician ever has. I think most Americans who are watching this tonight, they'll know what we're saying, they'll get it, and they'll feel that we have been more than candid.

Steve tried again:

KROFT: You're trying to put this issue behind you. And the problem
with the answer is it's not a denial. And people are sitting out
there, voters, and they're saying, "Look, it's pretty simple. If
he has never had an extramarital affair, why doesn't he just
say so?"

BILL CLINTON: That may be what they're saying. You know what I
think they're saying? I think they're saying, "Here's a guy who's
leveling with us."

But Don didn't think Clinton was leveling and told him so during a break
when the camera crews changed tapes. "I think at some point," he said,
"you're gonna have to be as candid as you know how. And then, from there
on, you say, 'I said it on *60 Minutes*. If you want to know what I think or say
on this subject, go get a tape and run it again. I've said it all.' I think you're
gonna have to, or you're not gonna shut those guys up."

Clinton never did get much more candid. But when the interview
started rolling again, it was Hillary who said something that neither she,
nor anyone else, would ever forget. Steve had asked if the Clintons' marriage was an arrangement:

KROFT: I think most Americans would agree that it's very admirable
that you had—have stayed together, that you've worked your
problems out, that you seem to have reached some sort of an
understanding and an arrangement.

HILLARY CLINTON: You know, I'm not sitting here, some little woman,
standing by my man like Tammy Wynette. I'm sitting here because I love him and respect him, and I honor what he's been
through and what we've been through together. And you know, if
that's not enough for people, then, heck, don't vote for him.

What the Clintons did that night did seem to be enough for most people. Bill Clinton went from getting just under 3 percent of the vote in the Iowa caucus that month to more than 25 percent in the New Hampshire primary two weeks after the interview. He went from virtually unknown to one of the front-runners. And when asked about the Gennifer Flowers allegations out on the campaign trail, he used Don's line: "Watch *60 Minutes*. I've said all I'm going to say, and I'm not going to say any more."

Don often said that interview got Bill Clinton elected. Hillary, though, was never so generous about it. She was angry, and Don thought she held a grudge for many years. She admitted to me fifteen years later that she did—against Don and against *60 Minutes*. She told the editor of Colorado's *Grand Junction Daily Sentinel* at the time that the questions Steve asked on the air were not the ones he had asked in the room, suggesting that he had been reshot asking the same questions with a harder, tougher tone. The charge was outrageous enough to get Don pretty fired up. He called Hillary to complain, and she eventually, at least publicly, backed off her claim.

Adding to the day's surreal quality was the disastrous production of the interview itself. Don had decided to ask our local CBS affiliate in Boston, WHDH, for a truck and technicians to tape and transmit the interview back to New York. Unfortunately, they didn't have much experience with this kind of high-profile interview. The Channel 7 team brought in big, bulky lights that overheated. One of them came crashing down in the middle of the interview, just missing the Clintons as they sat on the couch. Hillary jumped into her husband's arms. "Jesus, Mary, and Joseph!" she cried.

It was terrifying. And it was unfortunate, because when the light came down, Hillary had been in the middle of an answer about Gennifer Flowers that was too good to lose. Don must have known because he came running into the room to make sure Hillary wasn't hurt—and to ensure she wouldn't lose her train of thought or, worse, walk out of what had already been a tense interview. It was classic Don. "Are you all right?" he asked

A light narrowly missed hitting the Clintons when it crashed down during their *60 Minutes* interview.

and then added almost immediately, "Wow, that was the best thing you said, with you right at that point. The high point of the whole thing."

•   •   •

The Clinton interview will be remembered as one of the most significant television interviews of the decade. And with thirty-four million viewers, it was also among the most-watched stories of the season, in large part because it ran after the Super Bowl. But the very next week, *60 Minutes* landed another big interview, one that, ironically, also mixed sexual accusations, power, and politics. Anita Hill, who had accused Supreme Court nominee Clarence Thomas of sexual harassment in Senate confirmation hearings just four months earlier, gave an interview to Ed.

She had testified that Thomas had harassed her when he was her boss, using descriptive and obscene language while working together—probably one of the first, and certainly the most prominent, case of its kind, before American culture and workplace behavior started to change significantly.

Don Hewitt rushed to smooth things over with the Clintons after the light fell.

BRADLEY: People say, "Well, I sat there, and I watched her, and I wanted to believe her, but I don't understand how she could say nothing for ten years. I don't understand how she could stay with him. I don't understand how she could follow him to another job." How do you make those people understand?

HILL: I can't make those people understand. I really can't, not from my situation. But what I can do is really to share with those people what others have experienced. One of the things that women do when this happens is to examine themselves, and even to the extent of blaming themselves, their own behavior, their own actions, their own words. And so that is a factor: women not coming forward. Another thing that happens very often is that women are told either by their harassers or by others that they won't be believed if they come forward. And they know of enough experiences of other women where not only were they not believed but they were actually made to be the culprit in these situations.

BRADLEY: Do you think that's what, in essence, happened to you: that you came forward, and they didn't believe you; that in some ways you were made to be the culprit?

HILL: Yes, indeed, that is what happened. And I think that anyone raising a claim of sexual harassment has to understand that there is a great potential for that occurring. But what—what you can only ask for is what I think most of us would ask for: a fair hearing.

BRADLEY: Do you think you got a fair hearing?

HILL: No. I-I don't think that it was a hearing on the issue, and in that sense, no.

We finished the 1991–92 season in first place, something that hadn't happened in nine years. But Don, who told us never to rest on our laurels, didn't rest on his. Instead, in June he traveled to Moscow with Lesley and her producer, Rome Hartman, to interview Boris Yeltsin, the first elected president of Russia, just days before he was to arrive in the United States for a summit meeting with President Bush.

Lesley had done a lot of political interviews before, but the setting for this one was unusual. It was Yeltsin's tennis court, where he was playing Saturday morning doubles at his dacha outside Moscow. In between games, after his daughter wiped the sweat off his brow, he would answer a few of Lesley's questions. The interview got off to an innocent enough start, until Yeltsin alluded to stories that he drank too much, a subject Lesley admitted she didn't quite know how to bring up. Much to everyone's surprise, with cameras filming, Yeltsin accused CBS of doctoring a videotape to make him look drunk during a trip to Washington three years earlier. Nothing could have been further from the truth, and Don got all worked up, jumping out of his seat to deny it. Here's how that bizarre scene played out:

HEWITT: No. Not CBS.

YELTSIN: No CBS.

HEWITT: No. No. Not CBS.

YELTSIN: Cross yourself if this is true.

Don had never crossed himself before. He was Jewish. But he did it, and all was forgiven. The tennis match resumed, and so did the courtside interview. Until Lesley asked Yeltsin about the poor state of Russian health care.

STAHL: I did a story in Saint Petersburg. Children's Hospital Number One in Saint Petersburg. No medicine. We saw two babies die because they didn't have antibiotics.

YELTSIN: Then why don't you give us antibiotics?

STAHL: No bandages.

YELTSIN: You are a rich country. I have my own mother who had a heart attack. She's lying in a hospital ward with ten other patients.

Lesley Stahl interviewed Russian president Boris Yeltsin on the tennis court at his private house outside Moscow.

There's no medicine to treat her heart. I, myself, had to bring some medicine for her from Moscow, and this is the mother of a president.

With that, he stormed off furiously. The interview was over. But they had captured something quite extraordinary, as Don had predicted. Yeltsin came across as a bully who, it appeared, was tipsy and off balance. It was one of our most revealing portraits of a head of state.

SEASONS

25-26

1992 to 1994

I found that I think much better on a typewriter than I do on any other conceivable instrument, whether it's a pen or a computer or whatever. There's a kind of finger-brain connection that works well. Problem with computers is, you just breathe on them, and they'll write something for you that you don't want to even entertain. When you're typing, you really mean it.

—Morley Safer

At *60 Minutes*, there has always been an intense focus on the way we tell our stories. What Don Hewitt taught us, and what Fred Friendly taught him, is that it's the writing that keeps people watching, much more than the pictures.

The stories we report should never, ever be boring. Our job is to cover what's important and to make it interesting. Our stories, at their best, are written in the spoken word—crisp and sharp and imaginative, without unnecessary adjectives or adverbs—never underestimating the intelligence of our viewers but never overestimating their knowledge of the subject.

A memo from Fred Friendly to CBS employees in 1952 about an episode on the Korean War that aired on the program *See It Now* still describes the kind of storytelling that we strive for each week:

"It is not to be . . . an effort to flex our muscles, or to razzle-dazzle with fancy gadgets, exciting switches, or overproduced episodes. We are simply going to try to portray the face of the war and the face of the men who are fighting it. It is our attempt to narrow the distance between the dough foots out there and the people at home who may watch the show. We like to say, *See It Now* specializes in the 'little picture.'"

This is something we say a lot: keep your focus narrow, because a story about the little picture will help people understand the big picture. And always avoid gimmicks. We don't add music to affect the mood, and sound effects are forbidden.

Very few people in broadcast journalism have done all this as well as Morley Safer, who was a dream to work with. For four fulfilling years as one of his producers, I saw him take scripts that I had written and, graph by graph, turn them into poetry.

I remember the first story I worked on with him. I brought him the script, and within two hours, he had rewritten almost every paragraph,

Morley Safer with Jeff Fager, who produced for him for four years.

Morley used a typewriter until late in his life.

Some of Morley's most
memorable pieces were
produced by his best friend,
John Tiffin.

turning it into a Morley Safer story. It always seemed effortless. He would put the paper in his typewriter, look out the window for about ten seconds, and then start typing away. Two minutes later, graph done.

Midway through *60 Minutes*'s twenty-fifth season, in February 1993, Morley and John Tiffin produced a story called "Tango Finlandia." To this day, it holds up as a great story in every way, but the writing, in particular, was superb. One of the joys of our broadcast is doing stories about other cultures; pure adventures into another world. That's what Morley and John did best. They took us places viewers could never go themselves.

Finland is a land of shy, sullen people; a land where alcohol is often overconsumed and long, cold winters help produce the national mood. But leave it to our intrepid pair to find a respite amid the despair with a heart-warming story about tango dancing.

SAFER: This is not a day of national mourning in Helsinki, Finland's capital. These are Finns in their natural state: brooding, private, grimly
in touch with no one but themselves, the shiest people on earth.
Depressed and proud of it. We found that no one looks anyone in

the eye; so intensely private that to be noticed is an embarrassment, to take notice an affront. It's no surprise that Finland has one of the lowest birth rates and one of the highest suicide rates. A nation of Garbos, they all "*vant*," or want, to be alone, isolated by Arctic geography and a language of alphabet soup gone crazy.

So what do they do about this clinical shyness, this almost terminal melancholy? They come to places like this—there are two thousand of them in the country—pay their fifty markkas, that's about twelve dollars, and take part in what has become a kind of national obsession: the tango . . . The Finnish tango is not to be confused with the groin-grinding, passionate, Latin American version. The Finns have managed to neutralize all that—it's a sad shuffle in a minor key, with lyrics to reaffirm a couple's instinctive sense of hopelessness.

Morley knew how to use humor, one of the hardest things to do on television. There was usually also a touch of the absurd. Take this, from his profile of Anna Wintour, the icy and influential editor in chief of the fashion bible *Vogue* magazine:

"To an outsider, these shows are another planet: part dazzling, part *Rocky Horror Show*. Models who seem as angry as they are emaciated, wearing clothes fit for a cadaver."

This was from his story about the contemporary art fair in Basel, Switzerland:

"You can't tell the billionaires from the wannabes; the gawkers from the gawked at; the exhibitionists from the exhibitions. They come to celebrate the bonanza that contemporary art has become. The art market sizzles, while the stock market fizzles. This is where big disposable income comes to be disposed."

His observations always helped pull you into his story. This was about the great American conductor Michael Tilson Thomas:

"He stares down from the podium like some benevolent bird of prey, eyes staring past that great beak. It's all wonderfully choreographed, every gangly movement. But watch the eyes. The eyes of ninety-five musicians watching the eyes of the maestro. Portrait of a boy wonder all grown up, finally fulfilling the expectations of a fickle music establishment."

And this was about the opera singer Denyce Graves, whose story, Morley said, was as good as her voice:

"This is where she grew up: southwest DC. Guns made the music of the street, drugs were the currency, and the violence was not operatic."

Morley and I started season twenty-five with one of my all-time favorite stories, which we called "Mr. President," about Massachusetts State Senate president Billy Bulger. It was the first in a series of stories about the Bulger family we produced at *60 Minutes* over the next twenty years, mostly covering brutal and psychotic events in the life of Billy's brother, the notorious gang member James "Whitey" Bulger, the most ruthless and powerful mob figure in the history of Boston. This was the first story to introduce America to Whitey, who had just walked into the Massachusetts State Lottery headquarters with a winning ticket worth about $14 million. It was widely assumed that Whitey didn't actually pick the winning numbers but had instead forced the actual ticket holder to make him a partner. Then *Boston Globe* columnist Mike Barnicle was quoted in our story as saying the ticket holder was told "he had partners he could not live without—literally!"

Whitey's brother Billy, the senate president, was the most powerful politician in the state and his polar opposite. He was the good brother, not unlike in the classic movie *Angels with Dirty Faces*, starring Pat O'Brien as a priest and James Cagney as his gangster friend. The difference with Billy was that he used a tough guy approach to politics, albeit one mixed with his Jesuit education, fluency in the classics, and love for education, reading, and family. He was obsessed with the Boston Public Library and wouldn't allow a television set in the South Boston home where he and his wife, Mary, raised nine children. But he also appointed his South Boston pals to city jobs, challenged and poked fun at the Boston Brahmins with his Irish wit, and held court every St. Patrick's Day with a roast at the South Boston Social Club, where he led the singing of Irish anthems and took apart everyone who appeared before him.

Here's how Morley described it:

"Billy Bulger says he seeks no higher office, that he's unelectable outside of South Boston, that other world filled with Protestants and *Boston Globe* readers. But year after year, his colleagues reelect him as Senate president, afraid perhaps of that power, or of Whitey, or maybe they're just in awe of a masterful politician. The editorialists of Boston may call for his blood, but for Southie, it'll be some time before Billy Bulger's last hurrah is heard."

At his annual breakfast, which Morley and I covered for the story, the state treasurer, Bob Crane, said, "*60 Minutes* is here today. Can't wait to see that program." Then directing his comments at Bulger, he said:

"You'll wish it were 60 seconds."

Bulger made the best of the tension in the room:

British entrepreneur Richard Branson was profiled by Steve Kroft and producer Michael Gavshon in 1992.

Woody Allen, seated for a *60 Minutes* interview in his Fifth Avenue apartment, with Steve Kroft and Don Hewitt.

BULGER: Morley's going to be good to me, aren't you, Morley? That's how they all start out. "I'm your pal." What—what is it?

SAFER: You just remember I'm editing it.

BULGER: Grab your camera and get out of here!

It was Morley at his best, and he loved it. The subjects of our stories are always nervous about us. It didn't matter what kind of story it was, appearing on camera in a *60 Minutes* interview is intimidating. But Morley made people feel comfortable because he was likeable and fun and approachable.

$\cdot$ $\cdot$ $\cdot$

The 1992 political season produced another eccentric character who made for a good *60 Minutes* piece: businessman and self-made billionaire Ross Perot, who was running for president as an Independent. He dropped out of the race suddenly in July and then just as suddenly jumped back in come October. He told Lesley Stahl that month that he had decided to step aside because of a plan, hatched he said by high-level Republicans, to sabotage his daughter's wedding.

"This was run at the top," he insisted. "You know, everybody up there panicked in May and June when I was leading everybody in the polls, and they went crazy, and they lost their good sense, and they started doing things like this."

As crazy as that claim may have sounded—and it was never substantiated—Perot went on to win 19 percent of the popular vote, spoiling George H. W. Bush's chances for reelection.

Morley and I had profiled Perot the previous winter, after he announced that he was willing to spend $100 million of his own money to run for president as the ultimate antiestablishment candidate. Sound familiar? His campaign was remarkably similar to Donald Trump's, tapping into something other candidates didn't see: Americans were fed up with Washington and hungry for an outsider who promised to ride into town and shake things up.

Here's how Morley introduced him: "Can an independent possibly become president? Well, to quote the *Wall Street Journal*, this is a 'screwy year,' a year in which the outrage expressed by a crusty self-made billionaire might just catch fire."

SAFER: No one, particularly the president, is talking about the deficit.

PEROT: It's like a crazy aunt you keep down in the basement. All the neighbors know she's there, but nobody talks about her. She's kind of an unpleasant thing in the family, and nobody talks about it. If you were responsible for it, and you were trying to get reelected, how could you—you know, with all the handlers in the world and the best propaganda—Goebbels in World War II would envy the propaganda machine we have around the White House.

As Morley and I discovered, a great many Americans were seduced by Perot's straight talk and twangy Texan charm. So was Don Hewitt—though he later admitted it was a short-lived romance. But Morley had a blast being with him and writing about him.

"Perot's message is not a whole lot different from other men who've bashed away at a populist theme: long on what's wrong, short on details of how to fix it. That may trouble reporters and politicos, but it seems to please millions of Americans. And what Americans love most of all is a maverick, an untamed cowpoke, willing to ride in and clean up the town, especially one who's willing to blow one hundred million dollars for a job he says he doesn't really want."

> SAFER: Here you are in your early sixties, you've done everything a
> man can do. And you're just a little bored with success—
> PEROT: Oh, no.
> SAFER: —money, and the ultimate toy is back in Washington.
> PEROT: No. No, no, no. Absolutely not. I wouldn't give you three cents
> to go up there. It's phony. It's artificial. They put you in a bubble,
> and here's what happens so—it won't happen if I get stuck up
> there, I promise you that—they put you up there inside a bubble,
> and all these people start feeding you stuff inside the bubble, and
> pretty soon you don't know what's happening in real life.

60 Minutes ended that season as the most-watched television program in America, again.

• • •

Over the years, the correspondents of *60 Minutes* have turned up in all kinds of places and situations on camera, and a unique one came in the fall of 1993, when Ed Bradley showed up on the air wrapped in only a towel, in a hot sauna drinking vodka with the general in charge of Russia's nuclear missile program. That scene, as well as that trip into the underbelly of the Russian nuclear program and an entire series of reports over several years that tore the cover off some of the most fundamental secrets of the Cold War, was the brainchild of producer George Crile. The same George Crile who wrote the book (that later became the movie) *Charlie Wilson's War* about the US Central Intelligence Agency's covert operations in Afghanistan during its war against the Soviet Union. The same George Crile who produced a documentary for *CBS Reports*—*The Uncounted Enemy: A Vietnam Deception*—that alleged the US military deliberately misled the American public about the Vietnam War; this prompted General William Westmoreland to file a famous, lengthy, and ultimately unsuccessful libel lawsuit, though Crile's violation of CBS News reporting standards badly damaged his reputation—George had gone back to interview a subject for a second time, showing that person some of the material he had filmed from other interviews. It was and is a forbidden practice, similar to leading a witness in a courtroom. Despite that, George Crile was admired by his fellow producers and loved as a friend to many of us.

George was bold, debonair, charming, and a great raconteur. He could talk almost anyone into doing almost anything. Which is how Ed Bradley ended up in a sauna with a Russian general and a cameraman. Who else but George would have come up with that idea? And who else but George could have talked Ed into it?

When George died at the young age of sixty-one from pancreatic cancer in 2006, he left behind a body of work that had the kind of impact most producers can only dream about. And he is a good example of how important producers have been at *60 Minutes*, although their role is misunderstood by most people outside of the television news business. That's possibly because the title *producer* is a misnomer.

The job of a producer varies depending on the news program or company. At *60 Minutes*, there are about twenty-five producers, each of them responsible for at least four stories per year and usually more than that. The producer is primarily a reporter who chases down information, sometimes taking months or years in pursuit of a story. Often the producer is the one who has come up with the idea. Once an idea has been approved by the executive producer and the correspondent, the producer is involved in every aspect of the story: research and reporting, who should be interviewed, what they should be asked, what needs to be filmed, the choice of camera people, and so many other details. The process works best as a collaboration between producer and correspondent, right down to writing and editing the story.

George Crile described himself as a "glorified associate producer," but we all knew he was being modest. He would disappear for weeks on end—to rebel-held territory in Central America, the tribal regions of Pakistan, the streets of Haiti—and come back with boxes of videotapes, pages of notes, and a terrific story. His only problem was that he had difficulty putting it all together. That didn't matter much if he was working with a correspondent who could. Occasionally George would ask a friend for help, and as his friend and office neighbor in those days, he would often conscript me. That kind of collaboration is a big part of what has always made *60 Minutes* a great place to work. I loved working with George and learned a lot just by paying attention to how his brain worked. George, I thought, was one of the greatest interview producers at *60 Minutes*. He could come up with unique and important questions to ask in any setting.

Years before George wrote his book about Charlie Wilson, he produced a Harry Reasoner profile of the eight-term congressman from East Texas who had gotten the CIA to arm the mujahideen in Afghanistan, the same fighters who eventually morphed into Al Qaeda and the Taliban, in their holy war at that time against the Soviet Union. The war wasn't going well for the Russians and had turned, in many ways, into their own Vietnam. Wilson admitted to Reasoner that his support for the Afghan rebels was payback against the Russians for what they did to us in Vietnam—supporting the American enemy, the North Vietnamese, in that war.

REASONER: Is there, among some Americans, a sneaking understanding for what the Russians are going through, particularly the field troops? An enemy they can't understand, they can't defeat, that is being supplied by—in mysterious ways.

WILSON: There's a conflict, because nobody enjoys the anguish that a twenty-year-old kid from Leningrad goes through here. And nobody enjoys the fact of his death, because he didn't have anything to do with it. And that wars have been that way since time began. But, Harry, there were a hundred sixty-seven funerals in my district, and I went to some of them. And—

REASONER: Out of Vietnam?

WILSON: Yeah. One hundred sixty-seven boys from East Texas, from my little congressional district. A hundred sixty-seven. And they didn't have anything to do with it, either. And I love sticking it to the Russians. And I think most Americans do. They need to get it back, and they're getting it back. They're getting it back as we speak, they're getting it back. They're digging for the last stand at Gardez, and they're going to lose. And I loved it.

Harry Reasoner, on the right, interviewing Congressman Charlie Wilson for a profile that aired October 30, 1988.

George's most significant contribution to *60 Minutes* was coming up with original stories of great import. And few things were as important as intercontinental ballistic missiles capable of destroying every major city in America with the push of a few buttons. By October 1993, there was a recognition that the Cold War was over, that the old Soviet Union was gone, and that the Russians were supposed to be our friends, which is why the story George produced was called "Is the Nuclear Nightmare Over?" There was also reason to believe that Russian missiles were no longer pointing at American cities. Why? Because Boris Yeltsin said so.

In the few years since the collapse of the Soviet Union, Russia was in turmoil, and a constitutional crisis over power developed between President Boris Yeltsin and the Russian Parliament. It got violent and became a civil war when Yeltsin deployed the army to attack the parliament building and arrest the leaders of the opposition. In this atmosphere there was uncertainty about how it all might unfold.

Ten days after Boris Yeltsin regained control of his government, the *60 Minutes* team traveled four hours by train from Moscow to Bologoye, a Russian base, and home to forty-seven intercontinental ballistic missiles. There they met Major General Alexander Gribov, the commander in charge of the missile division.

> BRADLEY [*narration*]: The general told us that before he would take us to see the missiles under his command the next day, he would insist that tonight we enjoy an old Russian custom: a sauna, dinner in the room next door, and the traditional vodka.
>
> BRADLEY: To your health, General, and thank you for the sauna—very good Russian sauna.

Once the pleasantries were out of the way, the general took Ed and the *60 Minutes* crew on a tour of an underground command center that could launch ten intercontinental ballistic missiles. There they met two young launch officers who, as Ed put it, could have been ordered to fire missiles that would have destroyed a good part of the United States.

Ed Bradley raised a glass of vodka with Major Alexander Gribov after taking a Russian sauna.

General Gribov explained how that would work.

BRADLEY: If you get the word from Moscow, and all of the codes are
correct—the sequence of events is correct, all of the words are
correct, you're convinced that this is an order to launch—once
you've gone through everything, what's the final step here?

GENERAL GRIBOV: Basically, what they have to do to launch the missile
is turn two keys at the same moment. He has to turn the key over
there, and he has to turn the key over there at the same moment,
and simultaneously you have to push this button.

The launch officers told Ed the system was set up that way in part so
they would never have to bear sole responsibility for launching a nuclear
weapon.

BRADLEY: You never think that you'll be the first to push the button?

LAUNCH OFFICERS [*through interpreter*]: Basically, no.

BRADLEY: Does—does it seem strange today that—that our missiles
are still pointed at you, and your missiles here are still pointed at
America? Does that seem strange?

LAUNCH OFFICER: It really is strange. But I hope that in the near future it will come to a certain decision that'll change the situation
because it really is ridiculous.

That was a headline. And it came not only from the launch officer but also
from the commander of Russia's missile program, General Igor Sergeyev.

BRADLEY: What—what I don't understand is, if there is no threat
from the United States, why are there Russian missiles targeted
on American cities?

GENERAL SERGEYEV [*through interpreter*]: I agree with you. There's no threat. If there's no threat, we should stop targeting each other. Let's do it. I'm ready to do it.

The story hit home with the Americans in charge of the US strategic nuclear missile program, especially General Sergeyev's suggestion that Russia and the United States stop targeting each other. The general was promptly invited to the United States to visit its nuclear sites. *60 Minutes* was asked along too. George and Ed, along with a camera crew, became the only witnesses to a rare and fascinating attempt by military leaders to take the politics out of "mutual self-destruction" and bring some common sense to the conversation. Why are we targeting each other still? That was the question all of them wanted to answer.

Just one month after the Russia story aired, the cameras captured General Sergeyev aboard the Pentagon's top-secret airborne command center, which could launch nuclear missiles at Russia at a moment's notice. And there was the Russian general asking a group of American officers about how their system worked.

> OFFICER NUMBER TWO: He wanted to know if we could also change the target.
>
> INTERPRETER: Retargeting.
>
> OFFICER NUMBER ONE: Oh. Yes, we can do retargeting.
>
> GENERAL SERGEYEV: Yes. Mmm-hmm.
>
> BRADLEY [*narration*]: And getting answers that, not too long ago, the KGB would have spent a fortune to learn.
>
> OFFICER NUMBER TWO: Are we protected . . .
>
> INTERPRETER: Is there a—
>
> OFFICER NUMBER TWO: Not on this aircraft, no.
>
> GENERAL SERGEYEV: No.
>
> OFFICER NUMBER TWO: No.

General Sergeyev was given an all-access tour. He was even welcomed aboard Kneecap, the flying White House—a sophisticated communications plane that stayed near then president Bill Clinton. The general's host was Lieutenant General Dirk Jameson, the commander of all US land-based missiles, who was stationed at Francis E. Warren Air Force Base in Cheyenne, Wyoming. So imagine his surprise when Ed and George showed a clip of their earlier story about Russia's nuclear sites identifying just where its missiles were pointed: Warren Air Force Base in Cheyenne, Wyoming.

> BRADLEY: Where's your headquarters?
>
> LIEUTENANT JAMESON: My headquarters is in Wyoming.
>
> BRADLEY: And which base?
>
> LIEUTENANT JAMESON: It's at Cheyenne.
>
> BRADLEY: It's Cheyenne.
>
> LIEUTENANT JAMESON: Yes.
>
> BRADLEY: Warren?
>
> LIEUTENANT JAMESON: Warren.
>
> BRADLEY [*narration*]: With General Sergeyev standing next to him, General Jameson was not about to let that missile get in the way of his objective. What the American general was doing at the behest of the Pentagon was launching a new strategy for dealing with the men who control the missiles pointed at America.

George Crile knew he was on to something special, and Don Hewitt loved it. During the next decade, George continued to follow up with several meaningful and fascinating reports into the nuclear missile programs of both countries.

Holding on to a good story is not always easy. You have to win over the confidence of often high-placed subjects who will allow you in. And that is sometimes quite complicated. We never want to do a story that the subject will love just so we can keep coming back for more. The goal is to get to the truth. The subject might not always be thrilled about every part of our reporting, but if he or she considers our story fair and accurate, the relationship is usually secure. That truth is really at the heart of good reporting—although it doesn't hurt if the producer or reporter also happens to be likeable. Simple human courtesy goes a long way toward finding things out.

A producer will hold on to a good source forever. Most do so because they're curious people who like to have a wide circle of contacts. And who knows how a person might help with a future story. One of the best at holding on to relationships is Howard Rosenberg, a Washington-based investigative producer who possesses the skepticism, irreverence, and humor it takes to do the job well, with only a touch of the jadedness that can come from covering government for so long. He's also a true original, usually dressed in black and always with a string of press credentials around his neck and a mobile device in every pocket. I've often wondered why

Mike Wallace hitched a ride with Luciano Pavarotti near the opera star's villa in Pesaro, Italy, for a profile that aired September 1993.

he needs multiple iPhones, BlackBerrys, and iPads. Perhaps it's so all the sources he's cultivated and sometimes befriended over the years can find him, and he them.

In the spring of season twenty-six, one of those old acquaintances came through for Howard and Lesley Stahl, resulting in a *60 Minutes* story about a little boy with leukemia named Dwayne Sexton. In 1968, Dwayne was taken to a specially designed radiation therapy chamber at a clinic run by the Atomic Energy Commission in Oak Ridge, Tennessee. There, he lay in a hammock while massive doses of radiation flowed through the walls, ceiling, and floor. What the boy's parents didn't know at the time— and what Howard helped uncover, first for *Mother Jones* magazine more than ten years earlier—was that Dwayne was steered away from conventional chemotherapy, which was not nearly as effective for childhood leukemia then as it is today, so that he could be part of a human experiment being conducted on behalf of NASA and the Pentagon to determine how much radiation an astronaut or soldier could withstand and still function. Dwayne Sexton died, as did all of the children who were treated at Oak Ridge with total body irradiation.

Howard was able to gain access to the radiation chamber, which had since been converted to a storage room, and Lesley went there with Mary Sue Sexton, who hadn't been back since her son was treated there more than twenty-five years before.

MRS. SEXTON: This is the room.

STAHL: You remember?

MRS. SEXTON: Certainly I remember! I stood right here and watched.
    See, they've changed the panels here.

STAHL: Little Dwayne was just back in here all by himself?

MRS. SEXTON: By himself, yeah.

STAHL: Right in this little room.

MRS. SEXTON: Uh-huh.

Lesley Stahl in Oak Ridge, Tennessee, with Mary Sue Sexton, whose son Dwayne was the subject of medical experiments there and died.

STAHL: Oh, wow.

MRS. SEXTON: They've changed it just a little bit. There was a cot-like bed up here, and—with the nylon netting around the sides, and he would—he was sitting here looking at his coloring book or comic books.

STAHL: So how long?

MRS. SEXTON: Three hours.

STAHL: Three hours he would be in here with that high dosage?

MRS. SEXTON: Never stopping.

According to Bob Alvarez, a special assistant at the US Energy Department who investigated what went on at Oak Ridge, the doctors there knew not only that such high doses of radiation were dangerous to children, but that total body irradiation didn't really work.

MR. ALVAREZ: Well, I discovered by 1966 that an external review team of experts basically said that the use of total body irradiation was of little value.

STAHL: Of little value in terms of the cancer patient . . .

ALVAREZ: This is a report: the 1966 Medical Program Review Committee Report, done by the Atomic Energy Commission, of this program. The reviewers said the following: "Abundant data accumulated during the past ten years on total body irradiation has been uniformly discouraging." And they go on to say, "This type of experimentation could be criticized on ethical and possible other grounds."

STAHL: This review committee says it-it-it's uniformly discouraging, and it's unethical, and they did it two years later to this little boy?

ALVAREZ: Well, what's important about this particular review is that this same review also said this research should continue because of the national interests involved in collecting the information about the biological effects of the exposed patients.

STAHL: For NASA?

ALVAREZ: For NASA.

STAHL: For the military?

ALVAREZ: For NASA and the Department of Defense.

Uncovering questionable government practices and holding government accountable is our most basic responsibility; Howard and Lesley did just that again that season with an incredible story about government waste, showing how the Department of Energy was spending more money trying to clean up old nuclear weapons facilities than it took to run them when atomic bombs were still being built. It was a classic *60 Minutes* government boondoggle story—a genre that became a mainstay—that exposed the absurdity of the bureaucracy:

STAHL [*narration*]: At its thirty-five sites last year, the Energy Department spent an estimated two hundred million dollars just on overtime. And remember, they weren't making anything at any of the facilities. At the Rocky Flats plant, the contractor, EG&G, is supposed to be reducing the workforce, but instead, it keeps adding more and more white-collar workers, who spend their time writing work rules. Try this work rule: How many nuclear workers does it take to change a lightbulb at Rocky Flats? This is the work package spelling out the rules for that job, changing a lightbulb in a radiation area at that plant. It's three hundred seventeen pages long. Now, you're going to think we're putting you on, but it took forty-three people to change one lightbulb. It actually took only two electricians less than an hour to do the work, but it took forty-one people more than a thousand hours to put this little plan together.

Quite often, a *60 Minutes* story will have a measurable impact: a law passed, a policy changed, a person indicted or released from prison. In this case, the situation just kept getting worse—a sign, if ever there was one, that Howard and Lesley had gotten it right. The story was called "The $12 Billion Clean Up" because that was the estimate back in 1993 for how much it would cost to clean up the country's nuclear waste. But the cleanup is ongoing, and today it's estimated that the price tag could top $200 billion before it's finished in roughly seventy years.

·   ·   ·

Most producers who have worked at *60 Minutes* judge the success of a television season by how good the investigative stories have been. Nineteen ninety-three was a particularly good year, and Lowell Bergman produced some important stories, including a series of disturbing reports about California prisons that foreshadowed a lot of issues we're still dealing with twenty-five years later. He and Mike Wallace started out with a revealing look at Pelican Bay State Prison's Security Housing Unit, or SHU, a $250 million "prison within a prison" that housed inmates who had committed

Lesley Stahl breaking bread with Suha Arafat and her husband, PLO chairman Yasir Arafat, in Tunisia, for a profile of Mrs. Arafat that ran in December 1993.

crimes while incarcerated. James Gomez, the director of the California Department of Corrections, explained it: "If you commit five murders on the outside, you don't go to Pelican Bay. If you commit ten murders on the outside, you do not go to Pelican Bay. If you stab staff and you stab other inmates, you go to Pelican Bay. What Pelican Bay is for is to isolate those individuals who come into the prison system and cannot behave within the prison system."

The SHU had no windows and no bars, just specially designed automated steel doors. Inmates were held in cells for twenty-two and a half hours a day and under the control of heavily armed guards for twenty-four. They never got direct sunlight and never had direct contact with other inmates, which meant the SHU was eerily silent. When Wallace took a tour, he had to put on a special vest to protect not against bullets but against sharp objects such as spears, knives, and darts.

Mike spoke with two experts who told him that what went on at Pelican Bay was about as bad as it gets. It was cruel and inhuman, and amounted to psychological and physical torture. Dr. Stuart Grassian, a professor of psychiatry at Harvard Medical School who had studied the prison, told Mike that "a lot of the people who end up in Pelican Bay SHU

Ed Bradley and a *60 Minutes* team dressed in chemical suits to shoot a 1994 story on the shores of a radioactive lake in the Kazakh city of Semipalatinsk, where the Soviet Union had conducted secret nuclear tests for some forty years.

are the last people who ought to be there." He found that over a third were psychotic, meaning they needed hospital care and constant monitoring, which wasn't happening.

The story led Mike and Lowell to a similar unit in another part of California a few years later for a stunning report they called "The Deadliest Prison." This story was about the California State Correctional Institution in Corcoran, where the FBI was investigating prison guards for orchestrating inmate fights, betting on the outcomes, and then at times shooting—and in at least eight instances, killing—the inmates if the fights got out of control. The inmates had become gladiators, and the prison yard was their Colosseum.

The most chilling part of the story came from prison surveillance video Lowell obtained of a prison guard using a 9 millimeter rifle to shoot and kill an inmate, Preston Tate, who was involved in a fight that the guards themselves had instigated. Other inmates who were there at the time told Wallace that they were never told to stop fighting before the guards started shooting. Yet an official prison review found nothing wrong with the incident. The killing was characterized as "a good shot," and the review said that the twenty-five-year-old Tate had ignored orders to "stop his aggression on another inmate." A state corrections official admitted later to Mike that Tate had not been the aggressor in the fight, nor did he have a weapon. He wasn't even the shot's intended target. But the shooting was still justified by the Shooting Review Board, as were *all* the shootings at Corcoran.

As a result of some seventy fights in less than a month, including the one that left Preston Tate dead, the governor of California closed down the Corcoran prison yard, though only temporarily. At the time the story aired, a grand jury was investigating the killing of Preston Tate and was expected to hand down indictments. Eight Corcoran guards were eventually indicted for conspiracy and violating the civil rights of SHU prisoners. They were acquitted in 2000.

·　·　·

The start of season twenty-six in September 1993 meant that *60 Minutes* had turned twenty-five. Already it was the longest-running program ever on prime-time television, which seemed a good reason to celebrate. We did so on the air with a two-hour special broadcast hosted by the great Charles Kuralt and produced by Paul and Holly Fine. The special opened with Don and Mike in the screening room fighting on camera. They were always fun to watch, and when there were cameras present, they knew how to scale it up a little bit and lay into each other. A camera captured this argument in the screening room after Don questioned Mike's reference to the ultranationalist Serbian Vojislav Seselj, and suggested losing him from the story.

WALLACE: Why is Seselj important?

HEWITT: Mike. Mike. Mike. Mike . . .

WALLACE: Because he hates Croats, and Croats hate him.

HEWITT: Mike—Mike, you know that.

WALLACE: Oh, come on, Don. For Christ's sake, that's well known.

Now you're—you're—you're gutting the piece.

HEWITT: You can—then forget *60 Minutes*, and you don't get on this week.

Don and Mike loved to ham it up on camera, but this exchange was also indicative of the pull and tug that made us all proud. You could always disagree at *60 Minutes*; it wasn't personal. It was in the interest of making the story better.

Two days before the special aired, a lavish anniversary party was held at the Metropolitan Museum of Art. Dinner was served in the ancient Egyptian Temple of Dendur (Morley Safer wondered aloud if it was an Orthodox temple or Reform), followed by a presentation in the auditorium. Don said he didn't expect the broadcast would last twenty-five weeks let alone twenty-five years. Howard Stringer, president of the CBS television network, said that for more than twenty-five years he had watched Mike Wallace's hair go from black to really black. Mike Wallace explained why Don Hewitt had wanted him to be on *60 Minutes*: "He knew that Harry Reasoner would be the anchor, and he wanted me to be the bad guy. I said, 'This is a possibility.'"

It was a nice evening, even though the ending left us all scratching our heads a bit when pianist Van Cliburn launched into two long classical pieces, the second one dedicated to the recently departed mother of Walter Cronkite. None of us was sure how that fit a celebration of *60 Minutes*, but, then, put all of the producers of *60 Minutes* together in one room and you can expect some criticism.

The party was in mid-November. Just a few weeks later came a jolt: the upstart Fox network had outbid CBS for the rights to broadcast National Football League games. For the first time in nearly twenty years, *60 Minutes* would no longer benefit from the football lead-in. Our program had by then become synonymous with Sunday and the NFL and all that went with it: family and friends and beer and a good time had by all, brought to you by CBS. What would happen now?

SEASONS

27-28

1994 to 1996

WIGAND: It's a delivery device for nicotine.

WALLACE: Put it in your mouth, light it up, and you're going to get your fix.

WIGAND: You'll get your fix.

—Dr. Jeffrey Wigand

"Come on in, the water is fine." Don Hewitt said that a lot about any new program that went up against us. It was a kind of cocky way of saying "We are not afraid of you!" And for most of our first twenty-five years on television, we didn't have a lot to be afraid of. That was about to change.

After many years in the top ten and riding high on reputation, *60 Minutes* was about to go through its roughest patch since the show's creation. The loss of the football lead-in was bad enough; ratings dropped significantly. Then came criticism in the press for being old and out of touch, which might have provided some incentive for what happened in the spring of '96, when NBC launched a Sunday edition of its magazine

Ed Bradley interviewed Keith Richards in New Orleans for a profile of the Rolling Stones that ran November 13, 1994.

program, *Dateline NBC*. It became the first news broadcast to go directly up against *60 Minutes*. He might not have admitted it, but Don was afraid.

But the most explosive and difficult situation the program faced—and had ever faced—was a battle with our own company about a story that took on Big Tobacco. During our twenty-fifth and twenty-sixth seasons, there were several stories about tobacco, and tobacco companies protecting their businesses, that had a powerful impact on public health—and on us as a broadcast. It all came to a head when CBS—the corporation, not the news division—blocked a story featuring Jeffrey Wigand, an executive from Brown & Williamson, who claimed the tobacco company knew about the health risks from smoking but was actively denying that fact.

CBS, fearing a lawsuit, refused to allow the story to air. Wigand had signed a confidentiality agreement with Brown & Williamson: a promise not to say anything negative about the company. CBS lawyers told Don Hewitt that running the story would result in a claim that nobody at *60 Minutes* had ever heard of before: something called tortious interference, meaning that we had induced Wigand into breaking his agreement.

Wigand had come to producer Lowell Bergman's attention when he needed an expert opinion for a story he was working on about safe

Mike Wallace and tobacco whistle-blower Jeffrey Wigand.

cigarettes. Safe in this case just meant safe from starting a fire in a home. Wigand became a paid consultant on the story, making sense of some documents Lowell had obtained, and never appearing on air. After that story was broadcast, Wigand told Lowell he would be willing to participate in a much bigger story, not as a paid consultant but as an insider blowing the whistle. Lowell and Mike Wallace were excited about the possibilities and pitched the story to Don in the spring of '95. Don loved it and sent them on their way, expecting a big story to be ready for the following fall.

While Lowell and Mike started working on their bombshell story, Lesley Stahl and producer Howard Rosenberg reported a terrific tobacco story called "Confessions of a Tobacco Lobbyist." The main character was everything a *60 Minutes* reporter hopes for: candid, well spoken, and ready to reveal details that a lot of people would rather never be revealed. His name was Victor Crawford, and until he was diagnosed with throat cancer, he had been a lobbyist for the tobacco industry, hired to spin the facts about smoking.

> STAHL: You, yourself, said it wasn't addictive when you were smoking and knew it was addictive.

CRAWFORD: Sure. It's not a crime, because I wasn't under oath. It wasn't perjury. And it's what I was being paid to do.

STAHL [*narration*]: Victor Crawford was paid to make smoking seem okay.

CRAWFORD: Was I lying? Yes.

STAHL: And you knew it?

CRAWFORD: Of course.

STAHL: And there were no tugs on your conscience, no second-guessing yourself? No going to bed saying, "I hate what I'm doing. I feel dirty"?

CRAWFORD: Mmm-mmm. My job was to win.

Not only did the story shed light on some flat-out lies, but we were helping people better understand one of the oldest political occupations: the Washington lobbyist. Many DC lobbyists operate entirely respectable practices that are considered an important part of our democracy, but all of them have one goal in mind: the interests of their clients.

CRAWFORD: My job was to defeat legislation that was going to hurt the industry. If I couldn't defeat it, then the job was to wound it to the point where it wouldn't fly.

STAHL [*narration*]: And how would he do that? Well, Crawford says he would use evidence he didn't even believe in.

CRAWFORD: We used to bring a scientist out of the woodwork and have this particular lab do this, and we'd have a poll pulled by some cockamamy pollster saying this, that, or the other.

STAHL: You're walking around with a study, and you're thinking to yourself, "This study's totally bull, but I'm going to give it to this guy anyway"?

CRAWFORD: Oh, sure. Just to show them that the jury's still out, that you shouldn't take away anybody's civil rights until you're absolutely sure what you're doing. How can you be absolutely sure, when this XYZ world-famous laboratory—why is it world famous? Because I said it is, and nobody's checked.

STAHL: I have to tell you, it's shameful.

CRAWFORD: It happens. It happens every day. It happens in every legislature.

In the fall of 1995, all of the focus at *60 Minutes* was on tobacco—and the Jeffrey Wigand story. It was big, and it was traumatic, and it came at a time when Big Tobacco was under fire from many fronts for, as Don put it, "turning a blind eye to evidence of the harmful ingredients in tobacco products." Don dedicated an entire chapter to Big Tobacco in his autobiography. He wrote that the Wigand story had everything:

> An issue that touched almost every American and a lone voice in the wilderness ready to put his career on the line to be a good samaritan and "tell all"—all that he knew about the inner workings of the cigarette company he worked for.
>
> It never dawned on me that CBS, even though it was owned by

Mike Wallace interviewed Radovan Karadžić near Sarajevo in 2005, after the Bosnian Serb leader had been indicted by the UN war crimes tribunal for crimes against humanity. *60 Minutes* cameraman Norman Lloyd captured the encounter.

a man who also owned a tobacco company, would put any roadblocks in the way of doing this story. Boy, was I wrong.

Nobody expected the internal controversy. But for Don, Mike, and Lowell Bergman—and the entire staff, for that matter—it became an all-consuming nightmare that made the scrap with Larry Tisch over the Temple Mount story five years earlier seem almost insignificant.

The company wanted to kill the story. Ellen Kaden, the top lawyer at CBS, explained the company's position on the risk of a lawsuit for "tortious interference" in CBS News president Eric Ober's conference room that September. An ABC News story on tobacco had previously resulted in a $10 billion lawsuit by Philip Morris, the largest tobacco company in the United States. ABC News admitted a mistake in the story and settled the suit out of court for an undisclosed amount.

Mike and Lowell made the case that Brown & Williamson would never sue them. This story was different, they argued. Our trusted lawyers, Rick Altabef and Jon Sternberg, who had been screening all of our stories with possible legal issues for years, objected directly to their boss, Ellen Kaden. Rick and Jon were always our allies in working to get stories *on* the air, rather than keeping them off the air. They were as dedicated to the mission of *60 Minutes* as anyone who ever worked there. And when they raised concerns, about a story or something specific within a story, we listened. In this case they asked Kaden that the tobacco issue be taken to outside counsel for advice because they suspected there might be a different opinion. Apparently Kaden took their advice, and they remember being called to a meeting room to listen in on a conference call from an outside law firm agreeing with CBS and general counsel Kaden that there was a significant risk to the company.

CBS News president Eric Ober also agreed with the company's position, leaving Don without much choice. So Don came up with what he thought would be an acceptable compromise: tell the story of how *60 Minutes* was being blocked for legal reasons from running a story that was important to public health, without using any names and without showing the whistle-blower's face. The program would be just about the legal issues, with the substance of Wigand's story left out.

Here's how Mike reported the story on November 12, 1995:

We learned of a tobacco insider who might know the "whole story"; who could tell us whether or not the tobacco industry has been leveling with the public. That insider was formerly a highly placed executive with a tobacco company.

But we cannot broadcast what critical information about tobacco, addiction, and public health he might be able to offer. Why? Because he had to sign a confidentiality agreement with the tobacco company he worked for; an agreement that prohibits him from talking about anything he learned while he was employed by them. It even says that, quote, "All information acquired by you, including this agreement, cannot be divulged."

The management of CBS has told us that, knowing he had that agreement, if we were to broadcast an interview with him, CBS could be faced with a multibillion-dollar lawsuit. Fact is, we are not allowed even to mention his name or the name of the company he worked for. And, of course, we cannot show you his face.

WALLACE: Is your confidentiality agreement with [*censored*] still enforced?

UNIDENTIFIED MAN (WIGAND): [*Voice only*] Yes, it is.

WALLACE: So that—What?—What are they going to do? Sue you for making this appearance?

UNIDENTIFIED MAN (WIGAND): [*Voice only*] I would bet on it.

The story ended with a personal note from Mike Wallace that was about as gutsy as anything ever done on CBS:

We at *60 Minutes*, and that's about a hundred of us who turn out this broadcast every week, are proud of working here and at CBS News, and so we were dismayed that the management at CBS had seen fit to give in to perceived threats of legal action against us by a tobacco industry giant. We've broadcast many such investigative pieces down the years, and we want to be able to continue. We lost out, only to some degree on this one, but we haven't the slightest doubt that we'll be able to continue the *60 Minutes* tradition of reporting such pieces in the future without fear or favor.

The broadcast made things worse; most critics considered it a cop-out. And the bickering inside the building became intense. One of the characteristics of Don's management style was to create competing teams within *60 Minutes* to bring out the best stories. That worked well when the broadcast was soaring, but in unpleasant times, competition turned ugly. *60 Minutes* was in turmoil, and some of it spilled out publicly. Mike and Morley went on the *Charlie Rose* show together, and Morley, defending the story, said Wigand "wasn't paid, he wasn't threatened, he wasn't promised anything other than an opportunity . . . to exercise his First Amendment right."

But Morley, who had been on Mike's side, fighting CBS's decision to keep the story off the air, was not aware that Wigand had been paid $12,000 as a consultant on the story about safe cigarettes that had been broadcast the previous season. He also didn't know that Wigand had received assurances from CBS that his legal fees would be covered in the event that Brown & Williamson sued him, and a promise from Bergman that the interview wouldn't run without his permission. Morley was furious when he found out, and wrote a letter of apology to Charlie Rose, which he shared with the staff at *60 Minutes*. It said, in part, "I am dismayed that the principals involved in the story deliberately suppressed this information. Both their colleagues and the public had a right to know."

It was a bad fight that needed to be resolved. Within a few days,

Morley and Mike issued a joint statement to say they'd buried the hatchet, saying they had put "too many years of hard work into this broadcast to allow one story, about which we still have honest differences, to affect either the broadcast or our own relationship."

But the broadcast *had* been affected. There were questions raised internally and externally about our having caved in, about our program's mission, and about our future. Don and Mike were fighting. Lowell and Mike were fighting. And Don feared that Lowell was undermining the broadcast by telling everybody who would listen that *60 Minutes* was not what it used to be. To a certain extent, it wasn't: people were yelling, doors were slamming, and the atmosphere was tense. This went on for almost two months. It got so bad that Ed Bradley staged what amounted to an intervention at his Manhattan apartment. With all the correspondents present, he called for everyone to get along for the sake of the broadcast's survival.

Despite that, the very public nature of the dispute started to weigh on Don, and he wrote Mike a letter telling him so. It read, in part: "The

President Bill Clinton took questions in December 1995 from all five *60 Minutes* correspondents about his decision to send US troops to Bosnia.

obsessive nature of the pursuit of the Jeffrey Weigand [*sic*] story, with its strange twists and turns, caused us damage far in excess of any good that could have come to us from publishing it . . . Believing, as I do, in Shakespeare's admonition that discretion is the better part of valor, until the right moment presents itself, I would like to put the Jeffrey Weigand [*sic*] story on the back burner and get on with our business—which is reporting, not crusading."

In January 1996 Andrew Heyward, a well-respected veteran of CBS News, replaced Eric Ober as president. Later that month, the *Wall Street Journal* reported almost all of the Wigand disclosures. *60 Minutes* followed on February 4 with the entire story. Here's how Mike introduced it:

A story we set out to report six months ago has now turned into two stories: how cigarettes can destroy people's lives, and how one cigarette company is trying to destroy the reputation of a man who refused to keep quiet about what he says he learned when he worked for them. The company is Brown & Williamson, America's third-largest tobacco company. The man they've set out to destroy is Dr. Jeffrey Wigand, their former three-hundred-thousand-dollar-a-year director of research.

They employed prestigious law firms to sue him, a high-powered investigation firm to probe every nook and cranny of his life.

CBS management wouldn't let us broadcast our original story and our interview with Jeffrey Wigand because they were worried about the possibility of a multibillion-dollar lawsuit against us for "tortious" interference: that is, interfering with Wigand's confidentiality agreement with Brown & Williamson. But now things have changed. Last week the *Wall Street Journal* got hold of and published a confidential deposition Wigand gave in a Mississippi case; a November deposition that repeated many of the charges he made to us last August. And while a lawsuit is still a possibility, not putting Jeffrey Wigand's story on *60 Minutes* no longer is.

Then came the famous videotape of all the tobacco executives lined up and swearing before a 1994 congressional hearing, with the head of Brown & Williamson, Thomas Sandefur, testifying that he believed nicotine was not addictive. The following exchange between Wigand and Mike is what created all the fuss:

WIGAND: I believe he perjured himself because . . . I watched those testimonies very carefully.

WALLACE: All of us did. There was the whole line of people—the-the whole line of CEOs up there, all swearing that—

WIGAND: And part of the reason I'm here is I felt that their representation, clearly—at least within Brown & Williamson's representation—clearly misstated what they commonly knew as language within the company: that we're in a nicotine-delivery business.

WALLACE: And that's what cigarettes are for.

WIGAND: Most certainly. It's a delivery device for nicotine.

WALLACE: A delivery device for nicotine.

WIGAND: Nicotine.

WALLACE: Put it in your mouth, light it up, and you're going to get your fix.

WIGAND: You'll get your fix.

WALLACE [*narration*]: Dr. Wigand says that Brown & Williamson manipulates and adjusts that nicotine fix, not by artificially adding nicotine but by enhancing the effect of the nicotine through the use of chemical additives like ammonia. This process is known in the tobacco industry as "impact boosting."

WIGAND: While not spiking nicotine, they clearly manipulate it.

Finally, the story had aired. It seemed so strange that it had created such an issue internally. Wigand was a powerful witness to a massive corporate scandal with a devastating impact on public health—his was exactly the sort of story *60 Minutes* existed to tell. It seems even odder today that CBS would have been so obstructionist, and we still do not know why. Was it due to Larry Tisch's ownership of the Lorillard Tobacco Company? To CBS's looming sale to the Westinghouse Electric Corporation? Or was it for some other reason? We may never know.

Battered and bruised, the broadcast carried on. Some spirit and friendships may have been lost for a while, some more permanently, but even with hindsight, it's difficult to imagine how Don and his team could have handled things differently. When the company says you can't broadcast a story, your only option—short of hiring a small army to take the CBS Broadcast Center by storm and force the tape into a machine—is to not air the story. Don could have quit in protest, but that certainly would not have helped. Losing him in those circumstances could have been devastating.

Still, Don had regrets. Everybody did. He knew he wasn't as strong in fighting the company as he could have been. He was too anxious to put it behind him, and, in retrospect, he was mad at himself for that. He had always stood up for his team, and this one time, when it mattered a lot, he felt he had caved too easily. Nevertheless, although the broadcast faced withering criticism for having lost its way even before the tobacco-story debacle, most of the staff got back to work and kept turning out strong stories during that spring of 1996—two of them classics that hold up today as among the program's most interesting ever. Both, coincidentally, featured significant African American figures tied to Islam.

In March came a story called "The Greatest," Ed Bradley's profile of Muhammad Ali, produced by John Hamlin, that revealed the champ's lighter side as well as his battle with Parkinson's disease, which made it difficult for the once-outspoken Ali to say anything at all. It took John about six months to convince Ed that the story was worth doing. "How can we

Ed Bradley with Bruce
Springsteen on the Asbury
Park boardwalk in New
Jersey for a profile that aired
January 21, 1996.

do a piece on someone who can't talk?" Ed asked. John was concerned that the longer they waited, the worse Ali's condition would become.

Just when John had begun to give up hope that the piece would ever get off the ground, Ed surprised him. "John?" he said as they were walking through New York's LaGuardia Airport. "Float like a butterfly. Sting like a bee. Let's do Muhammad Ali." We don't know why Ed changed his mind, but it's a good thing he did.

The highlight of the story was Ali tricking Ed into believing that he would sometimes drift off to sleep in the middle of a conversation and start punching the air. Ali and his wife, Lonnie, had played the joke on John the first time he met them, and John persuaded them to do it on camera. It happened one day when Ed, Ali, Lonnie, and the champ's longtime close friend and official photographer, Howard Bingham, were having lunch, with the cameras rolling, in Cuba. At one point, Ali closed his eyes.

BINGHAM: [*Clucking*] Hey, Ali. Ali. Ali. Touch him. Touch him.

MRS. ALI: Sometimes he does that.

BRADLEY: Yeah?

MRS. ALI: It happened after the [Joe] Frazier fight in Manila.

BRADLEY: What happened?

MRS. ALI: I don't know. I wasn't there. But ever since the Frazier fight in Manila, Muhammad will—it's sort of like—like narcolepsy. He'll just start sleeping, but he'll have these flashbacks. And he'll have—it's like nightmares. And his face will twist up, like he's boxing, and he'll throw punches at people. And he does it at night sometimes. Sometimes—I figured out the thing. Whenever he starts snoring heavily, I have to get out of the bed because I know it's going to start.

BRADLEY: Is that right? So when he starts—

BINGHAM: This is his next round.

BRADLEY: He's not putting on when he's doing this?

MRS. ALI: No. This actually happens.

BRADLEY: Mmm-hmm.

MRS. ALI: And the doctor told us not to really try to wake him if that

Ed Bradley was a good sport when Muhammad Ali pranked him.

does happen because he might end up with a heart attack because it might frighten him. So I don't.

BRADLEY: Mmm-hmm. Mmm-hmm.

MRS. ALI: I just get up and move.

BRADLEY: Mmm-hmm.

Just as Lonnie described, Ali suddenly threw a punch.

MRS. ALI: That's—that's—that's the hard part. You have to sort of—

Then he lunged at Ed, who realized only then that he'd been had. It is always fun to watch a subject turn the tables on a correspondent, because the story was always better when unpredictable things occurred, and it had never happened quite like that before.

When Nation of Islam leader Louis Farrakhan sat down with Mike later that spring, he too tried to take control of the interview, but by antagonizing his interviewer rather than teasing him.

It was just six months after Minister Farrakhan had organized his Million Man March on Washington, a rally that drew an estimated 800,000 people to the capital for the purpose of drawing attention to the issues and difficulties of being a black man in America. Farrakhan had built his ministry around anti-white rhetoric, charging "the white man," in a 1959 documentary, with being "the greatest murderer on earth."

More recently he had gotten himself into some trouble by meeting with Iranian leaders and with Colonel Mu'ammar Qaddafi of Libya, one of the most notorious American foes in the Arab world, where Farrakhan was greeted as a hero. He also went to Nigeria, where the military was not allowing a democratically elected government to take control. When Mike challenged him for visiting one of the most corrupt countries on earth, Farrakhan called Mike on what he saw as Mike's hypocrisy—which Mike *loved*.

Mike Wallace interviewed Louis Farrakhan for a profile that aired April 14, 1996. Cameraman Norman Lloyd and soundman Al Feuerbach are in the background.

MINISTER FARRAKHAN: I will not allow America or you, Mr. Wallace, to condemn them as the most corrupt nation on Earth when you have spilled the blood of human beings. Has—has Nigeria dropped an atomic bomb and killed people in—in Hiroshima and Nagasaki? Have they killed off millions of Native Americans? How dare you put yourself in that position as a moral judge? I think you should keep quiet because with that much blood on America's hands, you have no right to speak. I will speak because I don't have that blood on my hands.

WALLACE: Mmm-hmm.

MINISTER FARRAKHAN: Yes, there's corruption there. Yes, there's mismanagement of resources. Yes, there is abuse. There's abuse in every nation on Earth, including this one. So let's not play holy to moralize on them. Let's help them.

WALLACE: I'm not moralizing. I'm asking a question, and I got an answer.

MINISTER FARRAKHAN: Why would you put it as the most corrupt regime in the world? That doesn't make sense to me.

WALLACE: Can you think of one more corrupt?

MINISTER FARRAKHAN: Yeah. I'm living in one. I'm living in one. Yes, you've done a hell of a thing on this Earth, so you should not be the one to talk. You should be quiet when it comes to moral condemnation, in my judgment. I didn't mean to be so fired up now.

WALLACE: Oh, no. That's good. That's good.

The Farrakhan interview was given extra airtime, and it was worth it. It was a wide-ranging interview about race in America with someone who had always been considered extreme—he had preached a separation of black and white—but who had earned credibility because of his ability to organize the Million Man March. In the interview, Farrakhan said racial issues in America were far from resolved.

WALLACE: Do you still believe in separation of the races?

MINISTER FARRAKHAN: I believe, Mike, that if we can't get along in peace, then we should separate. We have serious differences that are exacerbated now, over time, between black and white. The question that we have to answer: Are those differences irreconcilable?

WALLACE: Are they?

MINISTER FARRAKHAN: I don't know. Have we tried as hard as we could to reconcile them? And if we have and we cannot, then separation would be the best answer.

That conversation took place on the heels of one of the most racially polarizing events of our time: the trial of O. J. Simpson for the alleged murders of his ex-wife and a male friend of hers. From the day in June 1994 that some ninety-five million people tuned in to watch the live news coverage of police chasing that white Ford Bronco carrying Simpson—charged that morning with the double homicide and now a fugitive after having skipped out on his arraignment—along LA's freeways, to the not-guilty verdict nearly a year and a half later, virtually every media outlet in the country covered O. J. Simpson relentlessly. Except *60 Minutes*. The story was good for ratings, but Don wanted to stay above the fray.

However, in early 1996, months after Simpson was acquitted in a unanimous, and deeply controversial, verdict, Don agreed to let Steve Kroft and Howard Rosenberg pursue allegations of jury tampering. Their story, "The Letter," revolved around juror Francine Florio-Bunten, who, after five months on the panel, said she was prepared to find Simpson guilty. But Judge Lance Ito dismissed her after having received an anonymous five-page letter, purportedly from a twenty-year-old receptionist at a literary agency, saying that Florio-Bunten had negotiated a secret book deal during the trial—a violation of the rules.

Nobody involved in the case thoroughly investigated who sent the letter or whether it was real, but there were suspicions that it had come from someone close to the defense. After all, as Florio-Bunten told Kroft, if she hadn't been let go, the outcome would have been very different.

KROFT: Do you ever stop to think what would have happened if you had remained on the jury?

FLORIO-BUNTEN: Sometimes, yes. I mean, it's—I think that it probably would have been a hung jury.

KROFT: You were prepared to fight?

FLORIO-BUNTEN: Absolutely.

KROFT: Why?

FLORIO-BUNTEN: Because I-I don't think I would have been able to see-see it any other way. I mean, I—

KROFT: You think he did it?

FLORIO-BUNTEN: I think he did it.

KROFT: So you're saying that the jury—if you'd held out, O. J. Simpson would still be facing justice?

FLORIO-BUNTEN: Yes, I think so.

Steve then read her an excerpt from the letter.

KROFT: "I know for a fact that my boss has entered into an agreement with the juror and her husband. The working title for the book proposal is *Standing Alone: A Verdict for Nicole*." Any truth to that?

FLORIO-BUNTEN: None.

KROFT: Were you negotiating a book deal?

FLORIO-BUNTEN: No.

KROFT: Did you ever have any conversations with any publishers or literary agents—

FLORIO-BUNTEN: No.

KROFT: —about writing a book?

FLORIO-BUNTEN: Never. All—

KROFT: But you could have made money.

FLORIO-BUNTEN: Yeah.

KROFT: You could have written a book.

FLORIO-BUNTEN: Could have.

KROFT: Why didn't you?

FLORIO-BUNTEN: Because I didn't want to. That's—it—it—you know, I did—I—I don't want to. I don't like it. It—it bothers me. It bothers me that there are other people that do it. It's—it bothers me that it happens in other trials.

KROFT: Because?

FLORIO-BUNTEN: Because the justice system is not for sale. This is not why you go on jury duty.

KROFT: So you think this letter's phony?

FLORIO-BUNTEN: I know the letter's phony. It has to be phony. It never happened.

Kroft and his team tried desperately to get to the bottom of it. The associate producer, Rebecca Peterson, spent two weeks calling and visiting fifty-eight literary agencies in Los Angeles in search of a receptionist based on the details of the letter. Howard Rosenberg hired a forensic document examiner to analyze the letter and a private investigator to sift through the trash outside the office of Simpson attorney Johnny Cochran in search of handwriting and paper samples. Unfortunately, they weren't able to turn up any conclusive evidence, but they did turn out a good yarn.

· · ·

As good as those and other stories were that spring, the year from hell was not behind us. The same March night the Ali story was broadcast, NBC went on the air up against us with its Sunday edition of *Dateline*.

Dateline had been on television during the week since 1992. It got off to a disastrous start when it aired an investigative piece called "Waiting to Explode" in which a GM pickup truck, it was later determined, had been rigged to burst into flames during a test crash.

But while the program had not garnered much critical respect, Don was still concerned about the competition. And that first Sunday night, *Dateline* picked up 12.5 million viewers—a huge rating by today's standards. Still, 22 million viewers watched *60 Minutes* that night.

That first Sunday evening's *Dateline* featured a one-part "investigation" about an Oklahoma trauma patient in need of emergency surgery: the patient was turned away from a hospital and later died. Reviewers seemed to agree the story was a bit muddled. That piece was followed by a profile of an Olympic gold-medal figure skater whose husband and skating partner had recently died of a heart attack. Then there was a consumer alert about nutritional drinks such as Ensure and whether they really provide adequate nutrition. The *Washington Post*'s media critic, Tom Shales, characterized that piece as "thin and watery." He went on to write that *Dateline* "seems 80% packaging and 20% substance. At *60 Minutes*, those proportions are roughly the reverse."

But some media critics thought otherwise. Frazier Moore, a well-regarded reporter who wrote for the Associated Press, had some harsh words for *60 Minutes*. At the time of *Dateline*'s Sunday premiere, he wrote that the longer-running show seemed "out of step. Aging. Old." He also suggested that we would be better off without Andy Rooney. Naturally, Andy did not take that lying down. He responded on the air a week and a half later, urging viewers to write or phone Moore with their views. Which they did. In April Moore acknowledged that the AP had received some seven thousand phone calls and a couple of crates' worth of cards and letters, most of them pro-Andy.

Still, Don was worried. Part of the criticism had focused on the broadcast's stories being stale and not about the world we live in. Don was concerned this might be true, especially if we weren't covering a big breaking story and *Dateline* was. So he set up what was called the "crash unit" to quickly turn around news stories that would be shorter than typical *60 Minutes* reports. He also added three commentators for a new part of the broadcast: columnists Molly Ivins and Stanley Crouch, and political satirist P. J. O'Rourke.

None of it worked. The crash unit was putting out stories of mediocre quality, and the commentators were long and boring. *60 Minutes* ended the season in tenth place in television, down more than three million viewers.

SEASONS

29-30

1996 to 1998

But you just remember one thing: in our first meeting, you must be good to me.

—Tina Turner to Mike Wallace

One day Mike Wallace walked into producer Josh Howard's office and said, "I want to do a story about Willie Nelson."

At least that's what Josh thought he said. And as most producers did when Mike pitched them a story, Josh said sure, okay. He told Mike he would submit a blue sheet pitching the story to Don right away. Then Josh said, "But Mike, just curious, we usually do very hard stories together. Why do you want to do a story on Willie Nelson?"

"Willie Nelson?" Mike said in disgust. "Willie Nelson? I said *Winnie and Nelson*—as in *Mandela*!" And then with real attitude, he snapped, "Heard of them?" He ended with a classic Mike Wallace line: "Excuse me, I didn't realize I had wandered into the toy department." Mike then left the office and, walking down the hall, shouted back to Josh, "Good luck with your next career move!"

Mike, by the way, loved Josh Howard and considered him one of his best producers ever.

Mike Wallace was an imposing figure at *60 Minutes*. He was tough, edgy, fun, bighearted, occasionally mean, full of life, and difficult to work with. When he was around, everyone knew it. If you had gained a few pounds, he would remind you. If he didn't like your story from that past Sunday, he would tell you. If he liked it, he would tell you that too.

He kept everyone on their toes whether you were on his team or not. And if you were on his team—I was not—the rest of us regarded you with a mix of respect and pity. Mike expected his producers and associate producers to make him and *60 Minutes* the number one priority in their lives. He would call at all hours and be mad if they were with their families and unavailable. He would go out with them on a story and complain the entire time that the story was not good enough—certainly not as good as they had told him it was. He would second-guess, pull practical jokes, yell, laugh, and punish everybody around him: the producer, the subject of the story, Don Hewitt, his son, Chris, or his stepdaughter, my pal Pauline— little wonder that he married four times.

Bob Simon in 1997 with Winnie Mandela, ex-wife of then president of South Africa, Nelson Mandela, and *60 Minutes* cameraman Siphiwo Ralo, producers Michael Gavshon and Carolyn McEwen, and soundman Meshack Mokoena.

Mike would walk into an office, measure its dimensions, and inform the occupant that the office of her rival was two feet bigger. And yet here's the best part: most everybody loved being around him. He was a spark, an invigorating presence, and yet he had dark moments that we all knew to wait out. In his essence, Mike was a troublemaker, and he loved that role, on and off air.

And Mike's work was extraordinary. Nobody could conduct an interview as well as Mike. He worked hard at it. He knew how to listen and follow up. And by now, in his seventies, he had learned a lot and refined his techniques. Around this time in his career, Mike defined what he thought made for a good interview when talking about one of his favorite interviewers—Charlie Rose—on Charlie's PBS program:

> With good research you could embarrass anybody, make anybody squirm. You could do it to me. But if you are really after illumination of an interviewee's character—qualities, substance, texture—if you're really after that, you can ask very pointed questions. Questions— sensible questions to get them to talk. You can establish, what you do so well, a chemistry of confidentiality. That was what comes across the table, which, you dirty dog, you have done on a couple of occasions over the past and you got me saying things I have no intention of saying. And why? Because you're two people who know a little bit about the same subject. If the interviewee has respect for the interviewer and feels that the interviewer knows a good deal and is well prepared, you can ask anything and you'll find that the interviewee will be a co-conspirator with you.

By mid-1996, Mike had just come through one of the most difficult periods in his life—the tobacco-story debacle—which had been, to a large extent, out of his control. He hadn't done anything wrong, but his reputation—and the broadcast's—had taken a beating. He started the very next

Lesley Stahl interviewed then presidential candidate Bob Dole in August 1996, on the eve of the Republican National Convention.

season with a segment that gave him a real sense of redemption: a story about a witch hunt led by the FBI and enabled by bad journalism.

It was the story of Richard Jewell, the security guard falsely accused by the FBI and some members of the media of planting a bomb in Centennial Olympic Park at the Atlanta Summer Games of 1996. It was a story about how reporting based on incomplete information can bring great harm to an individual. It was a story that made all of us connected with *60 Minutes* very proud.

On July 27, 1996, the Centennial Park bomb went off in the middle of a crowd, killing one person and injuring more than a hundred others. But the toll could have been much higher. Jewell was at the park that night working as an AT&T security guard when he spotted what he thought was a suspicious-looking backpack and evacuated hundreds of people from the area, undoubtedly saving lives. But within days, the thirty-three-year-old went from hero to villain when the FBI targeted him as a prime suspect in the case, and his name was leaked to the press by anonymous sources. From that moment on, nearly every major newspaper and television outlet ran stories naming Jewell as a suspect, probing his background, exploring his motives, and questioning his character and mental health.

The *60 Minutes* story took a different approach. Tom Anderson, the producer, made it an example of what the broadcast did so well: challenging conventional wisdom to tell the story of a man who was found guilty in a public frenzy without even being detained, arrested, or charged with a crime. In our story, called "It's All a Lie," Jewell was adamant about his innocence; he claimed he had been libeled. He was preparing to sue, among others, the *Atlanta Journal-Constitution*, NBC News, CNN, and a local radio station. Our interview was considered a turning point in the public's perception of Jewell, who was a sad yet compelling figure. He was a simple person living at home with his mother, and he had become a target even though his actions were heroic. He wasn't the guy who did it; he was the guy who first spotted the bomb under a park bench.

Jewell described to Mike what happened next when he and some other security people called a federal agent over to have a look:

JEWELL: He crawled under the bench, and with his penlight—he was— he was lying flat on his stomach, and he was undoing the top of the bag with his hand, and he was doing his flashlight like this, and all of a sudden, he just froze. And he tensed up, and he just rolled— not even moving his arms—he just rolled out of the way. When he rolled out of the way, he jumped up and ran over to the other agents that were standing about ten feet away. What really made me think "Uh-oh, this is bad" is that there was like a little line in training that they taught you, that [they] would instill in you, and it was: if you see an ATF [Bureau of Alcohol, Tobacco, Firearms and Explosives] agent running, you better be in front of him.

WALLACE: So did you start to run, too?

JEWELL: No, sir.

WALLACE: You stayed there within ten yards of where the package was?

JEWELL: Yes, sir. We were just concerned with getting the people as far away as we could as quickly as we could. And, you know, what has been a real pain for me is several of the officers were my friends, and I had gotten to know quite a few of them. And when the blast finally did go off, these guys had put their bodies between them and the people in the benches that wouldn't move and the package.

Mike then showed Jewell a headline from the Atlanta paper: "FBI Suspects 'Hero' Guard May Have Planted Bomb." Jewell told Mike that all of this would haunt him for the rest of his life.

> JEWELL: People will never forget my name. People will be ninety years old that were at the Olympic Games and go, "Do you remember when that bomb went off, that Jewell fellow that they accused of that? Do you remember that?" And people'll be going, "Yeah, I remember that. Can you believe all that?" It will never end, sir.

Richard Jewell came across as an extremely sympathetic character. The real bomber, it was later learned, was Eric Rudolph—a far-right, anti-government, anti-abortion, anti-gay anarchist who also bombed an abortion clinic and a gay nightclub. He hid from authorities for seven years before he was tracked down in a wilderness hideout in the mountains of North Carolina. Rudolph pled guilty to avoid the death penalty and is serving four consecutive life sentences at the Supermax prison in Colorado. Ten years after our story aired, the governor of Georgia publicly thanked Jewell for saving lives that night. Just a year later, Richard Jewell died suddenly at age forty-four. He had suffered from a mix of illnesses, including advanced diabetes.

The week before the Jewell story aired, Mike scored another big interview, this one with the family of the so-called Unabomber, Ted Kaczynski. We have experienced so many random terror attacks in the years since that we hardly remember the Unabomber. But at the time, his acts were incredibly significant.

Mike Wallace and Lesley Stahl interviewed family members of the so-called Unabomber, Ted Kaczynski, including his brother and sister-in-law, for a report that aired in September 1996.

Kaczynski was a Harvard-educated mathematician with a PhD from the University of Michigan accused of killing three people and wounding at least twenty-three more in a series of mail bomb attacks over almost two decades. The FBI had finally caught up with him in a tiny, remote Montana shack in April 1996; his arrest was a front-page story. His younger brother, David, had turned him in, and that September, before Ted Kaczynski's trial, *60 Minutes* broadcast an interview with David and their mother, Wanda.

Oddly, the interview was conducted by both Mike Wallace and Lesley Stahl because, like a lot of people, Wanda was afraid of Mike and had asked that Lesley do the interview. But there was no way Mike was going to give it up, so they ended up doing it together in an unusual double team. The day of the interview, set up by our executive story editor Vicki Gordon, Mike asked about letters David had received from his brother that grew increasingly bizarre and hostile, especially against their parents.

WALLACE: He says, "So, generally, if I experienced any failure or showed any weakness, I found that I couldn't come to you for sympathy. You were simply using me as a defenseless butt on which to take out your frustrations. I was supposed to be your perfect little genius."

DAVID KACZYNSKI: Mike, this is not the same family that I grew up in; that *he* grew up in.

WALLACE: Hmm.

DAVID KACZYNSKI: This is not the same mother that he's describing here. This is a fiction or a fantasy.

Ted Kaczynski's fantasies included accusations that his parents had verbally abused and rejected him.

WALLACE: He claims that because of the rejection, he's shorter than David.

WANDA KACZYNSKI: Oh, well . . .

WALLACE: "The rejection I experienced at home and at school even affected me physically. In case you wonder why Dave is three inches taller than I, I have read of two different studies that purport to show that rejection during adolescence tends to stunt growth."

STAHL: Hmm.

WANDA KACZYNSKI: Well, I don't know. What do you do?

WALLACE: He wanted nothing to do with the family. For instance, in one of the letters, he says, "There is nothing that could ever be important enough so that you would have to get in touch with me. Even if Ma dies, I don't want to hear about it."

STAHL: Wanda, are you okay?

WANDA KACZYNSKI: I'm okay. I'm all right.

The Unabomber interview offered a glimpse of a kind of sociopath we didn't understand well in the nineties. But with hindsight, in modern times, he seems terribly familiar.

Mike Wallace couldn't get on the air often enough. That same fall, John Hamlin, a producer on Ed Bradley's team, couldn't get Ed interested in doing a story about singer Tina Turner. But there was Mike, ready to go, even though he rarely did stories about performers. Unfortunately, just like Wanda Kaczynski, Tina Turner was afraid of Mike—and her concerns ended up at the top of the story when it aired:

TURNER: But you just remember one thing: in our first meeting, you must be good to me.

WALLACE: Oh, I'm going to be good to you.

TURNER: Are you sure?

WALLACE: Why would I be otherwise?

TURNER: Just make sure you be good to me.

Mike lived up to his word. He admitted in the very next narration that it wouldn't be a chore being good to her because she was "a joy to be with offstage and simply stunning when she is on." He rarely showed that side of his personality on the air, but hard-assed Mike Wallace could occasionally be a real softie. But that doesn't mean all entertainment profiles on *60 Minutes* are tension-free. One of the classic examples is Steve Kroft's interview with the venerable actor, director, and Hollywood legend Clint Eastwood. In the middle of the interview, Steve, at the urging of producer

Mike Wallace spoke with Tina Turner at her home in the South of France for a profile that aired November 1996. Cameraman Jan Morgan shot the interview.

John Hamlin, decided to tiptoe into uncharted water and ask the steely-eyed Eastwood a few questions about his personal life.

> KROFT: One of the things I learned in doing research for this story was the fact that you have lots of kids.
>
> EASTWOOD: (*pause*) Yeah, I like kids a lot.
>
> KROFT: How many do you have?
>
> EASTWOOD: (*pause*) I have a few.
>
> KROFT: (*pause*) Seven kids with five women, right? Not all of whom you were married to?
>
> EASTWOOD: (*longer pause*) No.
>
> KROFT: (*pause*) You would agree that this was somewhat unconventional.
>
> EASTWOOD: (*awkward silence*) Yes, it's unconventional.
>
> KROFT: But how would you describe your relationship with those kids?
>
> EASTWOOD: I'm in touch with all of them.

The exchange was unforgettable not because of Eastwood's answers, but because of his expression: a long, cold, silent stare.

> KROFT: (*awkward silence*) When I ask the question about the family, I have to tell you, that is a pretty awkward expression you have right now.
>
> EASTWOOD: What?
>
> KROFT: I don't think I've ever had anyone look at me like that before. It's a real Clint Eastwood look. It's intimidating. You let me know, "Approach with caution."
>
> EASTWOOD: Well, 'cause . . . there are other people that are involved here, and they are vulnerable people. I can protect myself, but they can't.

Steve can give a long, cold, silent stare himself, as those of us who have worked with him know. He is very involved in every aspect of the process,

Steve Kroft got the Clint Eastwood stare in November 1997. *60 Minutes* cameraman Ray Bribiesca shot the exchange.

demanding of himself and others, and totally committed to making every story as good as it can possibly be even after others have concluded that it's good enough. He can be blunt, with a wicked sense of humor, and generous with praise, but Steve would be among the first to admit that a delicate bedside manner is not one of his talents. Sometimes we wondered if he took a course on how to be difficult from the master himself—Mike Wallace.

He is also very discriminating in the stories he chooses to do. When Phil Scheffler, the executive editor of *60 Minutes*, urged him and producer John Hamlin to do a piece on heroin trafficking, using dramatic parts of an award-winning documentary that was set to run on HBO's Cinemax, Steve initially resisted on the grounds that there was no way to verify the authenticity of footage showing a drug courier swallowing condoms filled with "heroin" and smuggling them into Britain. The documentary, called *The Connection*, was finally turned into a *60 Minutes* piece called "The Mule."

Unfortunately for everyone involved, the following year the British newspaper the *Guardian* discovered that the "documentary" had been staged. Three Colombians had been hired to portray the smugglers, and the "heroin"-filled condoms that were swallowed actually contained powdered sugar.

60 Minutes had been fooled before, but never like this.

When it became apparent that the story was a mistake and an on-air apology was in order, Don went from office to office trying to get a correspondent to step up and do it for him on the air. But none of them would. Kroft complained that he never wanted to do the story in the first place. So Don decided he would do it himself: go on the air, spell out in detail how it had all been faked, and apologize. It was something he talked about a lot: when you make a mistake, make an apology. People will understand, he said, that we aren't perfect, that we make mistakes, and that we are ready and willing to acknowledge them.

Here's how his apology went that Sunday:

"My name is Don Hewitt. I'm the executive producer of *60 Minutes*, and I am making a rare appearance on the broadcast this evening to apologize for this *60 Minutes* story that now turns out to be not what we thought it was when we broadcast it . . . Bottom line: we, you, and television viewers in fourteen other countries were taken. To make amends, we felt obligated to lay it all out in detail and ask you, please, accept our apology."

He was sincere and credible. And besides, we all knew that a part of him enjoyed the exposure of having to go on the air to clear things up.

• • •

It wasn't the only time *60 Minutes* was caught off guard that season. Ed Bradley and Michael Radutzky reported on Kathleen Willey's claims that when she went to the Oval Office to ask President Bill Clinton for help landing a job in 1993, he groped her and more. This is what she told Ed:

> WILLEY: He kissed me on my mouth and pulled me closer to him.
> And I remember thinking, "What in the world is he doing?" And
> I pushed back away from him, and—he's a big man—and he had
> his arms tight around me, and he-he-he-he touched me.

Ed Bradley interviewed Kathleen Willey about her allegations that Bill Clinton groped her, for a report that aired in March 1998.

BRADLEY: Touched you how?

WILLEY: Well, he touched my breast with his hand, and I was just startled. I was just . . .

BRADLEY: This wasn't an accidental, grazing touch?

WILLEY: No, no. And then he . . . he whispered in my ear, "I've wanted to do this ever since I laid eyes on you." I remember saying to him, "Aren't you afraid that somebody's gonna walk in here?" He said, "No. No, I'm not." And then he took my hand and he . . . put it on him. And that's when I pushed away from him and decided it was time to get out of there.

White House attorney Bob Bennett appeared in the story to tell a different version of events: that the president had hugged Willey and possibly kissed her on the forehead, but nothing else. The story then took on a new life the Monday after it aired when the White House released nine letters Willey, who was forty-seven at the time, had sent President Clinton after the alleged incident. In them, she asked the president for help getting jobs, including an ambassadorship, and referred to herself as his "number one fan."

Ed Bradley with Joseph P. Kennedy II, one of Robert F. Kennedy's six children who spoke in 1997 about growing up as Kennedys and the problems that had plagued their family.

The big exclusive had turned into a debacle. It was obvious that President Clinton's advisors had held the letters until after the story aired in an effort to discredit Willey. It was pretty calculated and, in retrospect, pretty clever. Clinton's approval ratings remained high after the interview ran, and *60 Minutes* received piles of letters from viewers who supported the president and thought the broadcast was out to get him. Andy Rooney took on that allegation a few weeks later, comparing the letters to those the broadcast received when it ran stories critical of Richard Nixon.

ROONEY: It's not my job to speak for *60 Minutes*, but there's something I want to say. I've known Don Hewitt since 1943, when we were both with the *Stars and Stripes* in London. Don can be a genius one minute and an idiot the next, but he's made *60 Minutes* what it is, and that's not bad. I've known Ed Bradley for fifteen years. He's a consummate professional and a gentleman. Both Bradley and Hewitt are absorbed by their work as journalists. They live for it. Politics don't interest them. They were not concerned about helping or hurting President Nixon, and they are

Steve Kroft interviewed Jerry Seinfeld on the set of his comedy in February 1997.

not concerned now with helping or hurting President Clinton. It's news stories that interest them. The Willey interview was a news story. If you think it fell short of *60 Minutes'* standards, you may be right, but don't suggest that anyone at *60 Minutes* had an ulterior motive by doing it, because you'd be wrong.

The end of the 1997–98 season meant the end of thirty years on the air. There was a special broadcast put together to mark the occasion, but the level of enthusiasm was a lot lower than on previous anniversaries. Don and company had been spending a lot of time in recent years navigating some very rough seas. It's a shame, because there was actually a lot to celebrate. *60 Minutes* had become one of the greatest success stories in all of journalism *and* in all of television. The correspondents and producers may not have thought much about that at the time, but we do now.

So although Don wasn't in much of a mood to appreciate how far his broadcast had come, this seems like an appropriate moment to go back to the beginning and take a look at how *60 Minutes* started: very modestly and with very low expectations.

DECADE

1

1968 to 1978

SEASONS

1-5

1968 to 1973

I hope to restore respect to the presidency at all levels by my conduct.

—Richard Nixon to Mike Wallace, October 1968

Harry Reasoner began the very first *60 Minutes* broadcast sitting alongside Mike Wallace and declaring the program "a kind of magazine for television." It was a sort of mission statement for a TV news show with "the flexibility and diversity of a magazine," meaning that there would always be more than one story and that each story would be in some way different from the others.

It was September 24, 1968, at ten o'clock on Tuesday night. The first story was a report on the presidential campaign pitting Richard Nixon, who had been out of politics since losing to JFK in 1960, against Vice President Hubert Humphrey. The story was put together with film from cameras Don had placed in Nixon's and Humphrey's hotel suites capturing each of their reactions to winning their party's nominations. There wasn't much journalism in it, but what really stood out is what didn't happen. Nixon congratulated

Harry Reasoner, Don Hewitt, and Mike Wallace on the set of *60 Minutes* in September 1968.

Harry Reasoner and Mike Wallace introducing the first story on the first *60 Minutes* broadcast on September 24, 1968.

Director Artie Bloom, seated in the *60 Minutes* control room next to Don Hewitt, helped create the program's timeless look.

133

his campaign staff and basically ignored his wife, Pat, who sat in a corner as if she had nothing to do with the moment of victory. Nixon never said a word to her; he didn't kiss her, hug her, or even go near her.

The broadcast continued with comments from European columnists about the American presidential election and ended with excerpts from an animated film on the history of human creativity. In between was an interview with US Attorney General Ramsey Clark about the deterioration of relations between cops and citizens in big cities—a story that would still be relevant today, fifty years later. In comparison with today's *60 Minutes*, or even the *60 Minutes* of thirty years ago, the early broadcasts were long and tedious. But compared with 1968's *CBS Reports*, an hourlong documentary program that tackled serious topics, the show moved along nicely.

Almost nothing in that first broadcast resembled the modern *60 Minutes*—with one exception. The director, Artie Bloom, ended the program with a shot of a stopwatch and the sound of it ticking to the end of the hour. Don, seeking some kind of signature sound but not really wanting music, liked it so much that he added the stopwatch to the top of the broadcast as well to signal to viewers this was the start of *60 Minutes*. It was brilliant branding. To this day, that *tick-tick-tick* is one of the most recognizable sounds in the world.

There was some debate in later years about who really deserved credit for the stopwatch. Bloom was only twenty-five when he joined up with Don as the first director of *60 Minutes*. He was so much like Don: full of energy and ideas, only on the production side rather than in editorial. He had a great eye and was responsible for the program's classy and understated look that has lived on to this day. He was probably the best director ever to work in the news business—*and* he was fun, a wonderful spirited character. Artie was one of my very best friends at CBS, and I never doubted that the stopwatch was his idea. Don didn't really start claiming the watch as *his* until late in life, but I think he was by then confusing who had the idea and who made it prominent.

The reviews of the first broadcast were mostly good. The *New York Times* called *60 Minutes* "something television has long needed" and wrote that while that program "explored just a few of the many possibilities open to an imaginative editor . . . it was a worthwhile introduction." *Variety* magazine's review was a bit cheekier, saying, "*Sixty* should easily capture the thinking men's homes in the Nielsen sample—both of them." There were doubts, as there are to this day, that a program tackling serious subjects could work in prime time.

If *60 Minutes* were just going on the air today, it would have been canceled after its first year on television. Maybe even after a few months. Of all the shows on the air at the start of the 1968 television season, the brand-new magazine program finished the year in eightieth place—not dead last but pretty close. Still, television was so relatively new that there was room for a broadcast that provided a public service, even if it didn't draw many viewers. And ratings for news programs were rarely discussed in those days. It was considered crass to do that even when I first joined CBS News almost fifteen years later.

Harry Reasoner dined with *New York Times* critic Craig Claiborne for a story about the finer points of dining out that aired on November 26, 1968.

60 Minutes averaged around nine million viewers in the early years when there were few options—just the three networks and a few local stations—so it was not unusual for many shows to attract three times as many viewers.

With that size audience, Don Hewitt had to use his considerable powers of persuasion to get people to join him on his merry ship, as Morley Safer liked to call it. He got some of the best. Who could say no to him? Unless you had a great job with Cronkite on the *Evening News*, joining up with Hewitt on his new program looked pretty good. The concept was very different, and there was an excitement to the endeavor.

At first, *60 Minutes* was given the ten o'clock time slot on Tuesday nights, alternating every other week with *CBS Reports*. Within a year, *60 Minutes* was going against one of the most popular new shows on television: the medical drama *Marcus Welby, M.D.*, starring Robert Young, on ABC. It was a throwaway time slot for CBS and a great opportunity to try something new.

From the get-go, *60 Minutes* took on the personalities of its reporters. Mike Wallace wore the black hat: he was the tough guy, never afraid to ask anything of anybody. Harry Reasoner wore the white hat: the gentleman who covered softer stories with an elegant touch. On just the second broadcast, Mike conducted an interview with Richard Nixon that is a classic to this day. Even with Mike's reputation for getting subjects to reveal things to the cameras, nobody could have known how ironic Nixon's words would turn out to be. "The most important thing about a public man," he told Wallace just a month before the general election, "is not whether he's loved or disliked but whether he's respected. And I hope to restore respect to the presidency at all levels by my conduct."

Nixon beat Hubert Humphrey that November by a narrow margin in the popular vote and a landslide in the Electoral College. Segregationist George Wallace, the former and future governor of Alabama, received more than 13 percent of the vote as an Independent.

Presidential candidate Richard Nixon was interviewed by Mike Wallace in September 1968.

It was the end of one of the most turbulent years in American history. The country was tearing itself apart with racial tension and the war in Vietnam. President Lyndon Johnson had announced soon after the start of the primary season that he would not seek reelection. Just four days later, on April 4, Martin Luther King was assassinated in Memphis. In June came the assassination of Robert F. Kennedy in Los Angeles. At that terrible moment RFK, a late entry into the presidential contest, seemed poised to win the Democratic nomination over Hubert Humphrey and Eugene McCarthy.

60 Minutes, which premiered three months after RFK was shot, didn't devote much reporting to any of these big stories, in part because the staff was so small. With just two on-air reporters and five producers, there wasn't much time or budget for the kind of in-depth investigations for which the broadcast would become famous. Don asked some of the CBS News correspondents from around the world to contribute, to broaden coverage, but a lot of what was original on the early editions of *60 Minutes* came from interviews like the one with Nixon.

At the end of the year, on Christmas Eve, came the program's first attempt to add something to the Martin Luther King story when Mike Wallace interviewed his family about life without him.

WALLACE: I think that some of us sit around sometimes and wonder if the death of Martin Luther King didn't leave the civil rights movement, for a lot of people, leaderless, rudderless.

MRS. CORETTA SCOTT KING: I don't think that this is so. I think that if we're looking for another Martin Luther King, we won't find him because he comes once in a century, maybe once in a thousand years, but there are many other persons now who will come forth, I believe, and assume leadership that they never assumed before, because they feel that there is this need.

WALLACE: But as far as black leaders are concerned, I think that you'll agree, we hear in the papers, see on television, more and more about the young black militants. We hear names like [Stokely] Carmichael and [H. Rap] Brown and [Eldridge] Cleaver and [Huey] Newton and [Bobby] Seale, and you begin to wonder if perhaps they aren't getting more followers than some of the older civil rights leaders.

Mike Wallace sat down with the family of the late Martin Luther King around Christmas in 1968.

MRS. KING: Well, there are those persons who don't—who at least say they don't—believe in nonviolence as a tactic, but I tend to feel that there are many more people who believe—who at least believed, or say they believed—in the things that Martin Luther King believed than there are those who believe in violence and destruction. I think we tend to hear those people who speak loudest, and sometimes they are persons whose message is exaggerated out of proportion. There is this determination on the part of many black people who are called militants that they want right now, and I do too, we want—Martin Luther King wanted—equality—

WALLACE: Now.

MRS. KING: —justice, right now. I think we all want the same things. Our goals are basically the same. But I tend to feel that those things that he gave his life for will become stronger rather than weaker, because he has become now a martyr for his cause, and many of the poor people whose rights he fought for have hope somehow. It's a strange thing, but they have hope that they didn't have before, even though he's not here.

A few weeks later, Mike interviewed Republican vice president–elect Spiro Agnew, the former governor of Maryland. And what a character he turned out to be. Once in office, he took on the press relentlessly, saying that "perhaps the place to start looking for a credibility gap is not in the offices of the government in Washington but in the studios of the networks in New York." His most famous line was calling the press "nattering nabobs of negativism."

During the campaign, Agnew had drawn a lot of negative attention for controversial things he'd said, including the use of ethnic slurs. The *60 Minutes* interview came just a few weeks before Inauguration Day, but Mike asked some very tough questions. It was already his calling card and a style—the toughness—that made him unique.

WALLACE: Are you in any sense a liability rather than an asset to Mr. Nixon? At this moment?

VICE PRESIDENT-ELECT AGNEW: You'd have to ask him. Mike, I think this is the answer that you're looking for. I fully feel that by the time a year has gone by, and I have been functioning in this expanded vice president's role that's been given me, particularly in regard to intergovernmental relationships and the cities, that what I do and what I stand for is going to be so obvious it's going to be very difficult for the people who are attempting to cast me in the role of Neanderthal man to continue to think that way.

It was not to be. On October 10, 1973, less than a year after he and Nixon had won four more years in a landslide over the Democratic ticket, Agnew became only the second vice president in US history to resign after he pled no contest to tax evasion, accused of taking $100,000 in bribe money during his time as Maryland's governor.

·   ·   ·

Harry Reasoner's big interview that first year wasn't very exciting. It was with the Duke and Duchess of Windsor, who gave him a tour of their country home outside Paris, having just put it up for sale. The interview offered a sad look at the onetime king Edward VIII, who answered Harry's questions about his having abdicated the throne after less than a year in 1936 to marry the American divorcée Wallis Simpson.

REASONER: This is a picture of you and your father and—
DUKE OF WINDSOR: My brother.
REASONER: How old were you then, when you became king?
DUKE OF WINDSOR: Forty-two.
REASONER: And you were king for—
DUKE OF WINDSOR: Ten months.
REASONER: Is that long enough to be king?

Don Hewitt (far right) with Richard Burton and Elizabeth Taylor, who were profiled on *60 Minutes* on March 24, 1970. (On the far left is Sara Taylor, Elizabeth Taylor's mother.)

DUKE OF WINDSOR: No.

REASONER: If you had not abdicated, how would that have changed history, do you think?

DUKE OF WINDSOR: As a constitutional monarch, I don't believe it would have changed it at all. I might have tried to exert some, say, advice or pressure, to try and avoid the Second World War, but it was very unlikely that I should have succeeded.

REASONER: So that the changes in your life and the big decisions have been personal rather than historical?

DUKE OF WINDSOR: Sure, yes, I would say entirely personal . . . I said in my book I was very sorry to leave. I wanted to stay. I did my best to stay. But it didn't work out.

The story was bittersweet and genteel, but there was something missing in the early days of *60 Minutes*: a reporter dedicated full-time to the program who could bring a new voice to the broadcast. So when Reasoner announced in the fall of 1970 that he was leaving for ABC to anchor the nightly newscast, Don saw it as an opportunity.

Don wanted his new correspondent to come from within CBS News. At first, he went to Charles Kuralt, who had already made a name for himself "On the Road" covering Americana for Walter Cronkite. But Kuralt turned him down. He was much too independent to give up what he had earned: the near-total freedom to cover anything he wanted for the *Evening News*.

So Don turned to CBS correspondent Morley Safer, who was based in London and had made a mark with his work in Vietnam, culminating in a report about American soldiers setting fire to civilian huts in the village of Cam Ne. "This is what the war is all about," he said.

The Johnson administration was so upset about Morley's reporting that it tried to get him fired. The president famously asked if Safer was a Communist. When told no, he was a Canadian, Johnson reportedly replied, "I knew there was something wrong with him."

It was not surprising that Don wanted Morley. He was among the very few who lived up to the archetype of the CBS gentleman correspondent set by the Murrow Boys. They were scholarly, experienced, tough, and elegant. Don may not have been one of them himself, but he never stopped admiring them. He knew Morley would dignify his young broadcast, and his experience covering the news would help fill a gap.

What *was* surprising was that Morley said yes. Who would give up covering the world for Cronkite's *Evening News*, the most prestigious position in broadcast journalism, to join a program that aired only twice a month and attracted a fraction of Cronkite's audience? He would, and one reason for it was Don Hewitt. Morley thought he was brilliant; worth taking a chance on. And *60 Minutes* would give him the opportunity to do longer-format stories and to work with Joe Wershba, a highly regarded and exceedingly humble producer who had worked with Fred Friendly and Ed Murrow for years—another man Don had brought to *60 Minutes* to elevate his fledgling broadcast.

And so Morley joined *60 Minutes*, although with one condition: his

Correspondents Morley Safer and Mike Wallace in 1970.

contract would stipulate that when *60 Minutes* folded, he could return to his post in London. That language didn't come out of his contract until the twenty-first century.

•   •   •

If Don and Mike were Lennon and McCartney, respectively, George Harrison had just joined the band. Morley was a straight-talking, whimsical character as strong and original as the other two, with an independent creative streak that would bring new ideas and new ways of doing things to the young broadcast. He proved his worth before he even arrived to start his new job: shooting his first story on the plane trip from London to New York, about how US Marshals were trained to deal with hijackings, which had become surprisingly routine in the late '60s and early '70s, particularly with planes commandeered to Cuba.

Just a few months later, he reported a story that was easily the most important in the three years *60 Minutes* had been on the air. It questioned the incident in the Gulf of Tonkin that had ignited America's full commitment to the war in Vietnam—and became as controversial as the war itself.

On August 4, 1964, two US destroyers, *Maddox* and *Turner Joy*, were said to have been attacked by Soviet-built North Vietnamese torpedo boats while patrolling international waters in the Gulf of Tonkin. The supposed attack led Congress to pass the Tonkin Resolution, which gave President Lyndon Johnson the power to go to war in Vietnam. Morley's report suggested that the administration had misled the American people by distorting the facts about what really happened in the attacks. It was the first time *60 Minutes* had taken on the government in such a big way, and yet the story hardly made a splash, in part because viewership was still relatively low. The exposé didn't cause the public outrage it might have if more people had been watching.

The backbone of the story came from Morley's interview with Captain John Herrick, the officer in charge of the destroyer division who was aboard the *Maddox* that night. The captain talked about the confusing events of the evening and about how Washington had pressed him to confirm that the *Maddox* had in fact been attacked. Herrick had his doubts, which he had conveyed in a number of cables.

SAFER: It's also been suggested that Washington was putting a great deal of pressure on you to come up with some positive answers to what happened that night. A positive answer being, "Yes, we were attacked."

CAPTAIN HERRICK: Well, I'm sure they needed one. And that's what we were trying to obtain for them, and we did and sent it in.

SAFER [*narration*]: By six o'clock that evening in Washington, President Johnson had given the final go-ahead for the bombing of North Vietnam . . . And yet, while Seventh Fleet pilots were preparing to attack, the Pentagon was still pressing the commander in chief of the Pacific, Admiral [Ulysses S. Grant] Sharp, to press Captain Herrick on the *Maddox* to, in [US Defense Secretary Robert] McNamara's words, "make damn sure there had been an attack."

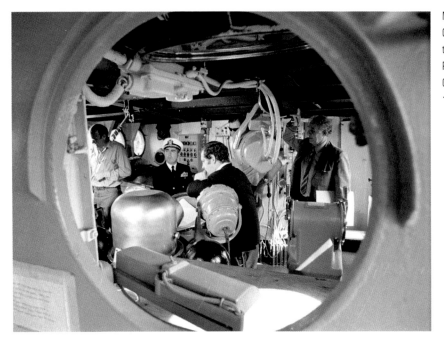

Morley Safer interviewing Captain John Herrick aboard the USS *Maddox* for "What Really Happened at Tonkin Gulf?," which aired on March 16, 1971.

"(1) Can you confirm absolutely that you were attacked? (2) Can you confirm sinking of PT boats? (3) Desire reply with supporting evidence."

Captain Herrick's final report shortly after eight o'clock at night, Washington time. He still had doubts: "*Maddox* scored no known hits and never positively identified a boat. No known damage or personnel casualties to either ship. *Turner Joy* claims sinking one boat and damaging another. The first boat close to the *Maddox* probably fired torpedo at *Maddox*, which was heard but not seen. All subsequent *Maddox* torpedo reports were doubtful in that it is supposed that sonar man was hearing ship's own propeller beat."

But by now it's all academic. President Johnson goes on television shortly before midnight to announce the bombing of North Vietnam.

Morley also interviewed William Fulbright, the longtime Democratic senator from Arkansas, who had been such a strong supporter of the Vietnam War that he helped steer the Tonkin Resolution through the Senate on President Johnson's behalf. As the war escalated, Fulbright was starting to have his doubts. Even before Morley's story aired on March 16, 1971, at a time when North Vietnam seemed to have the upper hand in the war, he led a movement, as chairman of the Senate Foreign Relations Committee, to repeal the resolution and investigate the incident at Tonkin.

> SENATOR FULBRIGHT: I am personally convinced in my own mind that no attack took place on the fourth. But, of course, it's impossible, really, in a way, for me to prove it negative. I'll put it this way: they most certainly did not prove the affirmative case, that there was an attack.
>
> SAFER [*narration*]: But on the night of August 4, 1964, hardly anyone doubted Defense Secretary Robert McNamara's official version.
>
> SENATOR FULBRIGHT: If one telegram, which we later found from Commander Herrick of the *Maddox*, had been made available to the committee at that time, I'm quite sure they would have had long hearings, gone into it thoroughly. And if they had been able to discover the facts as they actually were, I don't think they would have passed the resolution, because it was based on absolutely false, erroneous information. The events that they related then of August 4, 1964, were not true. It was not an unprovoked, deliberate attack. In fact, there was no attack at all.

More than two decades after the story aired, former defense secretary McNamara acknowledged that the Johnson administration was not justified in basing its military actions in Vietnam on the Tonkin Gulf incident. It makes you wonder if what happened in the 1960s could ever reoccur in modern times: Could something as serious as a war resolution be so flawed, so vulnerable to political tampering? But we know it did happen from our fifty years on the air. Both war resolutions in the two Bush presidencies—the one in 1991 to liberate Kuwait and the one in 2002 to invade Iraq—were fraught with questions of skirting the truth and deceiving the American public. And both were covered by *60 Minutes*.

But that would be years in the future. Back in 1971, Don and Morley and Joe Wershba were busy celebrating the Gulf of Tonkin story earning *60 Minutes* its first Emmy Award.

• • •

In May 1971, not long after Morley took President Johnson to task for the Gulf of Tonkin, Lady Bird Johnson took Mike on a dutiful and boring tour of the new LBJ Presidential Library, in Austin, Texas, the one highlight being when the former president stopped by for a brief interview about his legacy. He refused to talk about Vietnam but had something to say about the burden of war on the presidency:

> PRESIDENT JOHNSON: Throughout our history, our public has been prone to attach presidents' names to international difficulties. You will recall the War of 1812 was branded Mr. Madison's war. And the Mexican war was Mr. Polk's war. And the Civil War or the War Between the States was Mr. Lincoln's war. And World War I was Mr. Wilson's war. And World War II was Mr. Roosevelt's war. And Korea was Mr. Truman's war. And President Kennedy was spared that . . . because in his period, [Vietnam] was known as Mr. McNamara's war. And then it became Mr. Johnson's war. And now they refer to it as Mr. Nixon's war . . . I think it's very cruel to have that burden placed upon a president.

It was the only memorable part of the story.

The broadcast ended its third season finishing ninety-fifth among all the programs on television. But Morley had injected a new vitality into

60 Minutes; while the program still didn't have many viewers, there was enough critical acclaim that the CBS brass decided to put it on every single week of the year.

. . .

In June 1972 five men were arrested for breaking into the Democratic National Committee headquarters at the Watergate complex in Washington. The FBI discovered that the men had connections to the Nixon administration's fund-raising organization Committee to Re-elect the President, resulting in one of the biggest political scandals in US history, and the only one to end with the resignation of a president. The *Washington Post* did the lion's share of the reporting on the story that started as a bungled burglary and ended as a twisted web of conspiracies and cover-ups led by the president himself. Nobody will ever achieve what the *Post*'s Bob Woodward and Carl Bernstein did to uncover the details of the scandal—probably not in my lifetime, anyway. But CBS News and *60 Minutes* poured considerable resources into Watergate and ended up advancing the story in a few key places.

One of them was in Mike Wallace's memorable interview with John Ehrlichman, who'd been one of President Nixon's closest advisors until resigning on April 30, 1973. Ehrlichman seemed shifty and arrogant, but Mike didn't let up—and his timing was perfect. It was June 29, 1973, just over a month after the start of the Senate Watergate hearings, which had captivated the nation. There was gavel-to-gavel live coverage by the big three television networks. Mike asked Ehrlichman a series of questions based on what had come to light in the hearings that very week.

WALLACE: Did you see Senator [Lowell] Weicker enumerate a list of the illegal or unconstitutional or unethical acts committed by various persons, either in the White House or employed by officials of the White House?

EHRLICHMAN: No, I didn't.

WALLACE: Let me read them—a list of acts committed by people in the White House or employed by people in the White House or employed by people in the Cabinet: Breaking and entering, wiretapping, conspiracy to foster prostitution, conspiracy to commit kidnapping, destruction of government documents, forgery of State Department documents and campaign letters, secret slush funds, laundering money in Mexico, payoffs to silence witnesses, perjury, plans to audit tax returns for political retaliation, theft of psychiatric records, spying by undercover agents, bogus opinion polls, plans to firebomb a building, conspiracy to obstruct justice—all of this by the law-and-order administration of Richard Nixon.

EHRLICHMAN: Is there a question in there somewhere?

WALLACE: I'm just curious to know your reaction to it. How did it happen?

EHRLICHMAN: Point here is that to make a list like that and say, "How did 'it' happen?" or "How did that climate get created?" it seems

Mike Wallace interviewing John Ehrlichman for a story that ran June 29, 1973.

to me, is to misstate the association of a number of events. That has seemed to be the conscious tactic of some people in an effort to somehow or another make it tougher on the president and the administration. And it seems to me that he is entitled to a . . . a measure of fairness in the consideration of this whole thing that that kind of an approach doesn't give him.

That exchange captures the evasive and combative tone of the interview, in which a very sweaty John Ehrlichman told Mike that the White House had no interest in covering up anything. Two years later—several months after Nixon resigned the presidency rather than face certain impeachment—Ehrlichman was convicted of conspiracy, obstruction of justice, and perjury, among other charges, and served eighteen months in prison.

In the years that followed, *60 Minutes* conducted interviews with several Watergate coconspirators, beginning with G. Gordon Liddy. Known as a bit of a wild man, he was a former FBI agent and prosecutor who once fired a revolver into the ceiling of a courtroom. Liddy got a job in the Nixon White House and eventually became head of Nixon's so-called plumbers—a group of operatives in the president's 1972 reelection campaign tasked with chasing down damaging leaks to the press. Liddy orchestrated the break-in of the Democratic National Committee at the Watergate complex. To secure that interview, Don gave the go-ahead for something he said he would never do again: he agreed to pay Liddy $15,000. Such "checkbook journalism," as this is called, has been taboo for years because it calls into question the credibility of the source and the information. Mike Wallace acknowledged the payment on the air, though he didn't mention the dollar amount. He and Don thought Liddy would be sufficiently intriguing to viewers to justify the payment as well as a condition that Liddy had imposed, also accepted, that he would answer no question about Watergate that he considered to be "substantive." By the time the interview ran, Nixon had resigned. But the interview helped illuminate the type of person who had become a key operator in the Nixon administration. This was especially evident in the way Liddy spoke about White House counsel John Dean, the star witness in the Watergate hearings:

WALLACE: John Dean was the man who recommended you for your job at CRP [Committee to Re-elect the President]. What's your opinion of John Dean?

LIDDY: I think, in all fairness to the man, you'd have to put him right up there with Judas Iscariot.

WALLACE: Judas Iscariot? In other words, he betrayed Christ? Christ being Richard Nixon?

LIDDY: No, he being a betrayer of a person in high position.

WALLACE: And what do you think his motive was?

LIDDY: To save his ass.

WALLACE: That's all?

LIDDY: That's all.

Mike Wallace interviewed Watergate coconspirator G. Gordon Liddy at his home for a profile that ran January 5, 1975.

WALLACE: Shouldn't have said a word?

LIDDY: That's what I feel.

WALLACE: The best thing to do was to remain silent, let Watergate go on, if you will—the cover-up, the works?

LIDDY: I think John Dean should have remained loyal to the president.

WALLACE: Your boss at CREEP was Jeb Magruder. He describes you almost as a comic figure. A "cocky little bantam rooster," he called you, who liked to brag about his James Bondish exploits. Did you really threaten to kill Jeb Magruder?

LIDDY: I think that's one of the few truthful statements that Jeb Magruder has made.

Mike loved the interview. He was quoted saying he thought Liddy performed superbly: "He came off as the Nazi he wanted to come off as."

Just a couple of months later, another Watergate superstar, H. R. "Bob" Haldeman, Nixon's former chief of staff, sat down with Mike. The March 1975 interview was broadcast in the *60 Minutes* time slot—at six o'clock two Sunday evenings in a row—but it wasn't a *60 Minutes* interview. It was a CBS News Special that Don Hewitt had nothing to do with. Regardless, Don took a lot of heat after the *New York Times* reported that Haldeman had been paid roughly $25,000. (The actual sum was $100,000.) While it wasn't entirely unusual for news organizations to pay certain people for the exclusive rights to their stories—a practice since forbidden at CBS News—the fact that it came just two months after Liddy had been paid for his interview did not look good for CBS.

What made CBS look even worse was the interview itself—or at least that's what Mike wrote in his memoir *Close Encounters*. He had tried to justify the payment by arguing that it was no different from the book contracts and lecture fees the Watergate participants received, except that on *60 Minutes* they would be challenged in an interview by a reporter. Mike wrote, "I felt that the best, most effective answer to our critics was to deliver the kind of strong and incisive interview that would justify our venture into checkbook journalism. And it was precisely in that area that we failed."

Mike had expressed his concerns about the interview before he sat down with Haldeman. He was worried about giving a platform to a convicted felon, recently sentenced to two and a half to eight years in prison, who might not actually say anything of any value. And Mike's fears came largely true. Haldeman was evasive and sounded well rehearsed, probably because he had already been grilled so much by government investigators and at trial. If it had been an interview for *60 Minutes*, Don and Mike might have left much of it on the cutting room floor, but CBS News was locked into a contract with Haldeman, so he got his two hours of television and proclaimed his innocence on the air.

This is about as close as he came to contrition:

HALDEMAN: It's a puzzle to me that a man and a team as able as President Nixon and the people with him were could have started out from the very beginning—and I'll take a major part of the blame for this—with such bad judgment as to a matter, as I had—and I think all the rest of us had, at the top, at least—regarding Watergate. And I readily confess today, and I have not publicly done so before, but I readily confess to a serious failure in judgment as regards Watergate, and to a woeful lack of perception as the case developed.

WALLACE: Are you confessing to your own negligence in handling the Watergate matter?

HALDEMAN: I wouldn't say "negligence," because that would imply that I knew something and had failed to do something about it. My admission a minute ago was to a lack of, or a failure in, judgment, and I have to say that I—and I think this applies to all the rest of the top people at the White House and to the president himself—totally failed to perceive Watergate as a matter of major potential danger or of major presidential concern.

Nobody had much of anything good to say about the Haldeman interview, which didn't come as a surprise to Mike. He didn't think much of it either, but both he and *60 Minutes* managed to escape unscathed. Two years later, H. R. Haldeman entered Lompoc Federal Prison, where he served eighteen months.

SEASONS

6-10

1973 to 1978

Are you out of your mind? If you were a KGB agent looking for a place to hide, you couldn't find a better place than *CBS Reports*. Dan, Dan, Dan. Even Ed Murrow couldn't make *CBS Reports* fly. Come on. Don't be an idiot.

—Mike Wallace telling Dan Rather to leave
CBS Reports and join *60 Minutes*

Joining *60 Minutes* as a new correspondent in the early years was not an easy decision. Morley Safer had second thoughts before *and* after he decided to join up. In London, he had sat at the desk once used by Edward R. Murrow—and that *meant* something.

One thing Morley certainly hadn't anticipated about his new job in New York was a nightmare named Mike Wallace. Morley didn't get to see the fun, bighearted side of Mike. He saw the cut-throat, competitive side. It took him a few years to get used to working alongside him, particularly when Mike started stealing his stories. The incident that rankled Morley the most was when he began making plans to report a story about

Jean-Claude "Baby Doc" Duvalier, Haiti's "president for life," who, in 1971, at just nineteen, succeeded his late father, the brutal dictator François "Papa Doc" Duvalier. The day that Morley was scheduled to leave, he was told that Mike was already in Haiti doing the interview with Baby Doc. Morley had never experienced anything like it before; gentlemen correspondents didn't steal stories from each other. Welcome to *60 Minutes*.

Eventually Morley adjusted and accepted that he would win some and lose some. And he figured something out that would have a huge impact on broadcast journalism; a type of piece he could have all to himself: beautifully written adventures, profiles, and whimsical tales about anything at all that intrigued him. One of my favorites from this new genre was called "Last Train to Istanbul," a classic Morley Safer adventure aboard the Orient Express, produced by his best pal: producer and cameraman John Tiffin.

Early in the story, Morley delivered this line to the camera: "Just imagine, the porter has stowed your bags, the champagne is chilling nicely, and the Burgundian chef has prepared a light supper of oysters and stuffed partridge. And ahead of you lie eighteen hundred miles and three days to

Mike Wallace interviewed Haitian president Jean-Claude "Baby Doc" Duvalier for a profile that aired in April 1972.

Istanbul—three days of gourmet dining and deep concern for your comfort."

Nobody could steal that from him, because nobody else knew how to write like that.

·   ·   ·

In January 1974, Mike appeared with a story that became a prototype for many more to come: a piece challenging conventional wisdom and unafraid to take on some of our own, including, of all people, Walter Cronkite. The story, called "Press Junket," examined the practice of reporters accepting all-expense-paid trips and gifts in return for stories. Wallace interviewed the managing editor of the *Detroit News*, who had denounced the practice but was forced to admit on camera that he'd gotten a discount on a car. Mike also took a swipe at CBS, pointing out that while CBS News employees were forbidden from going on junkets, the CBS PR department set up junkets for TV critics.

Mike admitted having taken part in press junkets in the past, and producer Barry Lando surveyed some of the most well-known TV and print reporters of the day to see if any of them still did. Harry Reasoner didn't,

Morley Safer and producer John Tiffin (kneeling), while filming "How to Live to be 100," a 1975 story in Abkhazia, then a part of the Soviet Union, where many people live to age 100 and beyond.

and neither did Murrow Boy Eric Sevareid. But among those who had been on junkets in recent years was Walter Cronkite, who was said to have scoffed at the notion that his reporting could be bought.

It was the kind of story that got Don and Mike all worked up—they loved to stir the pot, even in their own house.

A week after that story aired, the *New York Times* published a review of *60 Minutes* in which Don provided a number of reasons for the show's growing success, including his belief that "the concept of a TV newsmagazine has been strengthened by the demise of or severe cutback of such print magazines as *Life* and *Look*. Also, he feels, Wallace and Safer represent the last of the 'globetrotting' reporter breed, hopping between international locales each week, even within a single program."

The review described the "Safer persona" as "one of almost friendly curiosity and deceptive casualness, neatly wrapped in dapper suits with a silk handkerchief in the breast pocket. The manner is generally amiable, whether Safer is examining a solar-energy project in Europe or the business of selling oil in the United States . . . Safer also excels on the 'lighter' pieces, where his writing style is at least as prominent as the subject."

First Lady Betty Ford gave a surprisingly candid interview to Morley Safer for a profile that aired August 10, 1975.

DECADE 1

On Mike Wallace: "The Wallace technique does not dabble too often in subtleties. It is direct, tough, and aggressive. Wallace is at his best when he is building to an inevitable zap. His manner is friendly and casual enough initially. Then the questions get shorter and are delivered more rapidly. Wallace's manner imperceptibly changes to something resembling reasonable neutrality. All he wants is the facts, ma'am. His subject usually ends up stammering or icily intransigent."

. . .

In December 1975 *60 Minutes* caught the biggest break of all: it was moved for the last time, to seven o'clock on Sundays. Until then, *60 Minutes* had been moved to more time slots than the number of years it had been on the air—never a good sign. There had been eight moves: from Tuesday night, to Sunday night, to Friday night, and back to Sunday night. Sometimes *60 Minutes* had been used as filler: to plug a prime-time opening in the summer while the network figured out what to launch in that spot come the beginning of the new television season in September. In the summer of 1975, the show was put on Sunday nights at nine thirty. That fall, it was taken off the air entirely, which was not unusual for a program that bounced around a lot. But it returned on December 7 in the new seven o'clock spot—a time period called the Family Hour, set up for family-friendly programs and public affairs—where it has lived happily ever since.

The move to Sunday at seven happened within a few months of another big change. Mike and Morley were still the only full-time correspondents on staff, and the two workhorses could no longer keep up the blistering pace. Don needed to add another correspondent, and there was no doubt in his mind that there was only one person for the job: Dan Rather. Dan was the most recognized young reporter at CBS News. He had it all: a powerful and recognizable voice, a real reporter with a tough attitude, and movie star good looks. He had built a reputation by standing up to President Nixon as a member of the White House press corps.

In his book *Tell Me a Story*, Don wrote about Mike making the first call to Dan, correspondent to correspondent. By then, Rather had left the White House to work full-time at *CBS Reports*.

"Listen my friend, we are going to have a third correspondent. We all want it to be you. There is no second choice." To which Dan responded, "I just don't know."

"Whaddaya mean you don't know?" Wallace asked.

"I mean, it sounds good and all that," Rather said. "But I am just beginning to feel good about *CBS Reports*."

To which Mike replied, "Are you out of your mind? If you were a KGB agent looking for a place to hide, you couldn't find a better place than *CBS Reports*. Dan. Dan. Dan. Even Ed Murrow couldn't make *CBS Reports* fly. Come on. Don't be an idiot."

There is no way to know if Don captured the conversation entirely accurately, but every bit of it is such vintage Mike—the choice of words and the way it was said—that the truth was probably very close to that.

Dan joined up. And that television season, *60 Minutes* took off.

The very first broadcast in the new seven o'clock time slot on December 7, 1975, resembled the modern *60 Minutes* in shape and style more

Dan Rather, rear left, the newest correspondent on *60 Minutes*, in an edit room with Morley Safer, Mike Wallace, and Don Hewitt in November 1975.

DECADE 1

than anything that came before. Mike Wallace and producer Paul Loewenwarter reported one of the most compelling stories we have ever broadcast—certainly on my top ten list. The subject was Clint Hill, a member of the Secret Service detail assigned to protect President John F. Kennedy on his visit to Dallas on November 22, 1963. He was the agent who was captured on film climbing onto the back of the limousine to protect Jackie Kennedy after her husband was shot.

In the interview, Hill described, for the first time, the events of that horrible day and the guilt he still carried twelve years later.

WALLACE: Can I take you back to November 22 in 1963? You were on the fender of the Secret Service car right behind President Kennedy's car. At the first shot, you ran forward and jumped on the back of the president's car—in less than two seconds—pulling Mrs. Kennedy down into her seat, protecting her. First of all, she was out on the trunk of that car—

HILL: She was out of the back seat of that car, not on the trunk of that car.

Mike Wallace with former Secret Service agent Clint Hill and his wife, Gwen, for a story that aired December 7, 1975.

WALLACE: Well, she had climbed out of the back, and she was on the way back, right?

HILL: And because of the fact that her husband's . . . part of his . . . her husband's head had been shot off and gone off to the street.

WALLACE: She wasn't trying to climb out of the car? She was—

HILL: No, she was simply trying to reach that . . . part of the head.

WALLACE: To bring it back?

HILL: That's the only thing.

At that point, Clint Hill started to cry. After he composed himself, Wallace continued.

WALLACE: In the twelve years since that assassination, undoubtedly you have thought and thought and thought again about it, and studied it. Do you have any reason to believe that there was more than one gun, more than one assassin? Was Lee Harvey Oswald alone, or were there others with him?

HILL: There were only three shots; and it was one gun, three shots.

WALLACE: You're satisfied Lee Harvey Oswald acted alone?

HILL: Completely.

WALLACE: Was there anything that the Secret Service or that Clint Hill could have done to keep that from happening?

HILL: Clint Hill, yes.

WALLACE: "Clint Hill, yes"? What do you mean?

HILL: If I had reacted about five-tenths of a second faster, or maybe a second faster, I wouldn't be here today.

WALLACE: You mean, you would have gotten there, and you would have taken the shot?

HILL: The third shot, yes, sir.

WALLACE: And that would have been all right with you?

HILL: That would have been fine with me.

WALLACE: But you couldn't. You got there in—in less than two seconds, Clint. You couldn't have gotten there. You surely don't have
any sense of guilt about that?

HILL: Yes, certainly I do. I have a great deal of guilt about that. Had
I turned in a different direction, I'd have made it. It's my fault.

WALLACE: Oh, no one has ever suggested that for a minute.

HILL: I—

WALLACE: What you did was show great bravery and great presence of
mind. What was on the citation that was given you for your work
November 22, 1963?

HILL: I don't care about that, Mike.

WALLACE: "Extraordinary courage and heroic effort in the face of
maximum danger."

HILL: Mike, I don't care about that. If I had reacted just a little bit
quicker—and I could have, I guess. And I'll live with that to my
grave.

You can watch the interview today, over and over, and still be moved by
it. Hill went on to tell Mike that his memories of that day led to his early
retirement and a "severe neurological problem" requiring psychiatric help.
It was a classic case of post-traumatic stress disorder, or PTSD, rarely
brought up in conversation until after the turn of the next century, which
made Clint an even more courageous figure in retrospect.

The Clint Hill interview is important for a number of reasons, one
of them being what it represented for journalism: the power of television.
In print, the interview does not have a fraction of the impact it delivers
on the screen. It took Mike a long time to get Clint Hill to open up, but
once he did, the impact was lasting. In all of our years on television since,
there has not been a single interview as powerful and meaningful, mostly
because Clint Hill told the story from the heart. It was a living testa-
ment to Mike Wallace's ability to get people to tell the truth—the whole,

emotional truth—which remains the ultimate goal of our broadcast even today, in large part because of the example Mike set.

On the same night as the Hill interview, Morley Safer and producer Phil Scheffler took a look at the changing face of the new volunteer army—the military draft had been discontinued in 1973—and how the military was training its newest recruits: women. The story is striking, looking back more than forty years later, and though the language is vintage 1970s in its typecasting of women, the story shows that the US Army was ahead of the times. Morley and Phil found men and women, living in the same barracks, subject to the same discipline, and doing many of the same jobs. Here's part of what Morley said at the beginning:

> SAFER [*narration*]: The fact is that the military is taking the role of the American woman more seriously than most of the other professions or trades or crafts. And every week here at Fort Jackson, South Carolina, two hundred new recruits graduate. Unlike the WACs [Women's Army Corps, established during World War II] of the past, they'll not automatically end up in the typing pool but will go on to just about every job the new army can offer. But first, they must face the test so familiar to generations of young American men: that calculated torture called basic training.
>
> SAFER: Well, when they come in, are they frightened?
>
> CAPTAIN BIDDLE: Yes, they're very frightened, some of them are, because they don't know what to expect. Their recruiter tells them something, and they expect only what they've been told, without realizing there's more to it than that. Some of them have grown up as an only child and have never had to share a room. Others have come from living with their husbands, and that's an adjustment in itself. They don't know how to live with a group of women. You get into a room with eight women, and one snores, you want to kill her. They get nervous if they do the least little

thing wrong. They get upset, and they cry about it. Or they just overcompensate and try to do the same thing over and over again.

SAFER: What happens when they become officers, Captain? Do they still cry?

CAPTAIN BIDDLE: Uh-huh, they still cry.

Can you imagine the angry mail we would get if that story aired today?

For his first story, Dan Rather paid a visit to the men on the front line of the Cold War: a nuclear missile complex in North Dakota.

RATHER [*narration*]: No need to dig foxholes along the front line; they're already dug. They're called "missile silos." The men in this foxhole have their finger on the trigger that will launch ten nuclear-armed missiles. If the order should ever come, Lieutenant Gene Moseley and Captain Leroy Wayman would each take a key from this red box; each would insert his key into keyholes twelve feet apart. Twelve feet apart makes it physically impossible for one person to operate both activating keys, and to blast off a missile, the two keys must be turned within two seconds of each other . . . Who are these men with their fingers on the trigger? Their average age is twenty-five. If that surprises you, it also surprised us. Despite constant psychological testing and retesting, they are ordered to keep a sharp eye on each other for any sign of emotional instability . . . Even when they're just alone, just the two of them, each man keeps a loaded pistol at his side.

CAPTAIN WAYMAN: The primary reason for it is in case you have visitors down in the capsule. And this is to protect your classified material that you have in your container, for the most part.

RATHER: But could it be that the guns are also for use against each other, in case one goes berserk and tries to disobey orders?

LIEUTENANT MOSELEY: Interesting theory. I imagine so, but I don't believe you'd ever find a crew having to go that far. A person doesn't just go insane, snap. The signs usually appear, and that's what we're always watching for. We're not authorized to use the weapon unless there's absolutely no other way. That is the last resort.

Dan, in his first appearance, already proved he belonged. He asked the questions all viewers at home might want to ask, and he asked them simply and directly.

The broadcast ended that Sunday as it had for the past year: with "Point-Counterpoint," a debate between newspaper columnists Jack Kilpatrick and Shana Alexander. Don Hewitt had experimented with the end segment from the beginning. There were some real flops, including one short-lived segment called "Digressions," featuring Andy Rooney and senior producer Palmer Williams in silhouette as characters named Ipso and Facto, who provided wry commentary on current events. In 1975 "Point-Counterpoint" with Jack and Shana, columnists of opposite ideologies—he, conservative; she, liberal—became a fixture at the end of the broadcast. The two were given access to the other's planned comments before they went to the studio so they could adjust their copy to be more personal.

In 1978 "Point-Counterpoint" inspired what became one of the most memorable regular skits on *Saturday Night Live*, launching *60 Minutes* into popular culture. Jane Curtin played Shana, and Dan Aykroyd played Jack. Aykroyd started all his commentaries with the same line—"Jane, you ignorant slut"—and the catchphrase stuck. It would be hard to find an American over fifty who doesn't know it. Don was never in love with "Point-Counterpoint" and was always looking for something different. But it became harder to kill after the *SNL* parody made Shana and Jack one of *60 Minutes'* best-known features.

·   ·   ·

In almost a decade on the air, Don Hewitt had proven he wasn't afraid of trying new and different, sometimes risky, approaches to get stories for *60 Minutes*—including the hidden camera. Hidden cameras weren't new to television news reporting; the great Fred Friendly had used them in the interest of capturing a story the public needed to see. But *60 Minutes* was about to take the concept to a new level of sophistication.

It happened for a February 1976 story called "The Clinic on Morse Avenue." Mike Wallace and producer Barry Lando had received a tip that medical labs were paying doctors illegal kickbacks to get their Medicaid business.

60 Minutes decided to set up its own medical clinic to see how pervasive the practice was. They rented a storefront on Morse Avenue for $450 a month and positioned a camera behind a two-way mirror installed behind the clinic's front desk. With investigators from a Chicago-based watchdog group posing as the clinic's directors, one of them named Pat Riordan—and Mike behind a door somewhere, listening—they secretly filmed meetings with representatives from eleven different labs, nine of which offered some kind of kickback.

The first people to visit were the owners of North Side Clinical Labs. Here's how the story unfolded:

Palmer Williams, left, and Andy Rooney in 1968 in a short-lived segment called "Digressions."

Dan Rather during the filming of a 1976 profile of actor-turned-environmentalist Robert Redford, who was protesting plans to build a power plant in Utah.

WALLACE [*narration*]: Standing behind the wall in the back room, I could hear what was going on in the front office. Part of the North Side offer was that if the Medicaid business the clinic sent them amounted to more than a thousand dollars a week, they would return fifty percent of that money to the clinic by leasing a small space in the back.

RIORDAN: So I could get five hundred dollars a week?

WALLACE [*narration*]: In other words, by renting a few square feet in the clinic hallway to the lab, the clinic could earn from that small space alone more than four times the rent of the entire clinic.

RIORDAN: We'd be getting in rent for that hallway two thousand dollars?

At that moment, Mike walked in.

WALLACE: Pardon me just a second, fellows.

He told them he had overheard the offer they'd made. They didn't deny it, and the camera came out into the open and filmed the following discussion about kickbacks:

LAB REPRESENTATIVE: It's a fact of life that in the inner city of Chicago it's done that way, and that's all I know.

WALLACE: And you know who picks up the tab? The taxpayer. Do you think that you can stay in business without—

LAB REPRESENTATIVE: No. We'd be out of business tomorrow. It's as simple as that. I've told you that already.

WALLACE: You'd be out of business tomorrow if you were not kicking back to doctors?

LAB REPRESENTATIVE: Right, right.

WALLACE: And you kick back to every doctor with whom you do business?

LAB REPRESENTATIVE: No, we do not . . . Some doctors, no. There are maybe one or two which don't and will not.

As *60 Minutes* gained popularity, it also started taking more heat. More and more stories dealt with tough or controversial subjects, and with bigger and bigger audiences, the stakes kept getting higher. Also in February 1976 Mike reported on America's nuclear power plants, interviewing a whistle-blower named Robert Pollard who had resigned from the US Nuclear Regulatory Commission claiming safety standards were not being properly enforced at the Indian Point plant north of Manhattan. Mike also interviewed the head of the Nuclear Regulatory Commission, a former US astronaut named William Anders. Mike asked if he had ever heard of Bob Pollard. He hadn't. Nor did he know that Bob Pollard had resigned, probably because he had handed in his resignation that very morning. The cameras captured the confusion that followed as Anders and his staff tried to find a way to respond to the accusations.

It was the kind of confrontation for which Mike Wallace became famous. He didn't jump out from behind a bush, but by ambushing Anders

Mike Wallace interviewed Egyptian president Anwar Sadat for a report that aired March 27, 1977.

For that same March 27, 1977, broadcast Mike Wallace also interviewed PLO leader Yasir Arafat.

with allegations he didn't know he'd have to answer, he might as well have. And while nuclear safety certainly deserved close examination, some questions were raised about whether this was the right way to go about it. The TV critic at the *New York Times* called the segment "rather sensational stuff" that raised "unfortunate but legitimate questions about the journalism of *Sixty Minutes*."

Dan Rather would later say those kinds of questions were the price the broadcast had to pay for its success. "When you're at the top, you expect this kind of criticism," he told the *New York Times*. "We expect to be on top for a very, very long time."

• • •

60 Minutes finished the spring of 1977 among the top twenty programs on television—officially making the broadcast a hit. Everybody was surprised by the success, which I believe can be attributed to several factors: the new time slot, the variety and chemistry of the correspondents, and the stories, which were getting better. Never had a news broadcast done so well, and that meant for the first time ever a news program was going to start making money. And there was a sense of invincibility. The numbers were going up and up, and viewers seemed to like what they were getting. Don and his team were ready to take on the world—which was probably what led to the decision to take on one of our own sponsors. And not just any sponsor, but the most important one: the Ford Motor Company.

The story, "Is Your Car Safe?," investigated a tendency of the gas tank on the Pinto to explode when rear-ended. *60 Minutes* reported that Ford was responsible for as many as two thousand deaths and ten thousand injuries, all in the interest of building a cheaper car that it knew was flawed.

Mike often said one of his favorite interviews was the one he did with pianist Vladimir Horowitz for a profile that aired December 26, 1977.

Ford participated in the story to tell its side of things but canceled all of its commercials the night the report aired in June 1978. By the next week, though, Ford was back with advertisements on *60 Minutes*. The company seemed to take it all in stride and probably calculated that its own advertising might make up for any negative impact. Don talked about that for the rest of his life: that Ford so valued its advertising spots on *60 Minutes* that it would let itself be criticized with hardly a complaint. By then, the numbers were too good to resist.

The broadcast finished the 1977–78 season in the top ten for the first time, ending its first decade on a high note.

DECADE

2

1978 to 1988

Imam, President Sadat of Egypt, a devoutly religious man, a Muslim, says that what you are doing now is—quote—"a disgrace to Islam." And he calls you, Imam—forgive me, his words, not mine—"a lunatic."

—Mike Wallace

In the summer of 1978, the start of the second decade of *60 Minutes*, a fifty-year-old CBS veteran decided it was time for a career change. He didn't seem a natural fit for *60 Minutes*. He didn't have a made-for-TV look or voice or delivery, nor did he have any experience in front of the camera, but he had a way with words and a good name for the job: Andy Rooney.

During the first few years of the broadcast, Andy had written for *60 Minutes*, occasionally experimenting with end pieces and occasionally working on Harry Reasoner stories. Harry was his pal, and when Harry

Don Hewitt surrounded by *60 Minutes* correspondents: Ed Bradley, Harry Reasoner, Morley Safer, Diane Sawyer, and Mike Wallace.

left CBS, so did Andy. He worked at PBS and ABC before returning to *60 Minutes* in 1978. (Harry also returned to *60 Minutes* that year.)

Still looking for a good way to end the broadcast, Don decided to give Andy a tryout that July for an original commentary spot called "Three Minutes or So with Andy Rooney." His first piece was a Fourth of July essay on death:

"On Fourth of July weekend in 1976, for instance, 758 people were killed in car crashes. A terrible figure. In April the weekend comes on the same four days of the month, and only 555 people were killed in cars. But now, here is the interesting thing about these figures: on those four days in April, a total of 21,700 people died of all causes; on the four days in July, 19,600 died—2,100 fewer."

Andy's point—which he made with several other statistics, including suicide—was that Fourth of July weekend was relatively safe. The piece wasn't good, but Don gave him another shot the following Sunday. This time his commentary was vintage Andy, making fun of the human instinct to grade things in life:

I rate things one to ten. One to ten ought to be our standard for rating everything. We need just one system, and that's the best. Most schools grade students' work as A, B, C, D, or F—five grades. Teachers aren't satisfied with five, so they start giving C-pluses and D-minuses. With a plus and a minus for five grades, that gives you fifteen. It's too many. Fifteen is for people who can't make up their minds how to rate something. Perhaps, you ask, what are some of the things you rate from one to ten? Well, I'll tell you some. *Charlie's Angels* I give a three. Wonder Bread, one. Zbigniew Brzezinski, six. Scotch tape, seven. Nixon's book, three. Howard Johnson's peppermint ice cream, nine. Golden retrievers, ten. Kleenex, eight. Schenectady, New York, five. General Eisenhower, ten. President Eisenhower, four. Vladimir Horowitz, ten. Rochelle Hudson, four. *MacNeil/Lehrer,* nine. Two-dollar bills, five. Howard Cosell, one. It's fun to do. You can sit around nights and make a game of it, making a list of things and rating them. *Time* magazine, Disneyland, the post office, California, airline food, *Star Wars*. I mean, the list is endless. If we all used a one-to-ten system of grading everything in our lives, it would make decisions quicker and easier. Prejudice has gotten a bad name recently, but prejudice is a great help to us in our lives. If we know what we think and where we rate things, we don't have to waste a lot of time thinking them through again. I rate liver one. I know I dislike liver, and I don't ever want to try another piece. The way to end a cute piece like this would be for me to give it a rating from one to ten. I rate television people who put endings like that on pieces like this, two.

With that, Andy earned a regular spot starting with the new season that September. His segment was called "A Few Minutes with Andy Rooney" and alternated every other week with "Point-Counterpoint."

Andy was not the only *60 Minutes* contributor in those years that brought the program to a new level. By the end of the 1970s, something was starting to happen that Don Hewitt never could have predicted: *60 Minutes* was becoming a destination for people who had something to say. If you wanted to tell your story to a big national audience, *60 Minutes* was the place to do it. This paid off with some terrific interviews: Katharine Hepburn and Johnny Carson, the Muppets and Pete Rose, Yasir Arafat and Fidel Castro. But the one from this era that still receives the most attention is Mike Wallace's interview with Ayatollah Khomeini.

It was 1979, the year the Shah of Iran was overthrown in a revolution led by Khomeini, who had become a popular revolutionary cleric living in exile in France for fourteen years. That November, Iranian student revolutionaries stormed the US embassy in Tehran and took fifty-two American diplomats and citizens hostage. Two weeks later, Mike Wallace and producer Barry Lando got a call that their request for an interview with the ayatollah himself would be granted. Just getting the interview was a surprise; they had requested it through an Iranian source who doubted it could happen. But when they got a call from him that they should fly to Tehran, they took off right away. What they didn't realize until they got there was that NBC, ABC, and PBS were offered the same interview. So much for an exclusive. All four were told to submit their questions in advance. Robin MacNeil of PBS dropped out and went home, apparently frustrated by the process. But the other three stayed and were given time with Khomeini.

Mike was frustrated with the interview. He thought the ayatollah spoke in a remote and toneless voice and that most of his replies were little more than the slogans and demands that had been heard on the streets of Tehran since the assault on the US Embassy. The *New York Times* thought so too. The day after the interviews aired, the paper accused the networks of being Iran's mouthpiece.

But Mike's interview was more than just an opportunity for the ayatollah to spew propaganda. He went off script and asked a question that wasn't submitted in advance—the only one that got what seemed to be an unscripted answer. It was a question about President Jimmy Carter's landmark accomplishment: the Camp David Accords, the most significant Middle East peace deal since the founding of Israel, signed by Israeli prime minister Menachem Begin and Egyptian president Anwar el-Sadat after twelve days of secret talks in 1978.

Mike sat down with Ayatollah Khomeini for an interview that ran November 18, 1979.

WALLACE: Imam, President Sadat of Egypt, a devoutly religious man, a Muslim, says that what you are doing now is—quote—"a disgrace to Islam." And he calls you, Imam—forgive me, his words, not mine—"a lunatic." I know that you have heard that comment.

KHOMEINI [*through an interpreter*]: A lunatic, madman, or . . . ?

WALLACE: Yes, that's what I heard President Sadat say on American television.

KHOMEINI: Yes.

WALLACE: That the imam is a disgrace to Islam—

KHOMEINI: Yes.

WALLACE: —and he used the word *lunatic.*

Mike never got tired of retelling how that played out in the room. He always got us laughing when he described the reaction of the interpreter, whose facial expression said, "*You're* the lunatic if you think I'm going to ask that question!" But he did ask it, and this is what Khomeini said:

"Sadat states he is a Muslim, and we are not. He is not, for he compromises with the enemies of Islam. Sadat has united with our enemies. Sadat knows well what is occurring south of Lebanon and with the Palestinians. He knows the crimes of Israel, yet he still considers Begin a friend and himself a Muslim. You must try to evaluate what he is doing then through Islam. The Egyptian people do not back Sadat."

The ayatollah was not alone in criticizing Sadat for compromising with the perceived enemies of Islam. That same year, Yāsir Arafat, chairman of the Palestine Liberation Organization (PLO), also took on the Egyptian president in an interview with Mike at his headquarters in Beirut, Lebanon.

WALLACE: Chairman Arafat, you say that President Sadat is a traitor to the Arab world, yes?

ARAFAT: Quisling, yes.

WALLACE: Quisling, traitor.

ARAFAT: Yes.

WALLACE: In many countries, the penalty for treason is death. So, if necessary, kill Sadat?

ARAFAT: It is up to them.

WALLACE: In other words, the Palestinians are not going to kill Sadat, but if the Egyptians want to kill Sadat for being a traitor, you say okay.

ARAFAT: Yes.

The Khomeini and Arafat interviews offered a window into how incendiary the Camp David Peace Accords had been for the Middle East. Just two years later, in October 1981, Anwar Sadat was assassinated in Cairo by fundamentalist Egyptian army officers.

· · ·

Of all the celebrity sit-downs over the past fifty years, Morley Safer's interview with legendary actress Katharine Hepburn in January 1979 stands out as one of the finest. We always crave one thing in an interview: a person who isn't afraid to say what's on his or her mind. A person who is overly careful and measured is not interesting on TV. If a world leader is bland, we often have no choice but to interview him or her, but if a celebrity is bland, we pass.

Katharine Hepburn was certainly *not* bland. She spoke her mind, and you realized while watching that she wasn't doing the interview to gratify her own ego. It was hard to figure out *why* she was doing it, actually.

Morley worked hard to convince her to do it. He worked on friends of hers he knew. He traveled to London, where she was shooting a movie, to convince her in person that he would be simple and fair. When she finally agreed, she told producer Jim Jackson she had one condition: Morley could interview her at noon on the dot at her Manhattan brownstone, but it would be called off if he was even just one minute late.

On the day of the interview, Morley got stuck in crosstown traffic. He jumped out of his taxi and ran the last few blocks, arriving at Hepburn's home at one minute before noon. When she answered the door, she said, "Mr. Safer, you are a very lucky young man."

Morley was nervous. You can tell when you watch the interview that he was occasionally at a loss for the right words as they discussed the quality of moviemaking in Hollywood, which Hepburn, who was about to turn seventy, called filth. She thought the movie business had reached all-time lows; she was "disgusted, because they are kidding themselves into saying it's an intellectual pastime."

"Bunk!" she said emphatically.

Morley admitted later in an interview with the Television Academy Foundation that she'd scared the hell out of him. Hepburn was a granite woman, he said, with strong opinions who might eat him for lunch.

SAFER: You are a legend to so many people—I guess just about everyone—because you do not give much of yourself publicly beyond
the films.

HEPBURN: You mean it's stupid of me to do this?

SAFER: I don't know, but—

HEPBURN: We'll find out [*laughing*]!

Morley Safer interviewed Katharine Hepburn in her New York City home for a profile that ran January 14, 1979.

SAFER: Do you feel like a legend? Do you feel like *the* Katharine Hepburn?

HEPBURN: No, I don't think anyone feels like anything, really. You know, I always felt they were out to get me—

SAFER: "They" being?

HEPBURN: —and that I'd better be good. And I still think I'd better be good, you know. I struggle to do my best. I've struggled for days to do my best for this, do you know what I mean? And I don't think you ever feel like anything. You feel like a bore [*laughing*]. You know, don't you? Or do you feel fascinating?

SAFER: No, no, I feel like a bore most of the time.

HEPBURN: Like a bore. Like a bore.

SAFER: Yeah.

HEPBURN: Then you think, "My God, they're going to find out what a bore I am, and then that'll be a terrible thing."

After the story aired, Morley called Hepburn to see what she thought—something he rarely did. He spoke to her brother, who told him that Hepburn didn't watch the interview! As soon as the stopwatch started ticking, she left the room and wouldn't come back in until it was over.

Morley was developing a reputation for interviewing leading ladies. He landed his next a few months later when he and John Tiffin teamed up for another classic *60 Minutes* story called "Backstage at the Muppets" about the Muppets and their creator, Jim Henson, and his collaborator Frank Oz. The interview with Miss Piggy could have come across as contrived and too cute, but it didn't—partly because Morley laughed the whole time, perhaps at the absurdity of it but perhaps also because he enjoyed Miss Piggy's flirtations. Here's how he told part of the story:

SAFER [*narration*]: From the moment you set foot on the Muppets set, you find yourself talking to the most monstrous of creatures: too

pushy, predatory pigs; no-talent bears; and other bits and pieces of foam rubber. Not just talking to them, but listening to them.

MISS PIGGY: Hello, Morley. [*Morley laughs.*] May I ask you a question? Please?

SAFER: Yes [*laughing*].

MISS PIGGY: Is your wife here?

SAFER: No, she's not.

MISS PIGGY: Great!

Mike's big celebrity interview that year was Johnny Carson, the ruler of late-night TV, who was every bit as memorable as Katharine Hepburn. What made the interview different was what made everything Mike Wallace did different: he was tough. The Carson interview was broadcast in two parts. The first, which aired in April 1979, dealt with a contract dispute between the *Tonight Show* host and the head of NBC, Fred Silverman. There had been rumors Carson might leave the network. Mike invited Johnny to address Silverman directly.

WALLACE: Is there anything you'd like to say to Mr. Silverman?

CARSON: I hope when this show is seen that you're still with NBC [*laughs*]. I'm as cruel as you are.

WALLACE: Is it a—is it a fact—

CARSON: What-what-what? Is what a fact?

WALLACE: Is it a fact that in the middle—

CARSON: Boy, you're getting warmed up now, aren't you . . .

WALLACE: Yeah. Is it—

CARSON: Takes you a while, but, boy, when that cruel streak starts to come up, you're murder [*laughs*].

The second part of the interview, which didn't air until the following September, was even better than the first. Carson played the drums for Mike, and they played tennis. They were a perfect match for each other, firing tennis balls and insults back and forth. It started on the court as Mike got ready to serve:

CARSON: What are you waiting for, your pacemaker to start? That thing has got to kick in just about when you serve.

WALLACE [*narration*]: He says he uses tennis, which he loves, as a kind of therapy to help get rid of his aggressions. And that goes double for his drums, a gift from Buddy Rich.

WALLACE: Some say that it helps you to work out your hostility?

CARSON: Sure.

WALLACE: True?

CARSON: Sure, it's like beating something. [*Bangs on drum.*] That's all it is. You ought to take this up, Mike. You've got a lot of hostilities.

WALLACE: I'd rather beat on you.

Mike went head-to-head with Johnny Carson in 1979.

WALLACE [*narration*]: If there is one universal comment from the guests who have appeared on *The Tonight Show*, it is that Johnny is a gentle man, a kind man. And by and large, that is true as well with the way he treats people in his nightly monologues.

WALLACE: Are you reluctant, in putting together your monologue, to go hard on a guy?

CARSON: Only when I sense the mood is—and which you can do from the audience, and I'll give you a perfect illustration. When Wilbur Mills had his problem with the famous Fanne Foxe and the Tidal Basin and so forth, it was amusing to most people, and you could do jokes about it.

[The incident in 1974 was as tabloid as it gets: the long-serving conservative Democratic congressman from Arkansas, a powerful chairman of the House Ways and Means Committee, caught driving while intoxicated in Washington at 2 a.m. with a stripper named Fanne Foxe in the car.]

CARSON: I stopped doing jokes immediately as soon as people found out that he was an alcoholic and had emotional problems, and in fact was dependent on alcohol. Then I think it would be a cheap shot to take, to still do jokes about it. So I immediately ceased doing jokes about that, because it was really unfair.

WALLACE: Of course, it takes one to know one.

CARSON: Aah! [*laughs*] Cruel. You're cruel.

WALLACE: But there was a time—

CARSON: What?

WALLACE: Come on. There was a time when—

CARSON: I used to have a little pop? I sure did.

WALLACE: That's right.

CARSON: I don't handle it well.

Don liked to say that a big part of the appeal for viewers was watching the adventures of our correspondents—especially when they revealed more of their own personalities, and viewers got to know them better.

•   •   •

In the spring of 1980, Dan Rather and producer Andy Lack capped a remarkable two years at *60 Minutes* with a story about the mujahideen fighters in Afghanistan, who were taking on the powerful Soviet military from their mountaintop bases. It was the trip that gave Dan the nickname "Gunga Dan." He put on the clothes of a mujahideen and took some heat from colleagues—and one prominent newspaper critic, Tom Shales of the *Washington Post*—for drawing too much attention to himself and the danger he was in.

But the story that Dan and Andy put together was remarkable. It captured what the American military would discover over twenty years later in the wake of 9/11: the enormity of the task of fighting an all-Muslim guerrilla army in a vast territory surrounded by the rugged mountains of

Dan Rather ventured inside Afghanistan for a report that aired April 6, 1980.

DECADE 2

Cameraman Mike Edwards in Libya, setting up an interview with Colonel Mu'ammar Qaddafi that aired March 23, 1980.

Afghanistan. The mujahideen were soldiers prepared to die for their cause, dedicated to keeping infidel colonial powers away. Their powerful enemy's planes and bombs would have a hard time even finding them in their hide-outs.

The story was broadcast at about the same time Dan won a famous battle with correspondent Roger Mudd to replace Walter Cronkite as anchor of the *CBS Evening News*. It was his swan song to full-time field reporting.

Dan was a real reporter, with experience covering every kind of story possible. But he had also become a news superstar who would have probably fled to ABC if he hadn't gotten the big job at CBS.

SEASONS

13-17

1980 to 1985

A crook doesn't believe he has made it as a crook until he has been on *60 Minutes*.

—Morley Safer

Starting in the late seventies and continuing into the early eighties, there was a parade of questionable or criminal characters on *60 Minutes*. As much as the broadcast had become known for landing big interviews, it had also developed a reputation for doing stories about crooks and con men.

Jimmy "the Weasel" Fratianno, produced by the veteran Marion Goldin, was among the most memorable. A member of the Mafia for thirty years, Fratianno went on to become one of the government's most valuable informants, helping to secure the convictions of high-ranking mobsters in New York and California. He also pointed the finger at Frank Sinatra, saying the singer had once asked him to break the legs of a former bodyguard who was writing a book about him. The story, "The Last

Mafioso," aired in January 1981. Because he was a protected witness under the guard of US Marshals, Jimmy the Weasel appeared in disguise. Mike did the interview at a government safe house in Virginia.

The story started with several minutes of pure interview.

Mobster Jimmy "the Weasel" Fratianno was disguised for his interview with Mike Wallace that aired January 4, 1981.

WALLACE: Jimmy, who was the first person you killed?

FRATIANNO: Frankie Nicoli.

WALLACE: Where did you kill him?

FRATIANNO: In my house.

WALLACE: How did you kill him?

FRATIANNO: We strangled him.

WALLACE: In your own living room.

FRATIANNO: Right.

WALLACE: And then he dirtied your living room.

FRATIANNO: A little blood.

WALLACE: A little blood and a little discharge.

FRATIANNO: Right . . . a little urine, yeah.

WALLACE: You smile when you think back about it.

FRATIANNO: Well, what are you gonna do?

WALLACE: After you shoved a gun up against Tony Brancato's head, you were apparently proud of yourself, because you say that you said, "Most guys just ain't got the stomach for it. They're squeamish. I can't figure them out." You remember killing Brancato?

FRATIANNO: Yes.

WALLACE: You take a look at this picture. Any emotion on seeing it? There's the two of them.

FRATIANNO: No.

WALLACE: Just a day's work.

FRATIANNO: Had to do it. I took a guy out of Vegas one time and killed him—just took him out of the Desert Inn. You know, there's different . . . different ways, different methods.

WALLACE: You were a good killer?

FRATIANNO: I just had the talent to . . . to do things like that. I never made any mistakes.

WALLACE: Matter of some pride.

FRATIANNO: No, just . . . some people are a little better than others, but I think it would bother me if I killed an innocent person.

WALLACE: What do you mean by an innocent person?

FRATIANNO: Well, you're an innocent person.

WALLACE: I'm glad to hear you don't have designs—

FRATIANNO: Well, I mean, somebody innocent, you know, that is not involved in criminal activities.

WALLACE: One gets the impression that mobsters are really animals.

FRATIANNO: Well, they're not animals.

WALLACE: No?

FRATIANNO: Some are, probably.

WALLACE: Jimmy, they're brutal, they're vulgar.

FRATIANNO: Yes, they are.

WALLACE: They're uncaring, they're animals.

FRATIANNO: Well, I'd say they're brutal. I don't say they're vulgar, all of them. I don't think I'm vulgar.

WALLACE: Well, you're very benign and you're smiling now—but you killed five men.

FRATIANNO: Yeah.

WALLACE: You garroted one man in your living room.

FRATIANNO: I'd say I'm brutal, yeah. I admit that.

It was one thing to get a crook to appear on *60 Minutes* and quite another to catch someone in the middle of a con. Sometimes these stories involved questionable methods, such as a *60 Minutes* staffer assuming a false identity. It became common to do ambush interviews where the correspondent would sneak up on a subject with a camera and start asking questions that tended to make the subject look guilty no matter the circumstances. While some of these stories were worthy, the methods raised questions. Was it good journalism or just good television? Either way, the stories delivered great ratings, and while it was still crass to crave better ratings, it was also intoxicating to be doing so well.

One story called "This Year at Murrieta" concerned the Murrieta Hot Springs health spa in California, which was selling "miracle" cures for cancer made from lemon juice and water. Mike Wallace and his team decided the best way to investigate this potentially phony clinic was from the inside. They went in undercover, with soundman James Camery pretending to be a wealthy investment counselor known as "the Colonel," who'd just learned he had leukemia. The cameraman, Greg Cooke, posed as his concerned nephew. Producer and amateur photographer Marion Goldin was the Colonel's longtime secretary.

The Colonel and his entourage rolled up to the spa in a rented Rolls-Royce, with the camera documenting as much of his charade as possible. The doctor at Murrieta looked in his eyes and diagnosed him with a "leaky lung" rather than leukemia. He was placed on a treatment regimen of distilled water and lemon juice, though Camery managed to sneak in a solid three meals a day and occasionally snuck out for dinner. The urine and saliva the Colonel submitted for testing weren't always his—he sometimes switched them with samples from other members of the team—but nobody on the Murrieta staff seemed to notice. He was told the results from a computer that analyzed urine and blood samples showed that his numbers were improving, especially during his supposed fast.

But the spa had more to offer than remarkable cures. The team captured the head of the Murrieta Health Clinic, R. J. Rudd, trying to peddle them a remarkable tax shelter. After nine days of undercover filming, Mike Wallace showed up and confronted Rudd.

Anybody who is old enough to have been watching *60 Minutes* that year will remember the interview, especially when Mike started asking Rudd about his training.

WALLACE: You're not a medical doctor?

RUDD: No, I'm not.

WALLACE: You're an economist?

RUDD: I'm a—I have a PhD.

WALLACE: In?

RUDD: In economics and one in philosophy. And I'm also a full-time ordained minister of the Gospel. Of my two PhDs, one came from the Tennessee University.

WALLACE: University of Tennessee?

RUDD: No, the Christian Tennessee University. And I got one from Florida . . . Tennessee . . . let's see—Trinity Christian College in Florida.

WALLACE: Where is that?

RUDD: I believe that now they're presently in Fort Lauderdale.

WALLACE: Well, [the diploma] says here it was signed and sealed at Brownsville, Texas.

RUDD: Okay, that was a branch of the operation, you see.

WALLACE: And this is the [diploma from] Tennessee Christian University. And where is this university? What town?

RUDD: It's—I believe that one is close to . . . let me think of the name just a minute. Chattanooga.

Rudd's diplomas were mail-order degrees from universities that didn't even exist. Diploma mills. And what about the mysterious computer that supposedly deciphered the urine and saliva numbers in patients' samples? Mike asked Rudd about that too.

> WALLACE: Where's the master computer?
>
> RUDD: It'll probably be somewhere in California here.
>
> WALLACE: You don't have it set up yet?
>
> RUDD: Oh, yes we do.
>
> WALLACE: Where?
>
> RUDD: In the Los Angeles area.
>
> WALLACE: Well, can we take a look at it?
>
> RUDD: No. We can't . . . let that out yet.
>
> WALLACE: Many would say there's a kind of con game operation going on at Murrieta Springs.
>
> RUDD: This is not a con game.

Well, it was. Rudd was later convicted of conspiracy and fraud.

Morley called that story and dozens of others like it "Mike jumping out of a closet" stories. He considered the role of the CBS News correspondent too dignified to engage in that kind of thing and largely refused to do them. And he objected to the practice on *60 Minutes*.

Dan Rather did his share, though, including a compelling story he reported with producer Steve Glauber called "Bum Steer," about fraudulent activities in the meat packing business. The segment revealed how a stamp intended to designate high-quality beef was being used on lesser-quality meats. Dan confronted the vice president of a large San Diego meat packing plant in a meat locker, armed with one of those stamps.

> RATHER: Could you explain to me what this stamp is?
>
> FRED CAMERON: I think what you guys ought to do is leave.
>
> RATHER: I don't understand.

Dan Rather grilled the vice president of a large meat packing plant in an actual meat locker for an investigation that aired September 11, 1977.

FRED CAMERON: Well, I—I don't think it's fair. I don't believe that that's at all fair.

RATHER: Well, I want to give you an opportunity to tell me how you think it's unfair.

FRED CAMERON: Well, I certainly will take the oppor—

RATHER: May I have that [the meat stamp] back?

FRED CAMERON: I don't know. Does it belong to you?

RATHER: Yes, it does.

FRED CAMERON: Where did you get it?

RATHER: I got it from someone who told me that you use that to put a different kind of stamp on the meat than the store buyer put on his own meat.

FRED CAMERON: Is that right?

RATHER: And I'll be happy to have you explain it.

FRED CAMERON: Certainly am disappointed in you. Really, I am.

RATHER: Yeah, and I'd like to have back that stamp, if you don't mind.

FRED CAMERON: Come on, and I'll give it to you.

RATHER: Well, now, could you tell me what it is? This is a phony stamp, is it?

FRED CAMERON: I don't know what it is. And I'm-I'm—

DECADE 2

RATHER: It isn't made out of metal, doesn't have a handle on the back.

FRED CAMERON: Boy oh boy, what a disgusting deal!

RATHER [*narration*]: We tried to persuade Cameron to come back and continue our conversation. He refused.

Dan got back the meat stamp, but he never saw Mr. Cameron again.

As often seemed to be the case, the ambush itself was just as important to the story as the details it uncovered. And while sometimes significant frauds were exposed, such stories often became more about putting somebody on the spot in an uncomfortable way. We rarely do stories like that anymore—at most, once every couple of years. I believe a decision to ambush somebody should be made of necessity, and only when holding someone accountable for something the public has a right to know.

. . .

During this period several *60 Minutes* stories brought claims of unfairness and shoddy journalism. Of those that became public embarrassments for the broadcast, the most infamous was a Dan Rather piece titled "It's No Accident," about false car accident insurance claims. Among other things, Dan and producer Steve Glauber revealed a bogus medical report that had been backdated and contained a list of examinations that had never taken place. The report appeared to be signed by a Dr. Carl O. Galloway. The doctor later claimed the signature was a forgery and sued CBS.

CBS won the trial that took place several years later. But the legal proceedings exposed techniques used by *60 Minutes* that proved embarrassing:

One involved changing an answer to a question Rather asked, editing in an affirmative answer, a "yes," from a different part of the interview. Another involved a "reverse question," in which the reporter is filmed asking a question to the camera after the interview is over, usually using the exact same wording but in this case changing the emphasis. The judge had ordered all of the film outtakes as exhibits, revealing that Rather asked some questions over again until it appeared he was satisfied that he had gotten

Dan Rather, with Don Hewitt, interviewed President Jimmy Carter in August 1980.

them just the way he wanted. After this came out, Don made sure that two cameras were sent on every interview so that the final cut could be compared against the unedited footage. A few years after the incident, reverse questions, which were mostly used because there was only one camera on most interviews, were banned from use in all CBS News reporting.

There was enough criticism of the program's methods over the years, both internally and externally, that Don decided to dedicate an entire broadcast to examining them. He brought in a panel of journalists and business leaders who reviewed several *60 Minutes* stories, including Murrieta and the meat stamp. On the resulting one-hour special, the decision was unanimous: *60 Minutes* was as interested in the entertainment value of the "gotcha" style as bona fide journalism. Don himself admitted that the technique "has been abused."

Mike, too, came to see this kind of reporting as unworthy of the broadcast. It generated "more heat than light," he said later, admitting, "We weren't getting a lot of information from those so-called ambushes . . . I have no doubt that what we started has become a plague."

In the years that followed—and in a tradition that continues to this day—*60 Minutes* became far more disciplined about reporting stories with shoe leather: chasing down details and victims and examples rather than trying to capture some kind of criminal drama on camera and *then* chasing down the facts. The hidden camera and the ambush are still used on occasion, but almost always only after in-depth reporting and repeated attempts to get a subject to comment on the record.

Dan Rather wasn't the only young star of CBS News known in the seventies and eighties for his epic reporting from far-off places. The other was Ed Bradley, who covered the war in Vietnam, the overthrow of the Cambodian government by the brutal Communist Khmer Rouge regime, the Paris Peace talks set up to end the war in Vietnam, and the fall of Saigon in April 1975.

Ed came back to the United States in time for the 1976 presidential campaign and then was assigned to cover Jimmy Carter's White House. His first appearance on *60 Minutes*, on June 24, 1979, was as part of a classic *CBS Reports* hour called "The Island," a powerful story filmed on an island off the coast of Malaysia on whose shores Vietnamese refugees known as "the boat people" were arriving to escape Communist Vietnam. The report included an unforgettable image of Ed wading out into the sea to help pull women and children to safety.

Ed Bradley, in 1979, helped refugees from South Vietnam, known as "boat people," as they arrived on the coast of Malaysia after crossing three hundred miles of the South China Sea.

When Dan Rather left *60 Minutes* to anchor the news, Ed was his natural replacement. But Ed was also unlike anybody who had been on the air at the broadcast. He was smooth and hip, and he moved in circles that included "gonzo" journalist Hunter S. Thompson, actor Harrison Ford, and musicians Aaron Neville and Wynton Marsalis. He was also African American. He never wanted to be typecast as the "black correspondent," but his perspective and his inner-city Philadelphia background gave *60 Minutes* much-needed diversity long before it became a priority at news organizations. Don Hewitt loved to tell audiences that he hired Ed because he was a minority: "a great reporter *and* a real gentleman, and if that ain't a minority, I don't know what is."

Ed was a great journalist, especially because of his interviewing

Don Hewitt in his office, going over a script with Ed Bradley.

abilities. He could get people to open up. His voice, charm, and neutrality put him on a level with Walter Cronkite. He was often rumored to be the next big anchorman and became the target of poaching efforts by the other networks. Because of all that, he became the highest-paid correspondent ever to work at *60 Minutes*.

Ed debuted as a *60 Minutes* correspondent in the fall of 1981. He did a few hard-hitting stories, including one on the Irish Republican Army (IRA), before making a lasting impression in reporting his first profile, of sixty-four-year-old singer and actress Lena Horne. The story was produced by Jeanne Solomon Langley, an excellent producer who worked with Ed and was based in London. In Ed's nearly three decades working at *60 Minutes*, that Lena Horne profile was his favorite—and one of the best we have ever done.

BRADLEY: Do you ever think of getting married again?

HORNE: No I'm too—

BRADLEY: Don't tell me you're too old.

HORNE: No. Well, no, I don't think that's got a lot to do with it, except that I'm so old and I'm set in a lot of ways I would hate to change. I'm spoiled.

BRADLEY: You wouldn't put that on anybody?

HORNE: I wouldn't lay that burden on anybody, no.

[*Video of Lena singing the show tune "Bewitched, Bothered and Bewildered."*]

Ed Bradley strolled through New York's Central Park with Lena Horne for a profile that aired December 27, 1981.

BRADLEY: You once said somewhere you didn't want to be an older woman singing songs about sex and all of that stuff.

HORNE: Yes, yes. And I don't, really, if I can avoid it now.

BRADLEY: Well, when you sing "Bewitched, Bothered and Bewildered"—

HORNE: Well, but it's funny to me. Don't you think so? Didn't you feel sorry for the old broad falling for that old-young thing?

BRADLEY: When you say that "I'm a rich, juicy, ripe plum again"?

HORNE: Yeah, but you can't help your sexual nature, you know. That's what that line means [*laughter*]. If a lady treats other people as she'd like to be treated, then she's allowed to go and roll in the grass if she wants to.

BRADLEY: Even if she's sixty-four?

HORNE: Even if she's sixty-four. Particularly then! [*laughs*]

Ed liked to say about that story, "If I arrived at the pearly gates, and Saint Peter said, 'What have you done to deserve entry?' I'd just say, 'Did you see my Lena Horne story?'"

Everybody who has worked at *60 Minutes* has one story they remember that fondly. For Morley Safer, it was a segment in December 1983 called "Lenell Geter's in Jail." This one fell into another of the program's favorite genres: calling attention to someone found guilty of a crime he or she didn't commit. Morley and producer Suzanne St. Pierre documented how impossible it would have been for Geter to commit the crime for which he was in prison: the robbery of a Kentucky Fried Chicken franchise in Greenville, Texas. The story exposed the flawed judicial process for an African American with poor legal representation. It was so convincing that the prosecutor abandoned his case: Geter was released from prison just four days after the broadcast.

For the rest of his life, Morley used the story as an example for young journalists to abandon any preconceived notions when reporting. "I wasn't on a mission to free this guy. That's the wrong way to go about telling this story," he said. "You've gotta go into the story just as skeptical about the defense as the prosecution. You know, and then you gotta just keep peeling away at that onion, and then something may emerge. If you go into the story believing the guy is innocent, I think you're sunk. Because you start ignoring stuff yourself."

Lenell Geter visited *60 Minutes* in 2016, some thirty-three years after Morley Safer reported on his case, leading to his release from prison.

Reporting a story like that one is difficult: time consuming and exhausting. A few months after completing the Geter story, Morley started filming one that was pure fun: a profile of comedian-actor Jackie Gleason called "The Great One," broadcast on October 28, 1984. At the time, Don said it was the best profile *60 Minutes* had ever done.

Morley gave full credit for that to the producer, Alan Weisman, who approached the story as if he were directing a film. He wanted the interview shot at a dark, smoky bar, and he wanted Jackie Gleason lit like Don Corleone in *The Godfather*, with one side of his face in shadow. And he rented a pool table, reminiscent of

Gleason's role as Minnesota Fats opposite Paul Newman in the movie *The Hustler*. He set it up next to a mahogany bar he had found under a dusty tarp at the Inverrary Country Club in Florida, near where Gleason lived.

Morley has said it was that atmosphere that put both him and Gleason at ease. "It really worked," he reflected. "And it was a conversation. Well, the best interviews are."

When the interview was over, Gleason and Morley played pool—among the most classic scenes in the history of *60 Minutes*. Morley, who was proficient but not brilliant at the game, spoke about it not long ago for our weekly webcast, *60 Minutes Overtime*. "I went first," he recalled. "And I did something I hadn't done for I don't know how long: I ran about six or seven balls. And Gleason thought he'd been hustled. He was looking over at 'em. And he would be angrier, angrier. And he is renowned for his temper. But I finally got so nervous, I blew the shot, the next shot. And then he just cleaned the table."

It seemed like a natural way to end the shoot. The cameras were broken down. Gleason started to leave. But Morley decided he had one more question. The cameras started rolling again:

SAFER: Tell me something. "The Great One." Where did that come from?

GLEASON: Well, Orson Welles called me "the Great One" first, and then Lucy [Lucille Ball] started to call me that, and I'm not really offended by it.

SAFER: Did you ever really believe it?

GLEASON: You just saw me play pool, didn't you?

With that, Gleason put down his pool cue and walked out of frame. And that was the end of the piece. You couldn't have scripted it better if you'd tried.

Morley Safer playing pool with Jackie Gleason for a profile that ran October 28, 1984.

• • •

In the fall of 1984—sixteen years after launching—the broadcast, which had been growing each year, finally reached its modern size, with five full-time correspondents each working with four or five producers. With more people on staff, each story received greater care, usually improving the quality of the reporting and storytelling—with special attention paid to fairness and accuracy. Each team could now also produce stories well in advance of air dates, although a trend toward stories that could air at any time was not necessarily beneficial for a news program.

The newest addition to *60 Minutes*, in 1984, was Diane Sawyer, the latest rising star of CBS. She was young—thirty-eight—beautiful, and incredibly smart. She didn't have as much general-assignment experience as Dan and Ed had when they joined, but Diane had excelled at each network assignment, beginning with covering the Three Mile Island nuclear disaster in 1979; then as the beat reporter at the US State Department; and then as co-anchor of the *CBS Morning News*, first with Charles Kuralt, followed by Bill Kurtis.

The *Morning* program's ratings were way behind NBC's *Today* show,

and Don was as anxious to get Diane over to *60 Minutes* as she was to leave morning television. He got defensive once when somebody suggested that he'd hired her because she was a woman, and—just as he'd had a line ready for questions about Ed being a minority—Don had a quip for this occasion as well: "Baloney," he said many times, "I would have wanted her on *60 Minutes* if her name were *Tom* Sawyer!"

Diane Sawyer and Don Hewitt in the *60 Minutes* control room in 1985.

Diane Sawyer interviewing Gloria Vanderbilt for a profile that aired in April 1985.

SEASONS

18-20

1985 to 1988

I think a mistake that too many interviewers make is that they're not comfortable with silence, and that they will rush in to fill the void.

—Ed Bradley, in an interview with the Television Academy Foundation

Don often said one of the lowest moments in CBS history came in 1971, when network founder and chairman Bill Paley let the great Frank Stanton retire from running CBS day to day by making him sign a contract as vice chairman of the whole company that included a mandatory clause to retire at age sixty-five. Stanton was widely respected for his taste and dignity. He ran the company as a creative enterprise first and a business second. The new people brought in to run CBS News after his promotion had experience in television but none running network news organizations. By the mid-eighties, some of them had come to resent Don, believing that he had become too big for his britches and too powerful. Others who worked at CBS News felt *60 Minutes* got special treatment and that the broadcast, while part of CBS News, was inaccessible and sometimes arrogant—a bitterness that had been growing ever since the program earned its success nearly a decade before.

All of this frustrated Don, who was close to Paley and had a great admiration for the way he and Stanton had run CBS for so long. He worried that the company, including CBS News, was now heading in a very bad direction: driven by profits and stock price and internal politics instead of a desire for quality television and news reporting. He never denied the fact that *60 Minutes* was a business. But he felt the new guys didn't understand that quality television was what brought in profits.

So Don came up with one of his craziest ideas ever. He got on the phone with all of the *60 Minutes* correspondents and anybody else who had money and a stake in the future of CBS News, and asked them to join him in an effort to buy CBS News away from the corporation. Once he got enough people on board, he took the idea to Gene Jankowski, the president of the CBS Broadcast Group. Jankowski told him the idea was crazy: CBS News was not for sale and never would be.

Diane Sawyer with fashion designer Calvin Klein for a profile that aired September 22, 1985.

When word got out that Don was leading what sounded like a coup attempt, the powers at CBS News got pretty upset. As Don remembered it, the president of CBS News, Van Gordon Sauter, called him "nothing but a destructive asshole" and an embarrassment. Don wrote in his book, "It was plain I was on his shit list, but then again, I can't remember a time when I wasn't."

Don tried to repair the damage with a letter to Jankowski, copying everyone involved and explaining that he meant no harm—and that from then on he would confine himself to his job as executive producer of *60 Minutes*. The rest of CBS News was none of his business. He was done: frustrated and fed up.

The episode has a postscript that could only come to pass at a place like *60 Minutes*, where practical jokes have always been the favored sport. Mike and Morley decided to let it leak to Don that the two of them were speaking secretly to a group of investors led by Don's pal Pete Peterson, a Wall Street investment big shot, about buying *60 Minutes* away from CBS. The deal would have one condition: Don not be part of it. They plotted the prank meticulously, to the point where they wanted to make sure Don thought he was hearing about it by accident.

The whole thing was diabolical even for these two rascals—and, if they stopped to think about it, far too mean-spirited to be considered a joke. But it worked. When Don heard about it, he went ballistic! He fired off calls to Morley and Mike, calling them traitors and backstabbers. He was so upset that they worried it could kill him. So they told him the truth: it was all make-believe. Or at least they tried to tell him that. This was Morley's favorite part of the story: when they told him it was all a joke, Don refused to believe them. It took them a good few hours to calm him down, and I don't think Don ever saw the humor in it.

He liked a good laugh, though. One day his secretary, Bev Morgan, told him she had a message from Ed Bradley: he was planning to change his name to Shaheeb Shahab. Don wasn't sure he believed it at first and hoped it wasn't true. But he was convinced when he confronted Ed about it. They agreed they should make a call to a reporter to break the story and get it over with. Don dialed columnist Kay Gardella at the *New York Daily News*, and just as he was about to tell her, Ed told him to hang up, that it was a joke. They both had a good laugh.

But between the moments of humor, the corporate uncertainty and instability did not go away. In 1985 Ted Turner announced his intention to take over CBS. It was a hostile bid by a flamboyant innovator who had changed television news by inventing CNN five years earlier. The acquisition might have proven to be of great benefit to CBS shareholders and employees, but the company put up a strong fight, and the Turner bid failed.

Don wanted to interview Turner for *60 Minutes*, and after a year of trying, in April 1986, Turner agreed. Interviewer Diane Sawyer asked him what he would have done if had taken control of CBS.

Actor Jack Lemmon was profiled by Morley Safer on January 5, 1986.

TURNER: There's too much sleaze and too much violence and too much materialism and too much stupidity in a lot of the network shows. Not all of them, certainly—some of them are okay, I'm sure.

SAWYER: So if you were network president right now, you'd take *Dallas* off the air?

TURNER: No, I wouldn't take it off the air; I would try and make it nicer . . . that might hurt the ratings, but it'd be a high-wire balancing act. I think the American people have been fed so much trash and violence for so long that they're addicted to it.

He even took a swipe at us, which Don loved:

"*60 Minutes*, I find out, has done a hatchet job on just about everybody of importance, every institution we have, over the last twenty years, and they have very few friends as a result of it."

• • •

It was a shock to learn from Mike Wallace upon his retirement in 2006 that during this period he tried to take his own life. There wasn't a very good understanding of clinical depression at the time. We've come so far since the mid-1980s in knowledge and awareness, and Mike was a big part of that. Later in life, he became something of an ambassador for mental illness, going very public with his history of depression.

The trigger for his suicide attempt was the libel suit that General William Westmoreland filed against CBS—naming Mike and producer George Crile—for the 1982 *CBS Reports* documentary *The Uncounted Enemy: A Vietnam Deception*, which suggested that at the height of the war, in 1967, the United States had purposefully underestimated the strength of the enemy in Vietnam, downplaying the strength of the enemy. The trial, which began in late 1984, revealed that mistakes had been made, mostly violations of our own CBS News standards. The trial made news almost every day, including on CBS newscasts. The case was eventually settled in February 1985, reportedly because the Westmoreland side realized that it would be difficult to prove "actual malice."

In the middle of the trial, Mike was hospitalized; everyone was told it was due to exhaustion. Only more than twenty years later did he admit to Morley Safer in an interview that his wife, Mary, had found him passed out next to an empty bottle of pills and a suicide note. Mike's own acknowledgment of his mental illness—along with incredible support from Mary, as well as some close friends who also suffered depression—helped him get through the most difficult period of his life.

Mike's interviews nearing the end of our second decade were as memorable as ever—and maybe even a little more thoughtful. His 1987 interview with playwright Arthur Miller was a spectacular example. The man who created the character of Willie Loman in the 1949 play *Death of a Salesman* was as introspective and honest about his own failings as anybody who ever appeared on *60 Minutes*. And Mike made the interview even better with his characteristic ability to move a conversation along and get the most out of it. It's a fine example of why Mike was so good at what he did. He knew, better than anyone, how to extract information and how to ask questions so their answers told a story.

The interview was timed to the release of the seventy-two-year-old Miller's autobiography and started with Mike asking him about one of his finest achievements, *Death of a Salesman*.

WALLACE: You wrote *Death of a Salesman* when you were thirty-three years old. How long did it take you?

MILLER: Well, the first act more or less was a matter of one day and a night. I then rested and worked about six weeks on the second act and put the whole thing together. But, of course, there's a lifetime in that play.

WALLACE [*narration*]: *Death of a Salesman* was a triumph for Arthur Miller. It won him both the Pulitzer Prize and the New York Drama Critics Award. The critics were comparing him to Henrik Ibsen and Eugene O'Neill.

MILLER: You inevitably begin to feel a kind of impact of power which

Mike Wallace interviewing writer Arthur Miller for a profile that aired November 15, 1987.

is sexual, it is financial, it is everything. You begin to shift and change, if you are not careful, which I wasn't. People were now talking to me differently: women, men. They were looking at me like an icon of some kind.

Mike prepared diligently for every interview he conducted. He would go over written questions and rework them to his liking. But he was never dependent on them. He was forever listening and following up on anything that came up unexpectedly, which is what you always hope for. With Mike, it even went beyond listening. He was observing his subject—body language, facial expression—as he did in this section about Miller's five-year marriage to Marilyn Monroe and their eventual divorce:

> WALLACE: Your face changes when you talk about her.
>
> MILLER: Excuse me?
>
> WALLACE: Your face changes when you talk about her.
>
> MILLER: In what way?
>
> WALLACE: Well I think you still, those were tough years . . . wonderful years and terrible years.
>
> MILLER: Sure they were. Oh, there was a lot of pain, certainly for her and certainly for me.
>
> WALLACE: Why? What did it do to you?
>
> MILLER: Well, it's a defeat. It always is.

The interview ended with a predictable question for profile stories, but the response is one of my favorites because it doesn't seem like Arthur Miller had one in mind. And so we, the viewers, get to witness his humility and his brilliance as he forms an answer before our eyes:

> WALLACE: You ever think about an epitaph?
>
> MILLER: Epitaph, never gave it a moment's thought.

WALLACE: Give it a moment.

MILLER: The first thought that occurs to me is, "He worked awful hard." But that's hardly a recommendation. Everybody does, or a lot of people do.

WALLACE: And what did he work for?

MILLER: Oh, some little moment of truth up on that stage that people could feel made them a little more human.

Ed Bradley also excelled at drawing people out. If he had to give a master class in reporting, he would ask his students to watch his 1984 interview with Richard Jahnke. At age sixteen, Jahnke, who was from Wyoming, shot and killed his father, Richard Jahnke Sr., after what he said were years of physical and emotional abuse inflicted on him and his sister, Deborah. The story, produced by Allan Maraynes, aired a little more than a year after the murder, and after the teenager had been convicted of voluntary manslaughter and sentenced to five to fifteen years in prison.

Jahnke spoke in a calm and controlled yet seething manner. The fascinating thing about the final product is that Ed barely had to ask a question. There are just shots of him listening intently—and that, he said in an interview with the Television Academy Foundation, was the point:

Ed Bradley with comedians Robin Williams and Jonathan Winters for a profile of Williams that aired September 21, 1986.

interviewing is all about listening and not trying to fill in the silence. "There were times," he said, "when I would ask Richard Jahnke a question, and there would be a minute of silence, a minute and a half of silence. And I think a mistake that too many interviewers make is that they're not comfortable with silence, and that they will rush in to fill the void . . . For me, it was one of the most riveting interviews that I've done in twenty years at *60 Minutes* . . . I can remember just sitting there waiting for him to say something, and when he said it, boy, it was amazing."

> JAHNKE: Just, you know, after the beatings he'd given us, after calling my sister a slut, after slapping her around, the Saturday before—because he was beating her because she had got up at eight thirty, and she just wanted some tea. He slapped her around for not combing her hair. That's the first time I went out there, and that's the first time I physically was able to do something against my dad. It was like a huge adrenaline rush. I just got out of my room, and I said, "Stop that!" I went in and grabbed him. My sister was on the floor, and he was grabbing her by the hair and slapping her. I just grabbed him. I was able to push him up against the wall. I gave him almost like an order. "Stop! Calm down!" And he did.
>
> BRADLEY [*narration*]: That night, his parents went to dinner. But before they left, according to Richard Junior, his father told him, "We'll find a way to get rid of you."
>
> JAHNKE: And I thought, "I just can't take this anymore." And I walked inside, and there was Deborah crying. She'd been through so much torture. That's when I decided, "I'm going to stop him! No more!"
>
> BRADLEY [*narration*]: Richard Junior decided in his own mind what he had to do. With Deborah waiting in the family room, he armed himself with a shotgun, a hunting knife, and a .38 caliber revolver, and waited in the darkened garage for his parents to return.

JAHNKE: I remember I was so afraid in the garage when the Volkswagen drove up and he starting walking up to the garage door. I wanted so much to just throw that gun down and when he opens up the garage to—to just hug him and say, "Dad, you know, we've got to stop this. We've got to do something. I love you." And I said to myself, "No! No more." And I just remember opening fire. I just remember those shots; they hurt so much. It was like—it really felt like I was being shot with him. And I heard . . . I thought it was a ringing in my ears, but it wasn't. It was my mom, just constant shrieking. I just had to get out of there.

Five months after Ed's story, "Dirty Little Secret," aired, Wyoming's governor commuted Jahnke's sentence to three years, enabling him to leave prison in 1985 at the age of nineteen. The governor said he felt compassion for him.

DECADE

4

1998 to 2008

SEASONS

31-33

1998 to 2001

It's worth remembering that the people who fretted that *60 Minutes* might be sullied by extending its brand name were all inside CBS. Viewers have no such misplaced sense of reverence.

—*New York Times*, January 15, 1999, reviewing the debut of *60 Minutes II*

In the thirtieth year of *60 Minutes*, Leslie Moonves, the new head of entertainment at CBS, had a problem: he had inherited a terrible lineup of losing shows. At the same time, newsmagazine shows were proliferating across other networks. One quick fix seemed obvious: Why not duplicate the best TV newsmagazine in the business? Why not launch another edition of *60 Minutes* to air during the week?

Andrew Heyward, the president of CBS News, started discussing the possibility with the *60 Minutes* staff, and it did not go over well from

60 Minutes II was launched in January 1999, with correspondents, from left, Bob Simon, Vicki Mabrey, Dan Rather, Scott Pelley, and Charlie Rose.

the beginning. Andrew admired Don; he said working with him was like walking into an airplane factory and finding the Wright brothers out on the assembly line. But Don could also be a handful. He would refuse to attend meetings, for example, especially budget meetings. Those of us who worked for him loved that about him—but it made situations such as this difficult. Don was worried the company would produce a cheap version of his broadcast and hurt the *60 Minutes* brand.

Les Moonves had a great admiration for the *60 Minutes* crew. A big part of why he wanted to add another edition of *60 Minutes* was to duplicate its high-quality storytelling.

Convincing Don to go along with a second edition of *60 Minutes* was something else altogether.

Things turned ugly when Les attended a birthday lunch being thrown for Mike Wallace, who was turning eighty. They gathered at Patron restaurant in Manhattan at a big round table.

Les remembers taking a beating from the entire crew of correspondents, all of whom seemed immovable. Ed Bradley was the most vocal, asking Les, "Why would you do this?" They all chimed in—relentlessly telling Les he would ruin *60 Minutes* if he went ahead with his plan. Les remembers feeling like he was arguing with Mt. Rushmore.

But the network needed the new show, and Les and Andrew convinced Don and the gang that *60 Minutes II* was going to happen one way or another; it would be better to accept it and insist that it be run by one of their own. That person turned out to be me. I had been running the *CBS Evening News* with Dan Rather since 1995, and we were having great success restoring the traditional CBS News values kept alive at *60 Minutes*, but I jumped at the chance of going back to *60 Minutes* after four years away.

In the summer of 1998, I set up headquarters on the opposite end of the *60 Minutes* floor, and we started work on building the new broadcast, with plans to premiere six months later. The first idea we had was to include "*60 Minutes* Classics": to revisit *60 Minutes* stories with significant updates. Everybody agreed it would help the quality of the new broadcast every week and guarantee that one-third of the airtime would resemble the original *60 Minutes* in quality and tone. As soon as Mike Wallace learned we would pay the *60 Minutes* correspondents a significant fee for each of these "classic" segments, he suddenly became the show's biggest fan.

To ensure that the other two-thirds of the broadcast would maintain the same standards, I hired the best veterans from *60 Minutes* who had left the broadcast or who would work on both. The original director, my good friend Artie Bloom, agreed to direct *our* broadcast as well, and Patti Hassler, another *60 Minutes* veteran who had left the broadcast a few years earlier, came back to be my number two. Mike Whitney, one of the best broadcast producers at CBS, came with me from the *Evening News*. We assembled a great team of correspondents, too. The first was Dan Rather, who was certain to add credibility every time he went on the air. Bob Simon, among the finest reporters ever to work at CBS News, was keen to join, as was Charlie Rose, one of the best interviewers in the business. We

Patti Hassler, who was Jeff Fager's deputy at *60 Minutes II*, eventually moved into that role at *60 Minutes*.

added Vicki Mabrey, a solid CBS News correspondent, and Scott Pelley, who had been covering the Clinton White House brilliantly through the long and strange investigation of the president by the independent counsel Ken Starr, and the impeachment process that followed the revelation that the president had lied about having an affair with the intern Monica Lewinsky.

Start-up broadcasts are never painless, but we had a model to follow, which made it much easier. We knew how to select and tell our stories; Don had taught us that. We didn't need to compose music; we had the *60 Minutes* stopwatch. There was no need to build a new set; *60 Minutes* used the artwork of the great Bob Corujo, superimposed behind the correspondents during their studio introductions. Bruce Jensen, our graphic artist, created a perfect little roman numeral *II* that appeared in the corner as the program began. Morley Safer pitched in and wrote our first promo: "Does America really need another newsmagazine? Yes, if it's *60 Minutes II*."

Our budget allowed us to hire the same number of producers as the Sunday program, as well as to fill what I believe is one of the most important jobs: senior editor in charge of fairness and standards. Esther Kartiganer had held that position at *60 Minutes* ever since the mid-1980s, when, in the aftermath of the lawsuit from Dr. Galloway, who had accused the broadcast of slander by suggesting he was involved in insurance fraud, Don had instituted measures to strengthen our editorial process. *60 Minutes* and now *60 Minutes II* were the only news programs with a member of the staff solely responsible for making sure that nobody's words or actions were taken out of context and that the subjects of our stories were treated fairly. It was no easy task, but I knew just the person for the job: Claudia Weinstein, who had, in her decade at *60 Minutes*, proven to be meticulous in chasing down details.

As we headed for our launch in January 1999, I remember one reporter asking if I wanted to beat *60 Minutes'* ratings. I answered by quoting John the Baptist, who said it was okay to be number two, because everyone knew who number one was. The next day Morley showed up in my office with a picture that he and Bob Corujo had designed. It was of Morley holding out a platter with my head on it. The quote beneath read: "The Punishment of St. Jeff the Baptist."

·   ·   ·

The advent of *60 Minutes II* gave the Sunday broadcast a wake-up call. There were now twenty-five new producers chasing similar stories, which made everything a bit more competitive. And *60 Minutes* got better because of it.

That 1998–99 season of *60 Minutes* delivered one of the program's most controversial and compelling stories: "Death by Doctor," about Dr.

Jack Kevorkian, a Michigan-based medical pathologist pushing for terminal patients to have the right to decide to die. Producer Bob Anderson started pursuing the story after Mike Wallace got a call from a journalist friend telling him of the existence of a 1998 videotape showing Dr. Kevorkian administering a lethal injection to a patient named Tom Youk. The poor man was in the last stages of amyotrophic lateral sclerosis (ALS), also known as Lou Gehrig's disease, a neurodegenerative disorder that eventually robs patients of the ability to control their muscles. Youk, like many end-stage ALS sufferers, was paralyzed and barely able to swallow or breathe.

Morley Safer's original artwork, "The Punishment of St. Jeff the Baptist," hangs in Jeff Fager's office.

Bob went out to meet Dr. Kevorkian, who wanted desperately for *60 Minutes* to air the videotape of him putting Mr. Youk to death so that he would be charged with euthanasia instead of the more severe charge of assisted suicide. Mr. Youk's death had occurred less than three weeks after Michigan enacted a law making assisted suicide a felony punishable by up to five years in prison, and the video proved that the doctor had played a big part in Youk's death. Kevorkian was sure he would beat the charges in court to establish a legal precedent allowing physicians to allow patients to end their own lives.

Mike interviewed Kevorkian and Tom Youk's widow, who had asked the doctor to help her husband die. He also interviewed a medical ethicist, who was appalled. When the first draft of the story was shown to Don, Bob Anderson remembers that "there was never any debate about whether we should air the tape of Tom Youk dying. After all, how he died was the point of the piece, and airing the tape was essential to reporting the story."

Here's how the interview with Kevorkian unfolded on the air, interspersed with footage from the tape of Tom Youk's death:

Mike Wallace interviewing Dr. Jack Kevorkian for a story about assisted suicide that aired November 22, 1998.

DR. KEVORKIAN: Tom, do you want to go ahead with this?

YOUK: Yes.

DR. KEVORKIAN: Shake your head "yes" if you want to go.

YOUK: [*Shakes head yes.*]

DR. KEVORKIAN: All right. I'm going to have you sign again your name, and we're going to date it.

YOUK: Okay.

DR. KEVORKIAN: And we're ready to inject. We're going to inject in your right arm, okay? Okeydoke.

[*Footage of the assisted suicide of Tom Youk.*]

WALLACE [*narration*]: First, the doctor gave him Seconal to put him to sleep quickly.

DR. KEVORKIAN: Sleepy, Tom? Tom, are you asleep? Tom, are you asleep? You asleep? He's asleep.

[*Footage of the assisted suicide of Tom Youk.*]

WALLACE [*narration*]: Then he injected a muscle relaxant to stop his breathing.

WALLACE: And this . . .

DR. KEVORKIAN: Paralyzes the muscles.

WALLACE: But he's still alive at this point.

DR. KEVORKIAN: He's still alive, but—and that's why . . .

WALLACE: Now I can see him breathing just a trifle.

DR. KEVORKIAN: Now you see . . . a lack of oxygen's getting to him now, but he's unconscious, deeply, so it doesn't matter.

WALLACE: Is he dead now?

DR. KEVORKIAN: He's dying now, because his oxygen's cut off. He can't breathe. So now I'll quickly inject the potassium chloride to stop the heart.

[*Voice-over*]: Now there's a straight line.

WALLACE: He's dead.

DR. KEVORKIAN: Yep. The heart has stopped.

Mike was uncharacteristically sympathetic in the interview, though he did challenge Kevorkian.

WALLACE: You killed him.

DR. KEVORKIAN: I did. But it could be manslaughter, not murder.

WALLACE: Yeah. Yeah.

DR. KEVORKIAN: It's not necessarily murder, but it doesn't bother me what you call it. I know what it is. This could never be a crime in any society which deems itself enlightened.

Even before the segment aired, it caused an uproar. Religious leaders condemned it, and five CBS affiliates refused to broadcast it. Afterward, the *New York Times* wrote that CBS went "beyond reporting the news . . . becoming complicit, the carrier of a death played for the cameras." By broadcasting the death, the article continued, "*60 Minutes* creeps closer not only to the Internet but also to the lowest and literally cheapest form of television, reality programming." National organizations of doctors and ethicists were also appalled, in one case saying the network had done nothing less than air a live execution.

The broadcast responded calmly that it was "a hallmark of *60 Minutes* to explore complex and often controversial issues in a fair and responsible way." In spite of the uproar, the atmosphere among the staff at the broadcast was remarkably serene. Looking back today, with so many states having legalized or considered legalizing assisted suicide, the segment was way ahead of its time.

Dr. Kevorkian was found guilty of second-degree murder and spent eight years in state prison. Shortly after his interview aired, a group of people with ALS demonstrated outside CBS News headquarters in New York; they felt the report implied that ALS patients should kill themselves. In speaking with some of the demonstrators, Bob Anderson learned of the heroic struggles some patients endure to remain alive. These conversations led to a compelling *60 Minutes* story called "Choosing Life," which aired a few months later in February 1999.

•   •   •

One of the great advantages of being a magazine is that we can shift from airing one of the most unsettling interviews to one of the most uplifting, which we did on the very same broadcast in the winter of 1999 when Bob Simon and producer Michael Gavshon profiled Roberto Benigni. The Italian actor was on the verge of winning the Oscar for best actor in *Life Is Beautiful*, a film he cowrote about an Italian Jew who guides his son through their time in a Nazi death camp with humor, courage, and love. In his interview with Bob, Benigni spoke, in broken English, about being summoned to the Vatican to screen the movie for the pope:

BENIGNI: There were some cardinals, some monsignors, and about ten nuns; very beautiful, elegant, in the green suit, really wonderful,

wonderful nuns. And then after half an hour, they told me, "Now he's arriving, he's arriving, now arriving," and we see this little, little figure. How do you say figure?

SIMON: Figure. Figure.

BENIGNI: Figure, white, with two people, two cardinals, very big, very big. And this little, little figure, so weak, feeble, and then he said a prayer to Jesus, and everybody with the knees.

SIMON: Did you get down on your knees?

BENIGNI: No, I didn't, because I am not used [to] it. I don't—I didn't know what to do. And I couldn't betray my nature. I jumped on him. Oh, oh, I was so full of energy and enthusiasm, and I called him "Dad," like Pinocchio, "*Babbo*."

SIMON: You jumped on the pope?

BENIGNI: Yeah, and I told him, "*Babbo*"—"Father"—in—how do you say?—slang. No, it's like, really, a little boy, "*Babbo*," which means "Dad." "Dad, finally found you again. I have been so bad in my life!" And I kissed him here and here and here, and everywhere I kissed him. And the cardinal told me, "Quiet, quiet, he's very old," because they were afraid I could—

SIMON: When you jumped on the pope, was he surprised?

BENIGNI: Very surprised. But he like it because he told me, "You are very Italian." Because of my enthusiasm.

Actor and director Roberto Benigni and Bob Simon in Italy for a profile that aired February 28, 1999.

The interview showed that Bob was meant for *60 Minutes*. He often added a touch of wit or irony in his interviews and did well at what was expected of *60 Minutes* correspondents: to listen and respond spontaneously with great questions. That's probably why Bob won an Emmy for best interview of the year with that one.

Bob Simon was the consummate foreign correspondent, with more experience covering conflicts around the world than anyone else at CBS News. He had been reporting four to five stories a year for *60 Minutes*, but the rise of *60 Minutes II* brought him into the fold full-time. It was the break he'd been waiting for—and he helped give *60 Minutes II* the quality control we wanted.

• • •

60 Minutes II debuted on January 13, 1999, with a broadcast that made all of us involved very proud. We started with a story called "The Secret City," about Krasnoyarsk-26, an isolated city in the wilderness of Siberia. The story was reported by George Crile and producer Neeraj Khemlani on the ground in Russia, mixed with interviews conducted in the United States by Dan Rather, produced by Tom Anderson.

It was a terrific team all around, turning out a stunning report about a Cold War city dedicated entirely to producing weapons-grade plutonium for the Soviet Union's nuclear weapons program—a place still cut off from the real world. Ours was the first American camera crew to gain access to the tunnels and reactors built deep into a mountain. The city still actively produced plutonium for Russia, and there was a real cause for concern that it could fall into the wrong hands.

Because of the doubts about launching *60 Minutes II*—both within *60 Minutes* and among those media reporters who covered the news business—enormous attention was paid to that first broadcast. We were on the front page of *TV Guide*, and just about every newspaper in the country wrote stories about our premiere, with reviews running the day after. Fortunately, the first broadcast was successful: the audience exceeded seventeen million viewers, and the broadcast received universal raves. Tom Shales of the *Washington Post*, who was well respected but also feared, wrote, "Tickticktickticktickticktickticktick . . . *Boom! 60 Minutes II*, the first offspring of the most successful magazine in TV history, got off to an explosive, riveting, spectacular start last night with a broadcast of substance and style." The *New York Times* suggested that the program was almost *too* much like the original but praised it nonetheless. The last line of the *Times* story was my favorite: "It's worth remembering that the people who fretted that *60 Minutes* might be sullied by extending its brand name were all inside CBS. Viewers have no such misplaced sense of reverence."

All of us working on the broadcast were thrilled to get so many positive reviews, but more important to us was making Don and the *60 Minutes* gang proud. And they were. *60 Minutes II* was broadcasting one powerful and original story after another.

In March 1999 Bob Simon reported a story we called "The Shame of Srebrenica," about the massacre of eight thousand Muslim civilians in a Bosnian town. The Serbian army did the killing, but the "shame" in our story belonged to the Dutch soldiers sent to Srebrenica as UN peacekeepers to protect the civilian population, only to witness the men being separated from the women and children and trucked away. Their bodies were eventually recovered from mass graves. Five years later, few had been identified.

Bob and producer Randall Joyce framed the story as a cautionary tale. There was a possibility at the time that the United States would send troops into Kosovo—then a province of Serbia, now its own country—as a peacemaking force.

Here's how Bob described what happened in Srebrenica:

SIMON [*narration*]: If you want a sense of the enormity of what happened in Srebrenica, there's no better place to come than here, to old mining tunnels dug into the Bosnian hills. This is where the bodies are stored, more than eighteen hundred of them—a small fraction of the missing, but more than any morgue on earth could handle. None of these bodies have been identified, so they can't be buried. In Bosnia, even the dead can't go home.

[*Footage of stacks of bodies in bags.*]

SIMON [*narration*]: The bodies are still coming in, evidence of a colossal war crime. The Dutch troops, whose mandate was to prevent the massacre, have been home for three years, and many are now speaking out.

WARRANT OFFICER WIM DIJKEMA: We came there to help. We came there to protect them. We came there with a will to do as much as we could, but we failed.

SIMON [*narration*]: Warrant Officer Wim Dijkema belonged to that Dutch battalion which was sent to Srebrenica to stop an attack on the town.

WARRANT OFFICER WIM DIJKEMA: When the war started and the shelling started, we had some of those people in our bunkers, and they cried and they begged us, "Please, help us."

SIMON [*narration*]: When the attack began, the Dutch tried to help. They called in air strikes. Dijkema filmed the Dutch hiding in the safety of their bunker while two NATO planes destroyed one Serb tank. That's when Serb general Ratko Mladic threatened to kill the UN peacekeepers if the air strikes continued. That's when the air strikes stopped, and the defense of Srebrenica was effectively over.

MAJOR ROB FRANKEN: We were beaten in every way.

SIMON [*narration*]: Major Rob Franken, the Dutch second-in-command, was in charge of the troops on the ground.

MAJOR FRANKEN: We got orders to defend Srebrenica from the UN in Sarajevo with all means. And we got the order not to bring body bags back to Holland, so security of our own personnel had priority.

SIMON [*narration*]: Now, one minute. You're getting orders not to bring body bags back to Holland?

MAJOR FRANKEN: That's correct . . . We had to defend the city. If you call it the definition of nonsense, I could agree with that.

You could hear the sorrow in the Dutch voices. They had witnessed the beginnings of a genocide and had done nothing. Now they were struggling with the consequences.

A few weeks after the story was broadcast, Bob and producers Draggan Mihailovich and Jill Landis reported another story of heartbreaking human drama. This one we called "The Lost Children," an epic post–World War II tale of English orphans shipped by the thousands to abusive orphanages in far-off Australia, only to find decades later that they had had families back in England.

SIMON [*narration*]: This story begins in postwar Britain, a nation victorious, but battered and broke; a nation burdened by overflowing children's homes, many of the kids put there by families too poor to raise them. What happened next is almost unfathomable in civilized countries or in modern times. The British government, in collaboration with churches and charities, developed a secret plan to clear out these children's homes, a plan which has only recently been uncovered. The kids were told that they would be adopted by loving families in Australia, and they were shipped off by the thousands. It was as simple as that. The first ship to sail in 1947 was the SS *Asturias*; cargo: 147 boys and girls.

JOHN HENNESSY: Oh, I remember this vividly.

SIMON [*narration*]: John Hennessy was on that ship. Only a few weeks before it sailed, some priests and bureaucrats showed up at his children's institution in England. They were rounding up kids to go to Australia. John was eleven years old.

HENNESSY: We thought Australia was down the street or it was around the corner. How did we know it was on the other side of the world? Well, anyway, they came with the stories, you know, that there's fruits there. Plenty of fruits.

NORMAN JOHNSTON: They said things like, "Well, if you go to Australia, you just hop on a kangaroo and ride to school."

SIMON: Did you know what a kangaroo was?

JOHNSTON: Barely, but, you know, it sounded good.

SIMON [*narration*]: Norman Johnston was seven years old and living in a children's home in Aberdeen, Scotland.

JOHNSTON: This was the image that was created about—well, as I now know that description to be—some form of a utopia.

MARY MOLLOY: I mean, when they first started talking about it, I was just barely six, seven.

They told of arriving in Australia six weeks and twelve thousand miles later, and being informed of the true purpose of their adventure.

SIMON [*narration*]: Not long after they disembarked, they received a lecture from a man in black, the archbishop of Perth.

HENNESSY: He said, "We welcome you to Australia. We need you for white stock," because at this stage, the white Australia policy was on. And we didn't know that we were part of the scheme to populate Australia with the white people. And the archbishop said, "The reason why we do [is] because we are terrified of the Asian hordes." Course, we didn't understand that.

SIMON [*narration*]: How could they? How could children understand that they were a commodity, that they were of value to a continent which was scared of Asians, that they'd been exported by a nation that had a surplus of white people? Who'd expect a child to understand that? If there was a single moment of truth for the kids, a moment when the dream darkened, it may have been when their fingerprints were taken and they were herded into lines.

MOLLOY: All of a sudden, we're standing together, and then there's three of us going one way, and one going another way, and, "Hey, what's happening? What's going on?"

HENNESSY: They grabbed the girls from their brothers, brothers from their sisters, screaming. And I can still hear the screams today.

SIMON [*narration*]: These children, who'd been plucked from institutions in Britain, were now trucked to their destinations in Australia: institutions. No parents were waiting for them, just picks and shovels, and for many of the boys, words of welcome from their new masters, the priests.

With stories such as this, Bob Simon earned his reputation as one of the best writers ever to work at CBS—the network famous for the best journalist-writers. And it was a great example of a lot of the stories that were showing up on *60 Minutes II*. While we were never trying to upstage the mother ship, we were determined to make everybody proud of the work we were doing, and the work was making a mark.

• • •

As could be predicted, though, it didn't take long for the two *60 Minutes* broadcasts to clash. There were all kinds of battles going on over stories. "We're not going to roll over and play dead for anybody," Don told the *New York Times*, "not even our kid brother."

Morley had a great line about the ruckus. "Who's going to win the competition when the two shows are going after the same story? *60 Minutes II*?" he would ask, holding up his index and middle finger. "No! *60 Minutes I*," he would say, dropping the index finger and leaving just his middle finger.

The most dramatic clash came in the fall of 1999 in the run-up to the 2000 presidential election. As the sitting vice president, Al Gore was the most prominent candidate. But it was indicative of a disorganized campaign that the Gore people said yes to Lesley Stahl at *60 Minutes* and to

Dan Rather at *60 Minutes II*—who both set out to do stories on Gore just a few months before primary season.

Andrew Heyward called Don and me to his office to try to work something out. Neither of us cared much, but we knew our correspondents did. Don started off the meeting by saying, "I don't really care how this turns out, but if it is decided that Lesley isn't going to win this, and she isn't going to get the story, let's just get one thing straight right up front: I ain't gonna be the one to tell her!"

Well, Lesley won. And when I told Dan, he was a gentleman about it.

•   •   •

With the new millennium came some big interviews for both *60 Minutes* broadcasts, beginning in the spring of 2000 with a segment on the Oklahoma City bomber, Timothy McVeigh. The domestic terrorist had been sentenced to death for the April 1995 bombing of the Alfred P. Murrah Federal Building in Oklahoma City, which killed 168 people, 19 of them children, and injured more than 600 others. It was the deadliest domestic terrorist attack in US history until 9/11.

Democratic presidential candidate Al Gore posed for a picture with Lesley Stahl and the *60 Minutes* team of producers and technicians after an interview that aired December 5, 1999.

Producer Michael Radutzky worked for months to land the interview for Ed Bradley. And he had to accept some conditions to make it happen. Since McVeigh was appealing the verdict, his attorney insisted that McVeigh would not discuss his role in the bombing; Ed was not allowed to ask if he was the Oklahoma City bomber. This was a difficult condition to accept, but Don decided that as long as this fact was reported as part of the setup to the story, the broadcast would go along in order to hear what McVeigh had to say. The hope was to glean some valuable information about how he could have committed such a horrific crime.

Here's how Ed told the story:

McVEIGH: Maybe one of the benefits of me talking to you today is that you'll see that maybe not everything is true that you've heard about me.

BRADLEY: For example, what's not true?

McVEIGH: Well, am I pure evil? Am I the face of terror, sitting here in front of you, or am I able to talk to you man-to-man?

BRADLEY: Most people in this country think you are the face of evil, don't they?

McVEIGH: They do. But sitting down here now—and let me make clear I'm not sitting here trying to influence you, and I'm not putting on a game face. I'm not conning anybody. I'm just being me. And maybe people will listen, as opposed to not listening at a trial.

McVeigh was a decorated veteran from the first Gulf War, when the United States set out to liberate Kuwait. But he said he was upset that he was forced to kill Iraqis during the war. He became bitter upon his return home and admitted to Ed

Ed Bradley interviewed Oklahoma City bomber Timothy McVeigh on death row at the maximum-security prison in Terre Haute, Indiana, for a story that aired March 12, 2000.

that after he had been imprisoned he had spoken with the Unabomber, Ted Kaczynski (who was also in prison), because they had common experiences.

BRADLEY: Did you ever talk to Kaczynski?

McVEIGH: I did.

BRADLEY: Do you think that you and he share similar concerns about how the government operates these days?

McVEIGH: We have somewhat different views. But there is some common ground there. I found that—in a way that I didn't realize—that we were much alike in that all we ever wanted or all we wanted out of life was the freedom to live our own lives however we chose to. And he expressed that one day. And it hit me that, well, you know, this labeling—he's far left, I'm far right—that's all out the window. There's a lot more commonality there.

BRADLEY: You both think you had lost the freedom to live your life the way you wanted to, and you think that the government took those freedoms from you?

McVEIGH: From my perspective, I believe that it's a problem with government. From Ted's perspective, he believes it's a problem with technology.

Ted Kaczynski, the Unabomber, is still serving his life sentence. Tim McVeigh was executed on June 11, 2001.

·　·　·

Mike Wallace scored the other big interview that year with the Chinese president, Jiang Zemin, on the eve of his visit to the United States. Zemin had not done an interview with an American television reporter for ten years, partly due to his conviction that Americans were unwilling to believe that the vast majority of the Chinese were satisfied with one-party rule. But Mike refused to avoid that subject. One of the interview's most spirited exchanges was over the use of the word "dictator."

WALLACE: You are the last major Communist dictatorship in the world.

PRESIDENT JIANG: You mean I'm dictatorship?

WALLACE: Well, of course. A developmental dictatorship is what we believe it is. Am I wrong?

PRESIDENT JIANG: Of course. This is big mistake.

WALLACE: You are, it seems to me, a dictator. An authoritarian.

PRESIDENT JIANG: No, but—but I—I—very frank speaking, I don't agree with your point I'm dictator.

WALLACE: I know you don't. I know that you don't. But there's an old American phrase about if it walks like a duck and quacks like a duck and so forth, it's a duck.

PRESIDENT JIANG: What means dictatorship?

WALLACE: A dictator is somebody who forcibly . . . whether it's free press or free religion or free private enterprise—now you're beginning to come a little closer to that. Father knows best, and if you get in the way of Father, Father will take care of you.

PRESIDENT JIANG: Your way of describing what things are like in China is as absurd as what the *Arabian Nights* may sound like. The National People's Congress selects the Central Committee of the Communist Party, and the Central Committee has a politburo, and the politburo has a standing committee, of which I am a member. And no decision is made unless all members agree.

WALLACE: But when we talk about dictatorship—I'm wagging my finger at the president of China—you know what? When I see the picture—

[*Footage from 1989 of a Chinese man standing in front of a tank.*]

WALLACE: —of that one young man in front of the tank in Tiananmen Square, that, to me, means Chinese dictatorship. That's a wonderful symbol that hits me in my heart about dictatorship in China.

PRESIDENT JIANG: I don't need translation. I know what you say.

WALLACE: I know.

PRESIDENT JIANG: I'm very willing to answer these questions.

WALLACE: You were a student protester in Shanghai.

PRESIDENT JIANG: Shanghai, that's right.

WALLACE: At the time of the Nationalists. "We want freedom. We want democracy." That was you.

PRESIDENT JIANG: That's right.

WALLACE: That's what those people in Tiananmen Square were saying: "We want freedom. We want democracy."

PRESIDENT JIANG: In the 1989 disturbance, we truly understood the passion of students who were calling for greater democracy and freedom. In fact, we have always been working to improve our system of democracy, but we could not possibly allow people with ulterior motives to use the students to overthrow the government under the pretext of democracy and freedom.

For an American audience, it might have been frustrating to hear Jiang dance around the question of what Tiananmen Square stood for. You never know what you are going to get in an interview with a leader of any country, but that a Chinese leader would even agree to such a conversation was a huge coup.

· · ·

60 Minutes II was also landing big interviews, which created yet more tension with the mother program. On December 5, four weeks past Election Day, Scott Pelley landed the first interview with George W. Bush. The result of the 2000 presidential race between him and Democrat Al Gore still had not been decided, with the state of Florida still too close to call and the US Supreme Court reviewing whether or not a recount should proceed.

PELLEY: Governor, thank you for taking the time. Are you the president-elect?

GOVERNOR GEORGE W. BUSH OF TEXAS: You know, Scott, I've asked my staff to call me Governor. This is a very extraordinary period in American history. We haven't had an election like this in a long time. And until it's over, I'll be governor.

PELLEY: Come on, Governor, you have 271 electoral votes, certified officially by all fifty states.

GOVERNOR BUSH: Right. Well, I feel like I have won the election. I feel like I've actually won it two or three times, but my opponent has made a decision to continue contesting, and I understand that. I can understand his anguish. I can understand the emotions involved, but he's pressing on. And until the election is final, I would hope that people would call me Governor Bush.

The Supreme Court's ruling in favor of Bush came exactly one week later. And just one week after that, Dan Rather scored another big interview for *60 Minutes II*: the exit interview with President Clinton, whose wife had just become the first First Lady elected to the US Senate, as the junior senator from New York. Dan asked the president if Hillary would one day run for the Oval Office but didn't get an answer. Nor did he get an answer when he asked what Hillary would be writing about in her memoirs.

RATHER: Well, I want to say this respectfully, Mr. President. Surely you don't want her writing about Paula Jones, Monica Lewinsky, and all those things again. Is she likely to do that?

PRESIDENT CLINTON: You ought to ask her. She can write about whatever she wants. In fact, I tell you, I bet it'll be a good book.

In the spring of 2000, Bob Simon was honored with a Peabody Award for a collection of his stories at CBS News. It was a big honor for all of us at *60 Minutes II*, and Bob came to New York to accept it.

Bob, who'd been living in Israel when he joined *60 Minutes II*, was

Jeff Fager and Bob Simon celebrating an Emmy win.

pleased when we didn't ask him to relocate, and he ended up doing almost all his stories overseas. His last US posting had been in Washington covering the State Department—the swashbuckling foreign correspondent confined to press conferences inside a stuffy bureaucracy. He became clinically depressed. His remedy: to get out of Washington. In 1982 he followed the secretary of state, Alexander Haig, to Argentina when Haig visited at the time of the brief Falkland Islands war between Argentina and England. When Haig's plane departed for Washington, Bob stayed behind to cover the war. He lived overseas for the next twenty-five years.

I always teased him that by the time we started *60 Minutes II*, he wasn't really an American anymore. For a kid who'd spent his early years in the Bronx, he couldn't tell you anything about the New York Yankees or any American sports team—or anything about popular culture, for that matter. Now here he was accepting one of the most important honors in the business—and he was about to prove me right. Just before getting up to accept the award, he spilled his entire glass of red wine over the front of his white dress shirt. He used his napkin to try to dry it up, and the woman sitting next to him was very kind. She worked hard to dab up the wine from his shirt, helping him disguise the mess with linen napkins. On his way back to his seat, he stopped at my chair and asked me who that nice woman sitting next to him was.

I said, "Bob . . . that's Oprah Winfrey."

SEASONS

34-36

2001 to 2004

Am I sad about leaving you guys? Yeah, but that's about the only thing I'm sad about. You can't have a "run" like I've had for more than half a century and not realize that, with the possible exception of William S. Paley himself, no one ever had a more fruitful, satisfying, and rewarding association with CBS than I've had.

—Don Hewitt, December 2003

September 11, 2001, began as a perfect late-summer day. I went for a run, as I often do in the morning, and was in the shower when my wife, Melinda, knocked on the door. She told me Scott Pelley was on the phone. I said I would call him right back, and she told me he said to get out of the shower.

When Scott gave me the news that a plane had flown into one of the Twin Towers, I rushed to get dressed, watching on TV as a second plane crashed into the second tower. It was difficult to comprehend the horror of what had just happened on live television, as was the instant realization that this was a terrorist attack of unimaginable proportions. Scott was already making his way to the World Trade Center. I called as many people as I could find on the *60 Minutes II* team who could also head down there, packed a bag for many overnights, and headed to Manhattan. Vehicles were blocked from going into the city, so I walked the last four miles from the Bronx, where I'd ditched my car, down Fifth Avenue—with hundreds of people on foot heading in the opposite direction and a direct view of the plume from the collapsed buildings soaring over downtown. The concept that one of the buildings had collapsed was impossible to absorb. How could that happen? How many people got out? Were the *60 Minutes* people I had sent down there all right?

CBS did outstanding work that day, with nearly every reporter in the building deployed to what would soon be called Ground Zero. But what distinguished the network was that months earlier, *60 Minutes* and *60 Minutes II* had begun the kind of in-depth reporting that would help explain the origins of this attack, and the entire staff of *60 Minutes II* was either at Ground Zero or working a related story somewhere in New

Scott Pelley near Ground Zero on September 12, 2001, the day after the attacks.

DECADE 4

York City. Some of the best reporting came from producer George Crile, who had captured stunning footage in Pakistan of people connected to Al Qaeda predicting the tragedy.

George had asked me if he could go to Pakistan in the spring and summer of 2001 to report for *60 Minutes II* on the anti-American sentiments that permeated the country. His trip had come on the heels of a powerful report by Steve Kroft and producer Leslie Cockburn about how Pakistan was becoming radicalized, its nuclear arsenal in danger of falling into the hands of Islamic terrorists—perhaps even Osama bin Laden, the Saudi-born founder of the Al Qaeda terrorist network. When the story won a duPont-Columbia award, the broadcasting equivalent of a Pulitzer, the committee that selected it called the segment "strikingly prophetic."

Crile went to Pakistan alone, as he loved to do, with a compact video camera and a good dose of curiosity. There he found a former Pakistani intelligence officer named Khalid Kwaja, who had been a teacher of Osama bin Laden and his comrade in arms for twenty years.

The interview was conducted two months before 9/11, most of it filmed while driving around in Kwaja's car.

KWAJA: America is a very vulnerable country. You're a very open country. I can tell you, your White House is the most vulnerable target. It's very simple to just get it.

CRILE: What do you mean the White House is vulnerable?

KWAJA: It's very vulnerable.

CRILE: Why?

KWAJA: Why? Why? Because—what is there after? Because you see how difficult it is over there to blow it up or something.

CRILE: I-I assume it's very difficult, or else someone would have done it by now.

KWAJA: US—see, this is the problem. Don't underestimate. It takes only maximum of one or two lives to have it. It's not difficult.

CRILE: And that's not difficult, to find two people prepared to sacrifice their lives?

KWAJA: Oh, no. Not at all. Not at all. For the cause, we have people available.

We didn't know if Khalid Kwaja had any inside knowledge of the impending attack. We assumed his banter was part of the general chatter among Al Qaeda supporters about how easy it would be to attack America.

George Crile also met a group of well-educated boys in an elite Pakistani prep school, all of whom, dressed in their perfect uniforms, with sweater and tie, were on bin Laden's side in his self-declared jihad against the United States. One of them used bin Laden's name as the screen saver on his computer. Crile brought up the cruise missile attacks President Clinton had launched against bin Laden in August 1998, just a few weeks after the near-simultaneous bombings of US embassies in Kenya and Tanzania that killed 224. Both acts of terrorism were soon linked to bin Laden.

CRILE: Are you proud of the fact that so far, America has been unable to get bin Laden?

BOYS: Yes.

BOY NUMBER FIVE: Yeah, we are proud.

BOY NUMBER SIX: Absolutely.

BOY NUMBER SEVEN: We are proud because they can't get him. They don't know where he is. They can't do nothing about it.

BOY NUMBER EIGHT: And they are superpower.

CRILE: The next time those missiles hit and they actually take Osama bin Laden out, then the problem is solved for the United States, correct?

BOY NUMBER NINE: But another Osama will come.

BOY NUMBER SEVEN: But you are going to kill one Osama; a thousand Osamas are still there.

BOY NUMBER TEN: You cannot stop us. . . .

BOY NUMBER NINE: Another Osama will come.

BOY NUMBER SEVEN: They're still waiting.

BOY NUMBER TEN: You think that we are children. But we are not children. We are mujahideen, and we can fight for the sake of Islam.

CRILE: There may be as many as ten others.

BOY NUMBER NINE: Yeah.

BOY NUMBER SEVEN: I'm just giving you that as an example.

BOY NUMBER ELEVEN: What we mean to say [is] that we Muslims are called lions who are asleep. If they wake up . . .

BOY NUMBER SEVEN: We're joined together.

BOY NUMBER ELEVEN: If they wake up, they are going to bust the world.

Steve Kroft was in New Orleans on 9/11, stuck there when commercial flights were grounded for three days. But he and producer Graham Messick found a story about airline security right there in the Crescent City. They interviewed a former Federal Aviation Administration (FAA) special agent named Steve Elson, who had been a member of an elite unit called the Red Team that conducted secret security probes at major airports and had been able to breach security 90 to 95 percent of the time. They had done so even when using something called a modular bomb unit, a replica of a sophisticated explosive device that a real terrorist might use.

KROFT: When you took this modular bomb out, how many people detected it?

ELSON: I went out originally and did fifty to sixty tests, and there was one detection, but I was able to talk my way out of it and get away without being caught. So I was one hundred percent successful as the bad guy.

KROFT [*narration*]: But it wasn't just the FAA's secret Red Team that was getting those results. In 1988 the FAA's deputy administrator for security, Cathal Flynn, hired an outside firm to conduct a vulnerability assessment at a major US airport which we agreed not to name because the results were so abysmal. It's all spelled out in this FAA memo.

ELSON: Well, according to this document—this is not a restricted or classified document, and it should be—but there were four hundred fifty tests conducted. The team was caught four times. That meant that the bad guys got through 99.1 percent of the time.

KROFT: According to the document, they got into baggage areas and passenger lounges, planting fake explosives in suitcases, carry-on luggage, and catering carts. They got into ramp areas and aircraft holds, and they breezed through metal detectors with no problem.

ELSON: And if you look further at the document, it talks about these people going through a screening checkpoint with pistols behind metal belt buckles seven times, and MAC submachine guns on their backs under their jacket.

KROFT: What do we call this kind of security?

ELSON: Nonsecurity.

There were the terrifying, big-picture stories and the heartbreaking, more intimate ones. The first Sunday after the attacks, Ed Bradley did a story about Summit, New Jersey, that brought home the terrible desperation the victims' families felt as the days unfolded without news of their loved ones. Summit—home to Ed's producer, Michael Radutzky—is a commuter town that lost ten of its residents. When one of Michael's neighbors, Debbie Rancke, asked for his help in finding her husband, Todd, who was at work in the World Trade Center's south tower when the planes hit, he asked if she might possibly be willing to let *60 Minutes* document her desperate search through New York City's hospitals and morgues. She said yes.

After three days, there was no sign of Todd anywhere. Ed asked Debbie Rancke what she was going to do next:

RANCKE: I ask myself that every day. What can we do next? And we regroup, and we keep calling hospitals, we talk to people who can put his picture out and—and continue to look for him, watch the news to see if anybody else has been found. And we come to New York every day looking for answers.

BRADLEY: I hope you find them.

RANCKE: We're a strong group, and we're going to get through this. I know that.

BRADLEY: I can see that.

Ed Bradley tries to comfort Debbie Rancke, center, who lost her husband, Todd, in the World Trade Center attacks.

Ed, usually so cool and collected on camera, had a hard time maintaining his composure during that interview. It was as if the gravity of what had happened sunk in as Debbie said those words. He got out of his chair to comfort her, but it seemed almost as if he needed comforting himself.

BRADLEY: Oh God, Debbie . . . I'm gonna do everything I can. Everything I can.

RANCKE: If you can help us in any other way. Just whatever you can do. Just help me find him. He's my whole life.

It took months to identify most of the victims who had been in the towers on 9/11 through fragments of DNA found in the wreckage. Todd Rancke was confirmed dead in April 2002.

For almost three months, the Sunday and weekday editions of *60 Minutes* devoted every broadcast to 9/11 and the context of the attacks. Both

Ed Bradley with members of the New York City Highway Patrol after 9/11. When someone in uniform was pulled from the wreckage at Ground Zero, this squad of police officers escorted the remains to the city morgue.

covered the impact on the financial markets and took a hard look at how the United States had provided a safe haven to the 9/11 terrorists. Both wanted to know what motivated Osama bin Laden. And both broadcasts asked if the United States was prepared to defend against bioterrorism, something that a lot of Americans were wondering.

·   ·   ·

Both broadcasts covered what happened next: the beginning of the longest war in US history. Less than a month after 9/11, in October 2001, President Bush set his sights on Afghanistan. The so-called Bush doctrine stated that any country harboring Al Qaeda was an enemy of the United States. Since Afghanistan, under control of the ultraconservative Muslim group known as the Taliban, had given bin Laden his base of operations, we expected a war to find him, kill him, and overthrow the Taliban government.

60 Minutes II covered that war regularly, mostly with reporting by Scott Pelley and Lara Logan. The skills Scott brought to *60 Minutes II* enabled us to do what we always wanted to: cover a story based on breaking news. Scott could get a well-reported, well-written, and compelling *60 Minutes* segment on the air in a fraction of the time that most of our stories took.

Like me, he grew up in an era of television journalism when speed was made more possible by videotape and satellite technology. We could get a story to New York from almost anywhere in the world in a matter of hours, and we all got better at doing that out covering the news for years.

As for Lara, she had been a stringer for CBS News radio in Kabul, waiting for weeks with the Afghan opposition group the Northern Alliance as its fighters prepared to invade the city and take on the Taliban-led government. The only CBS correspondent in the Afghan capital, she was perfectly placed to cover the beginning of the war. Within a few months, she was working for *60 Minutes II* and CBS News full-time. And like many war correspondents in the post-9/11 world, Lara soon ended up spending most of her time in Iraq.

Before the war in Iraq started in March 2003, *60 Minutes II* landed a groundbreaking interview that brought us a flood of criticism, although, in retrospect, the story seems weirdly prophetic. That February, Dan Rather and producer Jim Murphy interviewed Iraqi president Saddam Hussein, who vehemently denied having any weapons of mass destruction. "I think America and the world also knows that Iraq no longer has the weapons," he insisted. "And I believe the mobilization that's been done was, in fact, done partly to cover the huge lie that was being waged against Iraq about chemical, biological, and nuclear weapons."

We were clobbered for letting Hussein make that claim. But in a few months' time, we all learned that he had been telling the truth, and that the war predicated on the existence of weapons of mass destruction (WMDs) was fought on the basis of bad intelligence (at best) or manipulated press accounts (at worst).

Bob Simon and Michael Gavshon were among the first journalists to question the US government's premise for going to war. Their December 2002 story "It Pays to Advertise?" cast serious doubt on White House claims, including that the International Atomic Energy Agency had issued a report stating that Saddam Hussein was six months away from developing

Michael Gavshon and Bob Simon were the closest of friends and colleagues.

a nuclear bomb. David Albright, a physicist who had been a UN weapons inspector in Iraq in the 1990s, told Bob there was no such report:

SIMON: Why do you think the Bush administration has been exaggerating?

ALBRIGHT: Well, what I worried about, and this is why I personally got involved and why my institute got involved, is that we always fear that a government will use the nuclear card to increase support for a policy of what's, in this case, invasion of Iraq.

SIMON [*narration*]: And he says the administration has been making other unsubstantiated claims to beef up its case that Iraq is getting close to the bomb. Take this September *New York Times* article. Anonymous administration officials were quoted as saying that Iraq was trying to import "aluminum tubes." Those tubes, the officials claimed, could be used only in gas centrifuges to enrich uranium for a nuclear weapon. Hours later, the administration's top officials were on the Sunday talk shows trumpeting the story administration officials had just leaked . . . But the British government, which supports the administration's campaign against Iraq, had a different assessment. Its study on Iraq concluded "there is no definitive intelligence that the tubes are destined for a nuclear program."

ALBRIGHT: People who understood gas centrifuges almost uniformly felt that these tubes were not specific to gas centrifuge use.

SIMON: It seems that what you're suggesting is that the administration's leak to the *New York Times*, regarding aluminum tubes, was misleading?

ALBRIGHT: Oh, I think it was. I think it was very misleading.

Still, when it came to the question of WMDs, just about every news organization stumbled badly, including *60 Minutes*. A year before the start of the war, Lesley Stahl and Rich Bonin reported on the Iraqi National Congress (INC), a London-based group of Iraqi exiles who were waging a public relations campaign to get the United States into a war. As part of that campaign, the INC provided safe haven to a number of high-level Iraqi defectors who gave the organization specific details about Saddam Hussein's WMD program—information that was then passed on to the Pentagon.

The star of Lesley and Rich's report was Ahmad Chalabi, an Iraqi American who'd cofounded the Iraqi National Congress. Two years after the story aired—and a full year after the invasion of Iraq—the US government found that Chalabi had been deliberately misleading them. Lesley did a follow-up interview to pin him down on what he'd said previously:

STAHL: Here's what we were told: that in the intelligence community, they now believed that you, through these defectors, hoodwinked, spun, misled senior officials in the Bush administration, and that you coached these defectors.

CHALABI: We never coached any defector to say anything. We never told anyone to say anything.

STAHL [*narration*]: Specifically, his organization, the Iraqi National Congress, is charged with coaching this defector, Major Hareeth, who told US intelligence and *60 Minutes* two years ago that in order to evade the UN inspectors, Saddam put his biological weapons labs in trucks.

STAHL: I'm wondering if you spun me, if he spun me, if you all spun me.

CHALABI: We have not spun you.

Around that same time, a year into the war, Lesley and Rich landed a disturbing interview with President Bush's former terrorism advisor, Richard Clarke, who blamed the White House for not taking the proper steps to protect the country from threats by Al Qaeda and charged that the president and his Cabinet pressured him to find evidence to support a US war against Iraq.

> RICHARD CLARKE: [US Secretary of Defense Donald] Rumsfeld was saying that we needed to bomb Iraq, and we all said, "But no, no. Al Qaeda is in Afghanistan. We need to bomb Afghanistan." And Rumsfeld said, "There aren't any good targets in Afghanistan, and there are lots of good targets in Iraq."
>
> STAHL: But didn't they think that there was a connection?
>
> CLARKE: No. I think they wanted to believe that there was a connection, but the CIA was sitting there, the FBI was sitting there, I was sitting there, saying, "We've looked at this issue for years. For years we've looked for a connection, and there's just no connection."
>
> STAHL: Was Iraq supporting Al Qaeda?
>
> CLARKE: No. There's absolutely no evidence that Iraq was supporting Al Qaeda.

Richard Clarke told Lesley Stahl that the Bush administration failed to protect the country from Al Qaeda.

Similar to how we covered 9/11, *60 Minutes II* took a different, "boots on the ground" approach to the war in Iraq. Scott Pelley and Bill Owens headed for Kuwait to cover the war independently, meaning without being embedded with the US military, which is where most reporters were. The great newsman Larry Doyle, who was running CBS coverage out of Kuwait City, set them up at a farmhouse on the border with Iraq. I remember getting a call from Bill, who asked if we could purchase two SUVs so that they could drive straight into Iraq, dragging a satellite dish, to feed the material out.

On March 23, 2003, after twenty-four difficult hours of trying to get through some of the most impossible barricades to entering Iraq, Bill and Scott crossed the border just as the war was starting. They appeared on the air that Sunday night with the first television report from the front lines, filmed in the Iraqi port town of Umm Qasr. It was a remarkable effort that took real guts and resulted in some of the best war reporting in CBS history. Scott and Bill were joined by producer Mark Hooper, cameraman Sean Keane, soundman Paul Hardy, and Perry Jones, a savvy tech guy and satellite operator who had his work cut out for him with so much dust messing with the equipment. Those six fed us story after story from the front lines of the war, working their way through Iraq for five weeks straight until dust killed every piece of equipment they had. They then returned to Iraq several times more, once for a dramatic interview with Colonel James Hickey, one of the soldiers involved in the capture of Saddam Hussein in December 2003.

To make sure we were first with that story, we couldn't wait until the following Wednesday for *60 Minutes II*; it had to air on *60 Minutes* the Sunday right before Christmas. Scott and Bill had just a couple of days to shoot, write, and edit the story, but that was not unusual for them. It *was* unusual for Don Hewitt, who came in that Sunday to see their story and put it on the air that night. Don had never worked with them before because they were full-time on *60 Minutes II*, and he was nervous that they wouldn't finish the story in time. He wasn't used to such a quick turnaround on anything other than a straight interview and was stunned by their speed and performance. By the time it was done, the piece looked like it had taken weeks to produce—not less than two days. Don kept yelling into the phone, "You guys are like greased lightning!" He said it over and over: "Greased lightning!"

Scott Pelley and producer Bill Owens wearing protective gear and gas masks in Umm Qasr, Iraq, where chemical attack scares were frequent.

Scott Pelley went into the hole where Saddam Hussein had been hiding and where he was eventually captured by US Special Forces in December 2003.

The week before that story, Lesley Stahl interviewed Secretary of Defense Donald Rumsfeld. It was an important interview and happened to be the only live interview in a regular *60 Minutes* broadcast. We never did live interviews for a number of reasons, and probably the most significant is that we couldn't edit them. If a subject wanted to evade a question he could just run out the clock. Rumsfeld didn't try to run out the clock but he made some stunning comments. It was one day after Saddam Hussein's capture and Lesley asked the secretary about how they might get him to talk.

STAHL: Let-let me ask you—raise the whole question of-of—for lack of a better term—torture. Let's say he's not forthcoming. Would we deprive him of sleep? Would we make it very cold where he is, or very hot? Are there any restrictions on the way we treat him to get him to cooperate more than he has been?

RUMSFELD: You know, the—to even raise the word torture in terms of how the United States military would treat this person, it seems to me, is-is a—unfortunate. We don't torture people. And here's a man who has tortured to death tens of thousands of people, conducted rape and-and-and brutality the likes of which it would be difficult [to] find a-a-a-a more vicious and brutal dictator who—in-in-in our adult lifetimes. And I just told you that he would be treated according to the Geneva Conventions.

STAHL: Well, you know, some . . .

RUMSFELD: And—and to suggest that anyone would be engaged in torture or conduct inconsistent with the Geneva Conventions it seems to me is—is not on the mark at all.

STAHL: Sleep deprivation? No? You're ruling it completely out, is what you're telling us?

RUMSFELD: I'm not telling you anything other than I have just told you. He will be treated according to the Geneva Conventions, and given the protections of a prisoner of war.

Rumsfeld seemed so appalled that Lesley would ask the question, even though what were called "enhanced interrogation techniques" were being widely used at the direction of his Department of Defense. Within a few months of those comments we were tipped off to the most significant story we reported about over the entire course of the war—abuse at Abu Ghraib prison, where Iraqi prisoners were badly mistreated by American soldiers. We had obtained photographs of the mistreatment that soon became iconic images of a horrible moment in America military history.

The story was produced by Mary Mapes for *60 Minutes II*, but it had come to us because of an associate producer, Dana Roberson, who had established a relationship with an important source on a previous story. Like any good reporter, Dana earned his trust, and as soon as the source learned of the pictures of the Abu Ghraib abuses—which had surfaced in a court-martial of the soldiers involved—he called her. When we got our hands on the photos, we were stunned at what they showed: American soldiers in uniform posing with naked Iraqi prisoners stacked in pyramids or in poses meant to simulate sexual activity, and, in one instance, an Iraqi man standing on a box with his head covered and wires attached to his hands. He was told that if he fell off the box, he'd be electrocuted.

It was hard to believe American soldiers were committing such horrible acts. We didn't yet realize that the methods they used to break prisoners complied with their interpretation of the Bush administration's rules of how to treat prisoners in the post-9/11 world. Six soldiers ended up facing charges, including army reservist Sergeant Chip Frederick, who agreed to be interviewed over the phone from Baghdad, where he was awaiting court-martial. He told Dan Rather he was pleading not guilty and blamed his superiors for the abuse, saying the prison was understaffed and that he had never been properly trained to handle prisoners of war.

> RATHER: When you first arrived at the prison, Sergeant, what happened and what didn't happen?
>
> SERGEANT FREDERICK: Just everything. We had no support, no training whatsoever. And I kept asking my chain of command for certain things, like rules and regulations, and it just—it just wasn't happening.
>
> RATHER [*narration*]: Sergeant Frederick's letters and email messages home offer clues to problems inside the prison. Frederick wrote that he was helping the interrogators. Quote: "Military intelligence has encouraged and told us 'Great job!' They usually don't allow others to watch them interrogate, but since they like the way I run the prison, they've made an exception. We help getting them to talk with the way we handle them. We've had a very high rate with our style of getting them to break. They usually end up breaking within hours."
>
> SERGEANT FREDERICK: We had to use force sometimes to get the inmates to cooperate just like our rules of engagement said. We learned a little bit of Arabic, basic commands. And they didn't want to listen, so sometimes you would just give them a little nudge or something like that just to get them to cooperate so we could get the mission accomplished.

The most difficult part of reporting the story was vetting the photos to make sure they were what they appeared to be. That meant getting two people who witnessed the events to confirm them. When we finished the vetting after several weeks, we asked the US Army for a spokesman to respond.

We expected to air it the following Wednesday night. But the army spokesman asked us to wait a week out of concern for Americans held prisoner in Iraq who might face retribution when the story went public. We agreed to hold the piece, knowing that we were alone in reporting it. What we didn't expect was that the following week, Dan Rather took a call from Richard Meyers, chairman of the Joint Chiefs of Staff, asking that we hold the story another week. We weren't happy, but as Dan hadn't ever received such a request before, and since, as far as we knew, we still had the story exclusively, we agreed to hold it one more week.

But within a few days I was embroiled in unpleasant discussions with Donald Rumsfeld's Pentagon to secure the army interview. The defense secretary's people were unhappy we were doing the story and accused me of giving the photos to *New Yorker* writer Seymour Hersh. They didn't realize that by making this accusation, they'd tipped me off to the fact that the veteran investigative journalist was competing with us to break the news. I got into a shouting match over all this with one of Rumsfeld's top aides, Larry Di Rita. I told him there would be no more delay: we were going on the air with or without a spokesman to tell the army's side of the story.

Within a few hours, that interview was set up and on Tuesday, April 27, Dan interviewed General Mark Kimmitt, the deputy chief of coalition operations in Iraq, who said he was "appalled" at the soldiers' behavior. We put the story on the air the next night. We were surprised that the American news media gave the story very little play at first, because it made banner headlines in Europe the next morning. The following day, it made the front pages across the United States.

• • •

One day at *60 Minutes II* we were screening a Mike Wallace "*60 Minutes* Classic"—an updated version of a Sunday story from years before—when Don stormed into the screening room. "Is Mike here?" he yelled. When he saw Mike next to me, he started hollering, "You said this broadcast was going to be a distraction for me, and *you* end up being the one who spends all his time over here at *60 Minutes II*!" Mike *did* spend a lot of his time with us. And maybe Don was a bit envious of that, because he stomped out and kept yelling

Mike Wallace with Nancy Reagan, *60 Minutes* producer Debbie De Luca Sheh, and associate producer Keith Sharman in 2002 after interviewing the former First Lady about life with her husband, who had Alzheimer's.

all the way back to his office on the opposite corner of the floor. But the next day, he brought me the nicest note apologizing for the incident and asking me to please post his mea culpa on the board outside my office for all to see.

Don was always quick to apologize when he knew he had misbehaved—except when it came to his fights with Mike. The first time I witnessed them going at each other in the late eighties, I thought a lot of it was for show. But in later years, I realized some of it was real, which made me sad. They were brothers through most of their forty years together, but not by the end.

There's a written record of many of their fights. After a shouting match, often witnessed by dozens of people, they would try to resolve matters by sending each other notes—usually long, typewritten ones clarifying why the other one had wronged him. Here are a few samples, beginning with a note from Don to Mike a full thirty-two years into their relationship at *60 Minutes*:

Don to Mike, April 19, 2000

Dear Mike:

I am going to do both of us an enormous favor. As of this date, I am asking Phil [Scheffler] to represent me at Mike Wallace screenings. I have been to my last one. The personal attacks in response to professional opinions are more than I or anyone else should have to put up with. Mike, I have no problem with anyone questioning my judgment but attacking my character is quite another matter, and because you can't seem to separate one from the other, I have—more in sadness than in anger—opted to stay out of your way. If opting to do that doesn't restore the pleasure I've gotten from the last thirty-two years, I will—before letting myself become a bitter, sour old man—walk away entirely from the broadcasting miracle you and I and Harry Reasoner created at a low point in all three of our lives.

Mike scribbled a note on the top of the letter and sent it back to Don:

Don CRIPES—what a shit I apparently was. Throw away. Love, Mike.

Five months later, angry about a number of things, Don wrote this:

Don to Mike, September 20, 2000

I am open to any suggestion you have for healing the breech because one thing is for sure, this tension between us, brought on by I don't know what, is not healthy for either one of us and certainly not healthy for 60 Minutes.

Again Mike scribbled his response on Don's note, including a correction of a misspelled word, "breach":

Our disagreements, tobacco, Kissinger, and others stem from your belief that I'm too big for my (our) britches.
    I'd love to heal the breach, but I confess I don't know how at the moment.

Sometimes their notes were apologies. And sometimes the apologies were accepted, although the tension would remain, as in this note from Don to Mike in April 2003:

Dear Mike,

I accept your apology and would like to forget that what happened today ever happened. However, to avoid the wear and tear on both of us that my presence at a Mike Wallace screening invariably produces, I think the wisest course for both of us is for me to recuse myself from any future ones. Please know and accept that trying to persuade me to change my mind would be futile.

Let us be friends even though we can no longer be colleagues.

With respect and admiration.
Don Hewitt

Don was back screening Mike Wallace stories less than a week later.

Don's departure from *60 Minutes* at the end of May 2004 was difficult for everyone. He didn't want to leave, but there seemed to be a growing sense in the early 2000s that it was time. In his mind, he was doing as well as ever. His fights with the front office had always been a part of life, but recently they'd turned into fights about coverage. *60 Minutes II* was more aggressive about reporting big news, something Don and his number two, Phil Scheffler, had resisted doing despite pressure from within CBS. "That's not what we do," Phil would often say.

Don turned eighty in 2002, but age was no deterrent for him. "I plan to die at my desk," he would say. He went on CNN and said it. But eventually he gave in, and in January 2003, Andrew Heyward, the head of CBS News, announced that I would be replacing Don, although not for another year and a half.

Don wrote a letter to the staff just before Christmas that year.

Dear 60 Minutes:

On this, our last Christmas together, let me get a little "mushy" and say this morning what I wanted to say last night at our Christmas party but frankly didn't seem appropriate to the occasion.

Don Hewitt flanked by two men he liked to say were part of "Hewitt and Sons," Jeff Fager and Josh Howard, in 2004.

Am I sad about leaving you guys? Yeah, but that's about the only thing I'm sad about. You can't have a "run" like I've had for more than half a century and not realize that, with the possible exception of William S. Paley himself, no one ever had a more fruitful, satisfying, and rewarding association with CBS than I've had.

One of the more rewarding things about that long tenure is leaving this extraordinary broadcast and its offspring in the hands of two extraordinarily good guys—Jeff Fager and Josh Howard, who will soon become the new managing directors of a company I like to think of—even if no one else does—as "Don Hewitt & Sons."

Where will I be next year (and conceivably for a lot more years after that)? I'll be downstairs on the eighth floor in a corner office even bigger than the one I'll be vacating, with a fancy new title and a mandate to come up with new ideas for broadcasts and old ideas to improve the ones we already have—and trying, with all my heart, not to be a pain in the ass.

A few months later, in May 2004, Don called me down to his office. Outside the door, he handed me the key, wished me the best of luck, and walked out of the building.

SEASONS

37-40

2004 to 2008

I did a bad thing. I made a terrible moral error.

—former president Bill Clinton to Dan Rather, June 2004

Not until I actually moved into Don's office, the last week in May of 2004, did I fully appreciate how jarring this would be for the people who worked at *60 Minutes*. It felt jarring to me. It wasn't that I worried about not being up to the job. I felt very good about doing the job. I was confident I could bring new life to the broadcast and maybe even make it better. But that's different from occupying the space Don had lived in for thirty years. It wasn't that I was a stranger. I knew everybody well. We had worked together for years. It didn't matter. It was his den. I knew it would take time to get used to it, and I looked forward to these first months, or even the first year, being over and behind me.

The best way to do that was to get to work on stories. And we did. Right away.

The first story we broadcast after I took over *60 Minutes* was an extraordinary interview with former president Clinton at his home in Chappaqua, New York, coinciding with the publication of his memoirs. We devoted the entire hour to the interview, which we almost never did. This was the first time Mr. Clinton had answered questions about his impeachment and the scandal surrounding his relationship with a young White House intern named Monica Lewinsky.

This is how we started that broadcast, with the so-called tease—or preview—at the top of the hour:

PRESIDENT CLINTON: I did a bad thing. I made a terrible moral error.

RATHER [*narration*]: Bill Clinton likes to talk, but tonight you will hear him talk about things he has not talked about publicly before, including the relationship he had with Monica Lewinsky.

RATHER: The central question is "Why?"

PRESIDENT CLINTON: Just because I could. I think that that's the most—just about morally indefensible reason that anybody could have.

RATHER [*narration*]: So why is he talking now? Why else? His book is about to come out. But besides what's in his book, we also asked him if he thought he did enough to get Osama bin Laden and what he thought about President Bush launching the war in Iraq.

PRESIDENT CLINTON: I believe we made an error in not allowing the United Nations to complete the inspections process.

RATHER [*narration*]: We went with President Clinton to the towns where he grew up in Arkansas.

PRESIDENT CLINTON: That was my high school.

RATHER [*narration*]: To talk about his difficult childhood.

PRESIDENT CLINTON: You know, my mother was married five times to four men.

RATHER [*narration*]: And his early years in politics.

RATHER: You have accumulated nicknames as the years have gone by.

PRESIDENT CLINTON: [*Laughs.*]

RATHER: Which one do you like the least?

PRESIDENT CLINTON: Slick Willie.

NARRATION: Tonight, you will also hear President Clinton describe his worst day at the White House: the day he told his wife the truth.

PRESIDENT CLINTON: It was awful. But I had to do it.

But what was most interesting for those of us at *60 Minutes* was what happened once the cameras were turned off. As soon as the interview ended, Clinton got up, shook hands, took pictures with everyone, and then shouted, "Let's go in the kitchen and get some food!" We were having a good time, digging into a huge stack of sandwiches, when his assistant came in with a cell phone and whispered in his ear. He told us it was Hillary and that he would be right back. It was at least ten or fifteen minutes before he returned.

Dan Rather interviewed Bill Clinton at his Chappaqua home for a profile that aired in June 2004.

"She thinks I said too much . . . she thinks I screwed that up," he said. He looked at me. "You think I screwed that up?"

"No," I replied, "not at all. You did well!" As if it mattered what I thought! Hillary wasn't happy, but he seemed accustomed to being scolded like that because within a few minutes we were listening to him tell stories, laughing and eating sandwiches again.

• • •

We were preparing stories for my first fall in charge at *60 Minutes* when disaster struck *60 Minutes II*. The weekday broadcast was being run by Josh Howard, one of my best of friends, who was well respected and had started at *60 Minutes* in the late 1980s at the same time I started.

DECADE 4

In September 2004, *60 Minutes II* broadcast a story called "For the Record," which later became known as "Rathergate." In it, Dan reported that President George W. Bush had avoided service in Vietnam by landing a spot in the Texas National Guard. Central to the story were "newly discovered" documents written by a squadron commander suggesting that Bush was not a model pilot because, among other things, he went AWOL for long periods of time.

As soon as the segment aired, there were questions about the documents' authenticity. Not only were they photocopies, but the typeface appeared to be more modern than those used during the period of Bush's service in the National Guard. A week after the story aired, the commander's secretary, who would have typed the memos, said she had written memos similar to those in the story but that those particular memos were not hers. It was an instant crisis—one of the biggest in *60 Minutes* history because it involved strong accusations against a sitting president who was up for reelection in less than two months. It didn't help that after I left *60 Minutes II*, the show had its name changed to *60 Minutes Wednesday*, leading to real confusion about which broadcast had been responsible for the mistake.

The producer on the story was Mary Mapes of Abu Ghraib fame. She was riding high from that story, which had aired only five months earlier. Josh Howard expected big things from her. But for a number of reasons, some of them having to do with not wanting to miss the opportunity to break the news, they rushed the segment onto the air. To make matters worse, Dan did not tell viewers for nearly two weeks that there might be reason to doubt the documents' provenance or that a number of typeface experts had raised questions about their authenticity—some of them before the story had even aired.

Josh, who had been raised as I had been, in the Don Hewitt school of fessing up when mistakes are made, pushed all of those involved to apologize but was shot down.

It was a long and difficult period. An independent panel was convened. It was led by former US attorney general Dick Thornburgh and the former head of the Associated Press, Lou Boccardi, and for months, while they investigated the flawed report, a sense of gloom hovered over both programs. The controversy brought out tensions between the Sunday and Wednesday editions. Steve Kroft told the *Daily News* that he felt a "responsibility to draw a distinction between the two broadcasts."

In early January 2005, almost four months after the story aired (and two months after President Bush narrowly fended off the Democratic candidate, Senator John Kerry of Massachusetts, to win a second term), the panel released its devastating report. It carried evidence of sloppy reporting, of facts that went unchecked, and of executives who were inattentive. Three of them were asked to resign: Betsy West, the CBS vice president overseeing prime-time news; Josh Howard, the executive producer of *60 Minutes II*, and Mary Murphy, his number two. Producer Mary Mapes was fired.

All of us at both editions of *60 Minutes* were very upset. Mike Wallace was particularly angry that Josh, our friend and his former producer, had been let go. A few days later, when he ran into Dan Rather in the men's room, he confronted him, suggesting that Dan should have quit so that the others wouldn't be fired. Dan responded that they could agree to disagree. In November Dan had announced he was stepping down as anchor of the *CBS Evening News*. It was time for that to happen, but Dan's credibility had been damaged and it seemed that his departure as anchor was probably part of the fallout.

Mistakes in journalism often have one thing in common: a reporter's desire to confirm a story that he or she already believes is true. In this case, it may have been a belief that a young and privileged Mr. Bush was given a way to avoid Vietnam and then failed to meet the standard obligations while serving at home. The panel that studied the mistake concluded that there was no bias in the reporting; particularly no political bias against the president. But that point was debated within CBS News because many people did not agree with that conclusion. The bias that I belived did exist —the bias to corroborate a preconceived notion—is a more insidious problem in journalism, because anything that arises during reporting that could complicate the expected conclusion might be pushed aside or given short shrift. One of Bush's commanders had told Mary Mapes that, in fact, he remembered Bush asking if he could be transferred *to* Vietnam; apparently the request was denied because there was a surplus of pilots at the time. This anecdote was in Mary's notes but was not included in the segment, even though it would have made the story fair and accurate. It might even have made news. But it went against the narrative being pursued.

Jon Stewart, the popular and influential host of the satirical but topical *The Daily Show*, couldn't resist bringing up the Bush story in our interview with him that fall, telling Steve Kroft: "I can't believe that this National Guard memo scandal is the only scandal in four years that has gotten elevated to the status of having a 'gate' attached to it: 'Rathergate.' For God's sake, we launched a war based on forged documents. That doesn't get a gate. How do you not get a gate out of that? Dick Cheney's old company does business with Iran in an offshore Cayman Islands group. No gate, nothing."

The year before I took over *60 Minutes*, I remember hearing that *60 Minutes* had already completed almost half of the stories for the upcoming season before it even began. I thought that should have been a source of concern, not pride. Most of those "evergreen" stories could have run any week regardless of what was happening in the world.

In that same Jon Stewart profile, the comedian said something that stuck with me:

STEWART: Fox has the phrase "Fair and balanced." And journalists wring their hands about that. "How can they say, oh, those guys, they say fair and balanced, but they're not. I watch it. It's not. It makes me so mad!" Well, CNN says, "You can depend on CNN."

1 Scott Pelley interviewed two Texas game wardens who had traveled to New Orleans to help with the rescue operation after Hurricane Katrina ravaged the city in August 2005.

2 Lesley Stahl interviewed members of the cast of *Saturday Night Live* for a story that aired in October 2004.

3 Bob Simon spoke to eleven-year-old Elian Gonzalez in 2005 about being at the center of a custody dispute between the United States and Cuba five years earlier.

4 Ed Bradley went to Yankee Stadium with the team's star captain, Derek Jeter.

5 Producer Harry Radliffe, Ed Bradley, and producers Magalie Laguerre-Wilkinson and Michael Karzis leaving Louisiana after covering the New Orleans Police Department's efforts to restore order after Hurricane Katrina.

6 Mike Wallace sat down with actress Goldie Hawn and her partner, Kurt Russell, for a profile that aired in May 2005.

Guess what? I watch CNN. No, you can't. I watch it all the time.

So your slogan's just as misleading as theirs.

KROFT: We don't have a slogan.

STEWART: You actually do.

KROFT: What is it?

STEWART: "May cause drowsiness."

It was a funny line, and I wondered if there might be some truth to it. Had we lost some of our edge? *60 Minutes* had been losing viewers steadily, year after year, for some time. I think having too many "evergreens" might have been part of it.

I wanted *60 Minutes* to be more current. Each Sunday would be a little harder-hitting and a little more relevant. But staying relevant didn't mean covering developments in the Iraq War each week—it meant understanding that the war was going to be an important story for a long time. We could launch stories that would take months to produce but still feel relevant when they aired.

That was how we started the first two Sundays of my first full season: with stories about the war in Iraq, which seemed to be deteriorating into chaos—if not outright civil war—between Shiite and Sunni Muslims. Scott Pelley reported a story on just that: the fear of civil war, an outcome given little consideration when the US toppled Saddam Hussein. Scott also discussed some of the fiercest fighting involving American marines and the increasingly deadly Iraqi insurgency.

The following week, in the season's official premiere, Ed Bradley and producer Harry Radliffe delivered a report we called "Wanted: Dead or Alive," about Abu Musab al-Zarqawi, then considered the leader of Al Qaeda in Iraq. Zarqawi had taken terrorism to another level, torturing and beheading his enemies—some of them, as Ed reported, Americans:

"Eugene Armstrong and Jack Hensley, the two Americans who were beheaded this week in Iraq, are just the latest victims in a series of kidnappings, beheadings, murders, suicide bombings, and other acts of terrorism that have been attributed to one man, a thirty-seven-year-old Jordanian terrorist named Abu Musab al-Zarqawi. Zarqawi is said to run the most violent terror network among the many in Iraq. Who is he, and what are his beliefs?"

Ed interviewed the man in charge of national security for Iraq's interim government, Mowaffak Baqer al-Rubaie, who painted a disturbing portrait: "This man, I believe, he's a serial killer. I believe he's a sociopath bordering to a psychopath, and a massive killing. And he is a criminal before he superficially adopted Islam to justify his act of killing and his act of terror. So this man is capable of doing everything. What sort of Islam is this? This is total deviation from true Islam. Islam is all about mercy, it's all about love, it's all about peace, it's all about submission to God. Zarqawi has submitted himself to Satan, to the devil."

We didn't know yet that Zarqawi was building his own organization separate from Al Qaeda. He called it the Islamic State of Iraq and the Levant, or ISIL, known later as ISIS. Once again, *60 Minutes* had foreshadowed events to come. But Zarqawi didn't live long enough to see the group he created become a world menace. He was killed in June 2006 when the United States dropped two five-hundred-pound laser-guided bombs on the house where he was staying.

We had no idea that his organization would become so influential in the years to come and would set a new standard for human brutality.

• • •

Ed Bradley and I had worked together cheerfully for years, but both of us had to adjust to the fact that I was now the boss. Our relationship grew somewhat strained in October 2004. The Justice Department had reopened the almost fifty-year-old case of Emmett Till, a fourteen-year-old black boy who was tortured and murdered in Mississippi in 1955 after allegedly whistling at a white woman. The new investigation revealed that five people believed to have been involved in the murder were still

Ed Bradley spoke to Neil Armstrong in November 2005 about landing on the moon and the attention he received afterward and shunned.

living and could face criminal prosecution. So Ed and producers Michael Radutzky and Tanya Simon set out to find the suspects and revisit the case.

They had great material, but when they screened the segment, I didn't think they were telling the story well. It needed to begin with what had happened to Emmett Till rather than with the modern investigation. To do that required significant changes, and I walked them through how they could do it. It would not be a simple fix, and when Michael went back to Ed's office after the screening, he heard Ed say, "What the hell just happened in there?" Ed didn't think there was anything wrong with the story; he wondered whether I had asked for such dramatic changes simply to mark my arrival. But when they screened the revised story, I loved it—and so did they. Here's how the segment started:

BRADLEY: For many of you, the name Emmett Till may not sound familiar. But what happened to him in 1955 stunned the nation.

Emmett Till was a young black boy who was murdered in Mississippi for whistling at a white woman. And his death was a spark that ignited the civil rights movement in America. Two white men were put on trial for killing him, but in spite of strong evidence against them, they were acquitted in about an hour by an all-white jury. Why are we telling you this now? Because this past spring, the US Justice Department opened a new investigation based on evidence suggesting that more than a dozen people may have been involved in the murder of Emmett Till and that at least five of them are still alive. Those five could face criminal prosecution. And before we tell you about them, let us tell you what happened to Emmett Till.

One of the many compelling aspects to the story was Ed's interview with Willie Reed, who, as a seventeen-year-old sharecropper back on August 28, 1955, had seen Emmett Till in a truck with two white men the day of his abduction and later heard what he presumed were Till's screams coming from a barn. In an act of courage virtually unthinkable for a black man in the Jim Crow South at the time, he testified against the two white men, Roy Bryant, the husband of the woman who claimed to have been offended, and J. W. Milam, at trial. Almost fifty years later, Willie Reed told Ed he couldn't get the sound of those screams out of his head.

Ed Bradley in Ohio with Henry Lee Loggins, who for years was implicated in the abduction and murder of Emmett Till. He denied any involvement.

REED: I heard this screaming, beating, screaming and beating. And I said to myself, "You know, man, they're beating somebody in the barn." I could hear the beating. I mean the licks, I could hear it.

BRADLEY: Because you could hear the licks?

REED: Yes, you could. You could.

BRADLEY [*narration*]: According to Willie Reed and another witness, four white men came out of the barn, including Milam, who walked right up to Reed carrying a .45 caliber pistol.

REED: Milam was coming out of the barn. "Listen," he said, "did you all hear anything?" And I said, "No. I haven't heard anything."

BRADLEY: Why would you say that? I mean you had heard something. You had heard screaming. You had heard somebody being beaten.

REED: Yeah, somebody was being beaten. But then you see Milam come out with, like I say, khaki pants on and green shirt and [a] .45 by his side. Then he asks you . . . what are you going to say?

BRADLEY: You didn't hear anything.

REED: I didn't hear anything.

BRADLEY: You knew that's what he wanted to hear.

REED: Right.

BRADLEY: When they found the body, did you put two and two together and think that what you had heard going on in that barn that that was Emmett Till being beaten?

REED: I was sure. I was sure then.

BRADLEY [*narration*]: Fearing for his life after testifying against Milam and Bryant, Willie Reed was smuggled out of Mississippi. He went to Chicago, where he suffered a nervous breakdown and was hospitalized.

BRADLEY: You're a good man. You had a lot of courage . . . I think a lot of people would have walked away from it; wouldn't have said a word.

REED: No, I-I-I couldn't. I couldn't have walked away from that like that, because Emmett was fourteen, probably had never been to Mississippi in his life, and he come to visit his grandfather, and they killed him. I mean, that's not right. And I saw . . . in the pictures, I saw his body, what it was like; then I knew that I couldn't say no.

Bob Simon traveled to Pakistan in October 2005 to report on a team of medics from New York City who were helping victims of an earthquake that had devastated the country five weeks earlier.

The story, which meant a lot to Ed, won an Emmy. And going through the process of reworking a story that important with me as the editor ended up being very good for our relationship.

• • •

We kept up a steady stream of war stories because the wars in Iraq and Afghanistan had so pervaded our American experience, and we wanted *60 Minutes* to be on top of our most important stories.

"Under Fire" took Scott Pelley to the front line in Ramadi, Iraq, one of the most dangerous cities in the war. He and producers Shawn Efran and Kirk Spitzer, cameramen Sean Keane and Ian Robbie, and soundmen Paul Hardy and Manny Garcia spent two weeks with the Second Battalion of the Fifth Marine Regiment. The story brought home, in vivid detail, how difficult the war had become by the winter of 2004–05.

PELLEY: The battalion, known as 2/5 Marines, is on its second tour in Iraq. For these men, the resistance has turned out to be far deadlier than the invasion itself. Last week, Secretary of State Colin Powell called the war "a raging insurgency." That's what the marines are fighting, under fire in Anbar Province, the heart of the resistance.

Scott and the team spent two weeks with the marines as witnesses to an urban war where you couldn't see the enemy or anticipate an attack. But what they did see was heartbreaking. They went on combat patrol with Captain Pat Rapicault, sometimes called Frenchie by his men because he was born in France although raised in Mississippi; he had an accent from somewhere in between. Rapicault was thirty-four and married. Scott described him as someone who led from the front.

PELLEY [*narration*]: There was something we noticed about him. As he talked with us, he never took his eyes off the potential threats to his marines on the road. He told us the enemy was always watching, so you could never look away.

CAPTAIN RAPICAULT: We're constantly under observation from those guys. They know where we go. They know where we like to set up, and, of course, like anything else, it's to avoid any kind of repetition. Change your route, change the buildings you use. Otherwise they come at you to booby trap those buildings and try to blow them up.

PELLEY [*narration*]: We were with Rapicault's men, heading down Route Michigan, nearly back to Hurricane Point, when a car packed with explosives pulled up next to one of Whiskey Company's Humvees and exploded. That's what's left of the suicide bomber's vehicle. His target, the fully armored Humvee, was destroyed. A navy corpsman treated two survivors. But three marines were killed, including the man who helped us understand what the combat is like, the captain some called Frenchie, Pat Rapicault. In his company of about a hundred sixty men, there are now nine names in steel under the flag.

Morley Safer told me once that covering Vietnam was not as difficult as covering the insurgent wars in Iraq and Afghanistan, where journalists were considered targets as well. In 2006 we lost cameraman Paul Douglas and soundman James Brolin, who were filming a story with a combat unit in Iraq when a bomb exploded nearby; CBS correspondent Kimberly Dozier, who was with them, was critically wounded. This tragedy marked the lowest moment for CBS News in decades. We had such admiration for those we lost and for people like Scott Pelley and all those who worked with him, who kept returning to do story after story.

Lara Logan was one of them. She reported one of her most

memorable stories from the town of Tal Afar in 2006, accompanied to Iraq by producer Josh Yager, veteran cameramen Massimo Mariani and Ray Bribiesca, and soundman George Ionnides, who spoke perfect Arabic and was like a brother to me from years spent together in conflict zones. Tal Afar—a city of about two hundred thousand mostly Sunni Iraqis, fifty miles from Mosul—had been taken by Al Qaeda. The occupation had been surprisingly brutal on the civilian population: there were murders and intimidation and fearful residents imprisoned in their own homes. If this sounds reminiscent of ISIS-controlled cities in Iraq and Syria less than ten years later, that's because the "Al Qaeda in Iraq" terrorists holding Tal Afar were working under Abu Musab al-Zarqawi, the founder of ISIS.

Lara interviewed the impressive Colonel H. R. McMaster about his successful operation to liberate Tal Afar. Her report exposed the atrocities that had been carried out inside the city.

Lara Logan hitching a ride in Iraq while reporting on the city of Tal Afar, which had been an Al Qaeda stronghold until the US military took control.

LOGAN: What did it actually mean on a daily basis for people living there? What was life like?

McMASTER: Life was horrible in the city. They would leave headless bodies in the street. They kidnapped a young child on one occasion, killed the child, put a booby trap, and waited for the father to come claim the body, to kill the parent.

The Tal Afar campaign became a model for how to fight the rest of the war. McMaster went to work directly under General David Petraeus in leading the so-called surge of troops that helped turn the tide. Zarqawi's brutal regime seemed crushed—but it wasn't. ISIS started to grow back the moment the United States pulled out of Iraq in 2011. Tal Afar was taken back by ISIS a few years later. (Colonel McMaster was already a famous army intellectual for writing the book *Dereliction of Duty: Johnson, McNamara, the Joint Chiefs of Staff, and the Lies That Led to Vietnam*, about the breakdown of leadership during the Vietnam War. He was named national security advisor to President Donald Trump in 2017.)

The war in Iraq brought out the best in the curmudgeonly—bordering on belligerent—side of Andy Rooney. Our resident veteran reporter of World War II was not happy about "shock and awe," the phrase the Bush administration was using to describe the Baghdad bombing campaign. Not many people on television, let alone prime-time television going out to fourteen million people, had the stature to say something like this:

"Experts talk about precision bombing, but on the ground where bombs hit, it's not precise. People are killed, history destroyed. We didn't shock them and we didn't awe them in Baghdad. The phrase makes us look like foolish braggarts. The president should fire whoever wrote that line for him."

I loved working with Andy. In all his years with *60 Minutes*, he had never moved his office from the CBS Broadcast Center, which had been CBS News headquarters since the early 1960s, to our offices across the street on the ninth floor of the Ford building, where *60 Minutes* had been since the mid '70s. He liked being separate because it made him feel independent. He would cross the street once a week with his team—cameraman–tape editor Keith Kulin and associate producer Susie Bieber—to show me his weekly commentary. I rarely suggested changes, though when I did he was always responsive. Andy was a real reporter who wanted to show his stories to an editor with fresh eyes. When the screening was over, he would duck into Morley's office to catch up on some gossip before heading back across the street.

·   ·   ·

When the worst tsunami in generations hit Southeast Asia the day after Christmas 2004, we did not jump on the story right away. But when we did, Bob Simon and Michael Gavshon found a surprising way in: the story of the Moken people, who live off the coast of Thailand and survived the catastrophe because they knew it was coming. Here's how Bob described them, in a story that feels as though it takes you to another planet:

> SIMON [*narration*]: It's their intimacy with the sea that saved them. They're born on the sea, live on the sea, die on the sea. They know its moods and motion better than any marine biologist. They're nomads, constantly moving from island to island, living more than six months a year on their boats. At low tide, they collect sea cucumbers and catch eels. At high tide, they dive for shellfish. And they've been living this way for so many generations they've become virtually amphibious. Kids learn to swim before they can walk. Underwater, they can see twice as clearly as the rest of us and, by lowering their heart rate, can stay underwater twice as long. They are truly sea urchins. This old man decided he wanted fish for breakfast. It took him one toss of his spear. It was a puffer fish. If it's not cut properly, it can kill you. The Moken cut it properly.

There's an old Moken legend passed down over generations about a big wave that floods the earth and destroys it. Before it comes, the sea recedes very rapidly—which is exactly what happened before the tsunami.

> SIMON [*narration*]: It wasn't only the sea that was acting strangely. It was the animals, too. On the mainland, elephants starting stampeding toward higher ground. Off Thailand's coast, divers noticed dozens of dolphins swimming for deeper water. And on these islands, the cicadas, which are usually so loud, suddenly went silent.

Scott Pelley and cameraman Chris Everson on a melting glacier in Patagonia for a story about global warming that aired in April 2007.

Bob Simon interviewed a spear fisherman on a remote island off the coast of Thailand who predicted the giant tsunami of 2004.

Lesley Stahl went to India with Al Gore for a 2008 story about his campaign to end global warming.

An old Moken fisherman named Saleh Kalathalay told Bob (through a translator) that he saw the signs and warned everyone to leave.

SIMON: When you told people in the village and said something was wrong, did they believe you?

KALATHALAY: The young people called me a liar. I said we've been told the story of the wave since the old times, but none of the kids believed me. I grabbed my daughter by the hand and said, "Child, get out of here or you'll die!" She said, "You're a liar, father! You're drunk." I hadn't had a drop to drink.

SIMON [*narration*]: Saleh brought the skeptics to the water's edge, where they too saw the signs. Eventually everyone, the Moken and the tourists, climbed to higher ground and were saved. But the village itself? There's nothing left.

SIMON: Why do you think the tsunami happened?

KALATHALAY: The wave is created by the spirit of the sea. The wave had not eaten anyone for a long time, and it wanted to taste them again.

That same winter Lesley Stahl and producer Rome Hartman interviewed two young hotshots from a new company called Google. Thirty-one-year-old Sergey Brin and thirty-two-year-old Larry Page opened their doors to *60 Minutes* in January 2005, just eight months after the company had gone public. The company was worth more than Ford and GM combined at the time, and Brin and Page were worth a reported $6 billion each. The laid-back culture of Silicon Valley tech companies was still a novelty back then, and Lesley asked Brin about it:

BRIN: Our boardroom table was also our Ping-Pong table, so—it had the net and everything.

STAHL: And—and the dress code?

BRIN: Well, I'm probably a bit embarrassed when I look at the photos back then. I think we were pretty much disheveled students.

But Lesley's interview wasn't just about the look and feel of the place. It was about the enormity of what they had created, and she picked up on the motto they used from the beginning—don't be evil.

STAHL: Where did that come from and what does it really mean?

BRIN: We tried to boil it down at some point to a code of conduct, so to speak, for Google, well, how do we make all our decisions? For example, we don't mix our ads with our search results; we always label the advertising clearly down the side of a page.

STAHL: And that—that comes under "Do no evil"?

BRIN: That's right. There's no business relationship or anything that controls the search results.

That exchange took on new meaning as the years passed and their unprecedented power across the globe became apparent—reaching more than one billion users and owning information about their interests and habits.

Lesley's interview was the first major television interview they had done. And a few years later the same was true of her interview with Mark Zuckerberg, founder of another Silicon Valley company called Facebook, just four years old at the time. Produced by Shachar Bar-On, Lesley asked Zuckerberg if such a young man was capable of being CEO of such a big enterprise.

STAHL: Tell everyone how old you are.

ZUCKERBERG: I'm twenty-three right now. So that . . .

STAHL: And you're running this huge company . . .

ZUCKERBERG: It's not that big.

STAHL: You're twenty-three! Do you think that your age is an asset or a liability?

ZUCKERBERG: I mean, there's probably a little bit of both, right? I mean, there are definitely elements of experience and stuff that someone who's my age wouldn't have. But there are also things that I can do that other people wouldn't necessarily be able to.

STAHL [*narration*]: Like the founders of Google, Larry Page and Sergey Brin, Mark Zuckerberg is looked up to in Silicon Valley as a visionary. You seem to be replacing Larry and Sergey as the people out here who everyone's talking about. [*Long pause.*] You're just staring at me.

ZUCKERBERG: Is that a question?

• • •

By the end of my first full year at *60 Minutes*, things had gone reasonably well. But all was not well at *60 Minutes II*. The broadcast had been canceled. Rumor has it this was because of Rathergate, which might have been part of the reason, but a far bigger factor was the success Les Moonves, now in charge of the entire company, was enjoying. CBS was number one, which made it much tougher to keep a newsmagazine in a coveted and profitable time slot.

The only bright spot to the cancelation was that Les allowed me to keep on a large number of *60 Minutes II* staff, which infused even more life into *60 Minutes*, adding more tape editors and producers capable of turning a big news story into something unique.

• • •

Don Hewitt liked to tell the story of a toast given to his friend Al Neuharth, the founder of the national newspaper *USA Today*, when he retired at age sixty-seven: "He's too old to work at the newspaper and too young to work at *60 Minutes*." By the time of my second year in charge, Mike Wallace was eighty-seven years old, and Andy Rooney was eighty-six. I knew it would fall on me to guide the broadcast into a new era without them. Andy had told me not to let him stay too long, but with Mike it was not so easy. He knew it was time for him to scale back, but he had a hard time accepting it.

There was also the question of the top of the program, where each correspondent appears and says his or her name. For thirty-six years, Mike Wallace had been first; I thought that needed to change. Morley had already decided to cut his number of stories in half, so I wanted Ed Bradley to go first. Mike accepted this—until we got close to the Sunday when the change would take effect. Then he got upset. He told me he believed that I didn't want him around anymore, and he was egged on by some of the others on the floor. There was a bit of a revolt, truth be told. But we made the change, and when it aired, it looked and felt right—and we didn't get a call or letter about it from a single viewer. Ed was the senior full-time member of the team, and he deserved the top spot. The move made him incredibly proud.

In the year that followed, Ed took on one of the biggest investigative

Lesley Stahl in China for a report about that country's one-child policy, which resulted in the birth of more men than women, which in turn led to social instability and a rise in crime.

stories of his career: the Duke lacrosse rape case. Produced by Michael Radutzky and Tanya Simon, it concerned three white Duke University lacrosse players accused of raping an African American stripper who had performed at a team party in 2006. The story had already been a bombshell, with the players all but convicted in the court of public opinion—on campus and in the news media. But some of Michael's sources started telling him this judgment was rushed, and he approached Ed about doing a story that challenged the conventional wisdom.

At first, Ed wasn't comfortable with the idea. He was always careful when it came to stories that dealt with race, and this one was more racially charged than most. Michael remembers Ed saying that he needed to see some real reporting—not just a hunch—before committing to a story that would essentially defend a group of wealthy white athletes against the word of their black accuser. Michael came back with enough reporting to persuade Ed to take the story wherever it led.

In the fall of 2006, a full six months after the alleged rape, we turned the narrative upside down. The segment opened with Ed's introduction laying out our investigation, followed by his interviews with the three accused players: Reade Seligmann, Collin Finnerty, and David Evans. The Durham County district attorney who brought the charges, Mike Nifong, had waged a very public crusade against the players, calling them "a bunch of hooligans" whose "daddies could buy them expensive lawyers." We had become suspicious of the DA while reporting the story because he was playing up the racial aspects of the case while insisting his comments had nothing to do with the hotly contested election campaign he was waging in Durham, North Carolina, a city with a large black population. Nifong refused to sit down with Ed, but we used this quote from one of his campaign speeches, which shed some light on his mind-set:

"I am not going to allow Durham's view in the minds of the world to be a bunch of lacrosse players at Duke raping a black girl from Durham."

Our investigation was thorough and well detailed, poking holes in large parts of Nifong's case. We found that two of the accused players had credible alibis placing them elsewhere at the time of the alleged rape—evidence the DA didn't always want to see. We called the accuser's credibility into question through an examination of the conflicting statements she had given, as well as an interview with another woman who had danced with her that night and who contradicted most of her claims. We also found that the police lineup during which the accuser identified her alleged attackers was conducted in a way that violated local, state, and federal guidelines. We reported on the lack of DNA evidence and the inconsistencies in the accuser's medical records. The following year, the attorney general of North Carolina took over the case and exonerated the three players of all charges. But it was an outcome Ed didn't live to see.

We knew Ed was not well while working on the Duke story. He had told me six months earlier that a dormant case of leukemia had come out of remission, and he was starting chemotherapy to fight it. But on November 9, 2006, just a month after the Duke story was broadcast, Ed died at age sixty-five.

It was a terrible shock. The very afternoon we learned of his death, we went to work on an hourlong tribute to Ed to air that Sunday. We worked straight through the days and nights, dozens of us, unable to believe that

One of Ed Bradley's last stories was an investigation into rape charges that were filed against three Duke University lacrosse players, including team captain Dave Evans, on the right, pictured with his attorney, Bradley Bannon. The charges were eventually dropped.

Ed was gone. Hearing his voice resonating from one edit room to the next was oddly therapeutic.

We finished just in time for the Sunday broadcast. Morley started the segment with this:

> Last Thursday, this broadcast lost one of its pillars. Ed Bradley succumbed to CLL, a form of leukemia. Tonight we remember Ed the way we think he'd want us to, as a dedicated reporter who represented the highest standards of this craft; a man who inspired a whole generation of journalists with a calm elegance that was never an act. He was the genuine article. And so we begin with the extraordinary contribution he made to this broadcast: twenty-six years of rooting out the truth, exposing the dark side of the human condition and celebrating the best of it, and having a high old time along the way.

It was a wonderful way to remember him, with his favorite stories and our favorite Ed stories. The tribute ended with one of his friends, Wynton Marsalis, playing his horn and talking about Ed's love for music and New Orleans and a life well lived:

Supreme Court Justice Clarence Thomas has a reputation for staying quiet on the bench, but he opened up to Steve Kroft in an interview that aired in September 2007.

Ed Bradley, photographed after winning three Emmys at the 2003 awards, died in November 2006.

MARSALIS: I think, you know, that Ed, he wouldn't be too much for us crying over him, you know? Me and him actually have talked about that. He loved that funeral, New Orleans funeral. They play a little something sad. He said, "Man, that second line. Give me a tambourine."

Ed's funeral the next week was fit for a king. Two thousand people came to the glorious Riverside Church in Upper Manhattan, where Wynton led a vibrant New Orleans second line: a traditionally festive and upbeat funeral processional in Ed's honor.

It was a difficult year at *60 Minutes*. In the ten months preceding Ed's death, we lost two of my closest friends, director Artie Bloom and producer George Crile. Both of them had made significant marks on *60 Minutes*, and had done so with spirit, selflessness, and pure fun. They were both full of life; big personalities who died way too young from cancer: Artie was sixty-three and George was sixty-one.

Artie Bloom had been just a kid when he joined Don as the broadcast's first director in 1968, and he was still a kid when he died—a talented, fun-loving leader with impeccable taste. He gave *60 Minutes* its elegant look and was brilliant at making sure the focus was always on the correspondent, who would be lit perfectly in front of a simple yet elegant background. Artie deserves credit for so much of how *60 Minutes* looks and feels today, including our signature stopwatch.

George was an energetic and generous soul with an unending curiosity and a thirst for adventure. His extraordinary work about the rise of Al Qaeda and the nuclear cold war is well documented in this book. Both Artie and George have a great many friends who still miss them very much.

George Crile was dashing and debonair. He died in 2006.

•　•　•

The following winter, *60 Minutes* broadcast a rare and revealing interview with President George W. Bush. It was the first time we had conducted an interview at the presidential retreat Camp David, in the wooded Maryland countryside. We found him to be humble at a time when his approval ratings were very low, and he was calling for the surge of troops to try to end the war in Iraq. He admitted his administration had committed a lot of mistakes in conducting the war.

> PRESIDENT BUSH: Abu Ghraib was a mistake. Using bad language, like, you know, "Bring them on," was a mistake. I think history is going to look back and see a lot of ways we could have done things better. No question about it.
>
> PELLEY: The troop levels, sir . . .
>
> PRESIDENT BUSH: Could have been a mistake . . . And the reason I brought up the mistakes is, one, well, that's the job of the commander in chief, and, two, I don't want people blaming our military. We got a bunch of good military people out there doing what we've asked them to do, and the temptation is going to find scapegoats. Well, if the people want a scapegoat, they got one right here in me because it's my decisions.

Scott Pelley interviewed President George W. Bush at Camp David in Maryland in January 2007.

Valerie Plame, a former undercover agent for the CIA, spoke to Katie Couric about how her identity was made public after her husband criticized the White House about the Iraq War.

We didn't expect the president to be so self-effacing. A lot of our viewers didn't expect it either. Just two days after the interview, I received a note in the mail from President Bush congratulating me on a bet we hadn't made: I wanted to wager on the New England Patriots winning that Sunday just before *60 Minutes* aired, but he said he was not a betting man.

The very next month, February 2007, Steve Kroft met Barack and Michelle Obama and their two little girls in their Chicago home. He conducted the interview while Mr. Obama made tuna fish sandwiches for the kids. Obama had attracted a great deal of attention for his keynote address during the 2004 Democratic National Convention. He won a US Senate seat in a landslide that November. So in February 2007 he had only been a national politician for two years, and he was already running for president. It was a story we thought worthy of a *60 Minutes* profile.

KROFT: What makes you think you are qualified to be president of the United States?

OBAMA: You know, I think we are in a moment in history where probably the most important thing we need to do is to bring the country together. And one of the skills that I bring to bear is

being able to pull together the different strands of American life and focus on what we have in common.

Over the next decade, Steve reminded the president about that answer and it is still central to a debate about his presidency. Did Mr. Obama, in reality, lack the skills to bring people together, or did his opponents make doing so impossible?

Steve Kroft took a walk in West Hollywood with two members of the Eagles, Glenn Frey on the left and Don Henley on the right, for a profile of the band that aired in November 2007.

Steve Kroft met Michelle and Barack Obama and their two young daughters at lunchtime in their home in Chicago, just as the Democratic senator from Illinois was announcing his candidacy for president.

DECADE

5

2008 to 2018

SEASONS

41–43

2008 to 2011

I still wait for the phone to ring and hear those words, "Kid, I've got a great idea for you."

—Leslie Moonves, Chairman and CEO of CBS, at Don Hewitt's memorial service

If you asked most people what happened on Monday, September 15, 2008, they might not remember—but it was a historic day. It was the day that Lehman Brothers failed, the low point of the worst economic crisis since the Great Depression. One of Wall Street's largest and most prominent investment firms, established in 1850 and valued somewhere around $600 billion, filed for bankruptcy. The company had taken excessive risks in complicated and shaky home mortgage investments—and it wasn't alone in doing so. Nearly all established Wall Street firms were in over their heads with the same weird and risky investments.

Don Hewitt at his desk at *60 Minutes* in 2001.
He died in 2009.

The markets crashed that day. The Dow Jones Industrial Average dropped more than 500 points, a loss of around 7 percent.

Just two days later, we found ourselves in Elko, Nevada, interviewing Senator Barack Obama for a special edition of *60 Minutes* about the race for the presidency for that Sunday's broadcast. We interviewed Senator John McCain of Arizona two days later in Green Bay, Wisconsin. It was a perfect way to start the season, with a huge economic story looming in the middle of the presidential election, and we were with the two candidates. We had planned that Sunday's broadcast—airing forty years to the week since the very first episode of *60 Minutes*—as an issues-driven hour. But most of our focus ended up being on one issue: the state of the economy.

Steve Kroft interviewed Senator Obama inside a terminal building at the tiny Elko airport. Looking back nearly a decade later, this one exchange is particularly interesting:

KROFT: Why do you think you'd be a good president?

SENATOR OBAMA: Well, I think that when you think about the challenges we face, these are challenges that require us to look forward and not backward. When it comes to the economy, I think we have to recognize that we're now in a global economy. How—

KROFT: Yeah, I just—why you? I mean, why do you think you would be a good president?

SENATOR OBAMA: Well, I was going to get to that.

KROFT: Go ahead.

SENATOR OBAMA: I think both by training and disposition, I understand where we need to take the country.

KROFT: But what is there specifically about you? You mentioned disposition. What skills and traits do you have that would make you a good president?

SENATOR OBAMA: You know, I'm a practical person. One of the things I'm good at is getting people in a room with a bunch of different ideas who sometimes violently disagree with each other and finding common ground and a sense of common direction, and that's the kind of approach that I think prevents you from making some of the enormous mistakes that we've seen over the last eight years.

Bill Owens, our number two in command at *60 Minutes*, felt strongly about covering the financial crisis with the same resources and intensity as we had the wars in Afghanistan and Iraq. And we did. We stayed on the story almost every Sunday for the next several months, beginning the very next week when Scott Pelley and producer Henry Schuster landed the first big interview with the secretary of the US Treasury, a man very much in the hot seat: Hank Paulson, the former chairman and CEO of the giant investment firm Goldman Sachs.

Modern financial institutions had become so big that their tentacles spread into just about every part of the economy. They were, as the phrase became, "too big to fail." So if more of these institutions were to fail, as Lehman Brothers had, the country could face a full-on depression; a collapse of the American economy. In response, Paulson had started to orchestrate a bailout, asking Congress for a $700 billion fund to save Wall Street. This was an outrage to many Americans—and Scott asked Secretary Paulson if he found this anger justified:

Bill Owens became the number two in command at *60 Minutes* in 2008, the fourth person in that role since the broadcast's inception.

PELLEY: Shouldn't the price of failure be failure on Wall Street?

TREASURY SECRETARY PAULSON: Failure and the market discipline that goes with it is the right thing. But unfortunately, we have a system that is way out of whack, where institutions are too big to fail. We don't have the regulatory authorities and structure in place to protect the American people.

PELLEY: You can't be proud of Wall Street.

TREASURY SECRETARY PAULSON: I'm not proud of a lot of things. You

Treasury Secretary Hank Paulson took time out from managing the nation's economic crisis to take Scott Pelley on a tour of his office for a story that aired in September 2008.

know, as I go around the world right now representing the United States of America, it's a humbling experience.

Paulson showed Scott around his office at the Treasury, overlooking the White House, and told him the scariest moment of the crisis had come two days after Lehman Brothers failed, when banks stopped lending money to one another, and there was a rush to snap up Treasury notes, always a safe investment. It was an emergency that played out in front of our *60 Minutes* cameraman Phil Geyelin. Henry Schuster had arranged for him to be a fly on the wall of the Treasury for almost two weeks as a handful of people there drew up a three-page document outlining the biggest bailout in US history.

Just a week after they finished, President Bush signed the Troubled Asset Relief Program, or TARP, giving Paulson more power than any modern Treasury secretary, with $700 billion at his disposal to save Wall Street. In the end, $420 billion of that money was spent, all of which was reimbursed as the investment firms recovered.

That was just the beginning. Over the next few years, *60 Minutes* reported dozens of stories on the financial crisis and the Great Recession.

There were segments about the big banks and how they made bad bets using credit default swaps that amounted to insurance without any funds to back up the bets. There were stories about the so-called subprime mortgages that had lured low-income people into mortgages with ultralow teaser rates that would eventually balloon and ruin them. And there were stories about small banks that were failing across the country. In one instance, we were allowed to bring our cameras to record the federal government actually shutting down a bank.

Some of the human stories we reported in these recession years were heartbreaking, particularly the two that fell under the title of "Hard Times Generation" in 2011. They were stories straight out of John Steinbeck: struggling American families doing anything they could to stay afloat. In the first, we reported that the poverty rate for children in America could hit 25 percent. Many kids were already homeless and living with their parents in cheap hotels, where the school bus would collect them. Scott Pelley and producers Bob Anderson and Nicole Young gathered about twenty such kids in one Florida school for a group interview:

PELLEY: Who can tell me what it's like to feel hungry?

[*Almost all of them raise their hands.*]

BOY NUMBER ONE: It's, like, hard. You can't sleep. You just go to sleep for, like, five minutes, and then you wake up. Because it is like your stomach is hurting, and it doesn't have any food in it.

GIRL NUMBER ONE: Usually we eat macaroni, or we don't, or we drink water or tea.

GIRL NUMBER TWO: We have to sometimes take food from a church. It's hard because my grandmother is also out of work, and we usually get some food from her.

GIRL NUMBER FOUR: It's kind of embarrassing because the next day, you go to school asking kids . . . if they have cereal, and they haven't opened it yet; you go ask them if they want their cereal.

The next time Scott went to Florida, the kids and families he met weren't living in hotels but in vehicles. This second story followed an extraordinary fifteen-year-old girl named Arielle Metzger, who was forced to live with her dad, an unemployed carpenter, and her twelve-year-old brother, Austin, in a small truck after foreclosure took their home.

PELLEY: How long have you been living in this truck?

ARIELLE METZGER: About five months.

PELLEY: What's that like?

ARIELLE METZGER: It's an adventure.

AUSTIN METZGER: That's how we see it.

PELLEY: When kids at school ask you where you live, what do you tell 'em?

AUSTIN METZGER: When they see the truck, they ask me if I live in it, and when I hesitate, they kinda realize. And they say they won't tell anybody.

ARIELLE METZGER: Yeah, it's not really that much an embarrassment. I mean, it's only life. You do what you need to do, right?

Arielle Metzger and her brother, Austin, talked to Scott Pelley, standing next to the truck they were forced to live in after losing their Florida home.

DECADE 5

When the story aired, we were inundated with mail and phone calls from people who wanted to help Arielle and her brother. Both received pledges from a Florida college to cover their undergraduate education in full.

. . .

On Tuesday, November 4, 2008, Barack Obama was elected president. That night, we traveled to Chicago to hear his victory speech in Grant Park amid fifty thousand of his supporters celebrating and witnessing history. Later that evening (or, rather, early the next morning), Steve Kroft interviewed the people who ran Obama's campaign for that Sunday's broadcast. We called the story "The Inner Circle." It was well after midnight when we rolled tape with David Axelrod, David Plouffe, Anita Dunn, and Robert Gibbs. They were exhilarated and exhausted. Gibbs that night was off to a difficult start as the president-elect's spokesman: he was so hoarse we could barely hear him.

The Obama team told us about how they built a campaign without ever having to worry about what their candidate's message would be, because Obama took care of that himself.

The following week, we spoke with the president-elect and his wife, Michelle, in their first interview since the election. The broadcast drew the largest *60 Minutes* audience in a decade, with twenty-five million people tuning in.

Barack Obama's "Inner Circle"—Robert Gibbs, David Axelrod, David Plouffe, and Anita Dunn—sat down after midnight on Election Night 2008 to discuss the historic campaign they ran.

KROFT: So here we are.

PRESIDENT-ELECT OBAMA: Here we are.

KROFT: When was the first moment it began to sink in that you were president of the United States? Do you remember?

PRESIDENT-ELECT OBAMA: Well, I'm not sure it's sunk in yet.

KROFT: Have there been moments when you've said, "What did I get myself into?"

PRESIDENT-ELECT OBAMA: You know, surprisingly enough, I feel right now that I'm doing what I should be doing. That gives me a certain sense of calm. I will say that the challenges that we're confronting are enormous, and they're multiple. And so there are times during the course of a given day where you think, "Where do I start?"

Steve covered just about all of the big subjects: the troubled economy, two raging wars, Guantánamo Bay. And then Michelle joined in to talk about the enormity of what had taken place.

MICHELLE OBAMA: I'm not sure if it has really sunk in, but I remember we were watching the returns, and on one of the stations, Barack's picture came up, and it said, "President-Elect Barack Obama." And I looked at him, and I said, "You are the forty-fourth president of the United States of America. Wow. What a country we live in."

PRESIDENT-ELECT OBAMA: How about that?

MICHELLE OBAMA: And . . . yeah.

PRESIDENT-ELECT OBAMA: Yeah. And then she said, "Are you going to take the girls to school in the morning?"

MICHELLE OBAMA: I did not. I didn't say that.

We will never know if this was intentional—although my guess is that it was natural—but here were the president-elect and his First Lady in an interview badgering each other about domestic life, about taking the kids to school, and the laundry, and the dishes, and smoking. It was part of their appeal: they sounded like everybody we knew.

Steve finished his questions and then looked back at the team of producers—Frank Devine, Michael Radutzky, and me—to see if he had missed anything. I shouted to Steve that he hadn't asked what it meant to be the first black president. The cameras started rolling again.

KROFT: The emotion of that night was fueled in part by the fact that you were the first African American ever elected. Did you feel that?

PRESIDENT-ELECT OBAMA: There's no doubt that there was a sense of emotion that I could see in people's faces. And my mother-in-law's face. You know, I mean, you think about Michelle's mom, you know, who grew up on the west and south sides of Chicago, who worked so hard to help Michelle get to where she is, her brother to be successful. She was sitting next to me, actually, as we were watching returns. And she's like my grandmother was: sort of a no-fuss type of person. And suddenly she just kind of reached out, and she started holding my hand, you know, kind of squeezing it. And you had this sense of, well, what's she thinking, for a black woman who grew up in the fifties in a segregated

Michelle and Barack Obama with the *60 Minutes* team in Chicago after sitting down for their first joint interview following the 2008 election. Pictured from left to right: Jennifer MacDonald, Maria Gavrilovic, Matthew Magratten, Jeff Fager, Steve Kroft, Michael Radutzky, and Frank Devine.

Chicago to watch her daughter become First Lady of the United States. You know, I think there was that sense across the country. And not unique to African Americans.

MICHELLE OBAMA: That's right.

PRESIDENT-ELECT OBAMA: I think people felt that it was a sign of the enormous progress that we've made and the core

decency and generosity of the American people. Which isn't to say that, you know—there were a number of reasons that somebody might not have voted for me. But what was absolutely clear was that, whether people voted for me or against me, that they were making the judgment based on "Is this guy going to lead us well? Is this guy going to be a good president?" And that was my assumption walking in, and that's how it turned out. And that felt good.

This was Steve's sixth interview with Obama since the beginning of his candidacy nearly two years earlier, and the relationship we were developing with the new president was going reasonably well. His team appreciated that we didn't take his statements out of context—Obama was so loquacious that editing interviews down to size without losing his meaning was a real challenge. It wasn't that he rambled—his language was precise, his words well chosen—but he didn't finish his answers until he covered a question's every angle. Steve built a strong, professional relationship with the president, who knew Steve would be tough but also appreciated that *60 Minutes* allowed him to make his points to one of the few mass audiences left in America.

Mrs. Obama was a different story. We tried, over the next eight years, to interview her again, but it didn't happen. Michelle had always been ambivalent about her husband's run for office, and she sat for very few interviews with mainstream news organizations. We were told she wasn't unhappy with our interview but that she had been through some rough stuff during the campaign, especially being tagged unfairly as an "angry black woman." I think this made her extra cautious during her White House years.

• • •

In March, after the new president took office, Scott Pelley flew to Washington to interview the chairman of the Federal Reserve, Ben Bernanke. It was the first time a sitting Fed chairman had come on *60 Minutes*, and the timing was perfect: we were in the middle of the recession.

To convince Bernanke to do the interview, we had gone to lunch with him in his dining room in the Eccles Building, where the news media, at least those not part of regular Fed coverage, is ordinarily not welcome for fear that we could report something wrong and cause the markets to go haywire. Bernanke is a mild-mannered man from South Carolina, but, boy, did he get worked up about the need to bail out the firm AIG, which had set up Wall Street's bad "insurance" bets against mortgage investments without enough money to pay them off if they failed. Here's how that conversation went in the interview:

PELLEY: There have now been four rescues of AIG for about a hundred and sixty billion dollars. Why is that necessary?

CHAIRMAN BERNANKE: Let me just first say that of all the events and all of the things we've done in the last eighteen months, the single one that makes me the angriest, that gives me the most angst, is the intervention with AIG. Here was a company that made all kinds of unconscionable bets. Then, when those bets went wrong, we had a situation where the failure of that company would have brought down the financial system.

PELLEY: You say it makes you angry. What do you mean by that?

CHAIRMAN BERNANKE: It makes me angry. I, you know, I-I slammed the phone more than a few times on discussing AIG. It's just absolutely—I understand why the American people are angry. It's absolutely unfair that taxpayer dollars are going to prop up a company that made these terrible bets, that was operating out of the sight of regulators, but

Scott Pelley interviewed Ben Bernanke at Ohio State University, where the chairman of the Federal Reserve was giving a lecture on economic development.

which we have no choice but to stabilize or else risk enormous impact—not just in the financial system but on the whole US economy.

With the death of Ed Bradley some two years earlier and the retirement of Mike Wallace a few months before that, *60 Minutes* had openings to fill. I asked Bob Simon to move back to the United States for the first time in almost twenty-five years, but that still left us short by about twenty of the hundred stories we produced every year. To fill that gap, we brought on a few new contributors. Lara Logan, who had previously reported for *60 Minutes II*, added about five stories per year, still primarily covering the wars in Afghanistan and Iraq. Anderson Cooper, while still working at CNN, added another five stories, just as CNN's Christiane Amanpour had done years earlier; and David Martin, who covered the Pentagon for CBS, also began contributing on a regular basis. Katie Couric, who had joined CBS as anchor of the *Evening News*, planned to report about five stories per year for *60 Minutes*.

•   •   •

In January 2009 a plane landed in the middle of the Hudson River in full view of our windows on West Fifty-Seventh Street. Bill Owens called the news desk right away to report what had happened. Someone on the desk told him they'd heard it was a movie shoot. Bill responded this was no movie shoot; there were passengers climbing out onto the wings.

At a time when the news was filled with one depressing story after another about the economy and the wars and things that weren't going well, the story of hero pilot Chesley "Sully" Sullenberger was a gift from the news gods. The veteran pilot had safely landed the US Airways jet in the water with 155 people aboard after a flock of birds flew into the two engines, knocking out power in both, shortly after the flight took off from LaGuardia Airport. Now everybody wanted to interview Sully. We probably had a few dozen people calling everyone they could in search of a way to get to him. Lori Beecher, a producer working with Katie Couric, outsmarted everyone by connecting with the pilot's union in hopes that someone there might persuade Sully to speak to *60 Minutes*. Sully, it turned out, was a hard-core union guy, and it did the trick.

We met Sully at his home in the Bay Area just a few weeks after the crash. What I remember most about him, aside from his being decent and genuine, is that he was struggling. We all assumed he must have been riding high from the praise he'd received, but he wasn't. Sully was losing sleep and second-guessing himself, going over the accident moment by moment.

Katie Couric and Captain Chesley "Sully" Sullenberger chatted in the pilot's Northern California kitchen in February 2009.

CAPTAIN SULLENBERGER: One of the hardest things for me to do in this whole experience was to forgive myself for not having done something else, something better, something more complete. I don't know.

COURIC: But it had such a good ending.

CAPTAIN SULLENBERGER: Yes, it did.

COURIC: And it could have had such a terrible ending.

CAPTAIN SULLENBERGER: I know.

COURIC: But do you play this over in your head?

CAPTAIN SULLENBERGER: The first few nights were the worst, when the what-ifs started. The second-guessings would come, and it made sleep hard.

COURIC: Like what?

CAPTAIN SULLENBERGER: Just replaying it, you know, the flashbacks. You know, were we aware of everything we could have been aware of? Did we make the best choices? You know, all those kinds of thoughts.

But whatever Sully was going through personally, he had saved 155 people because of his cool and deliberate actions that day. All of them knew it, too, and said so when we gathered a group of them together in a hangar in North Carolina.

At *60 Minutes*, we like to follow a difficult, serious story with something inspirational or some kind of fun escape. What happened that day on the Hudson was both: a news story with inspiring human drama and an honest-to-God hero.

That same season, Bob Simon and Michael Gavshon found a story that took us on an escape with a different kind of hero: Dame Daphne Sheldrick, who ran an uncommon orphanage in Kenya—an orphanage for elephants. I loved how Bob set up the story in the studio introduction:

"Can you imagine an orphanage that's a happy place? We couldn't. But then we found one. The kids don't arrive here smiling. Like orphans all over the world, they've been abandoned, they're hungry, sad, and desperate. But after a few years, they're healthy, well fed, and, well, happy. The orphanage is in Kenya, outside Nairobi. And we might as well tell you now: it's an orphanage for elephants. They've been orphaned because their parents—their mothers, mainly—have died or, more likely, been killed in the bush."

Bob Simon looking up at an elephant at the David Sheldrick Wildlife Trust in Kenya.

Bob, the veteran war correspondent, took over the wild kingdom beat at *60 Minutes*. He liked to say animals were more fun than humans because they didn't bog you down with politics and bullshit. Michael Gavshon, who produced "The Orphanage," recalls that Bob spent as much time as he could off camera quietly watching the elephants. "I don't remember him ever being happier on any shoot," Michael reflected. "His favorite elephant was one named Emily. For months after the shoot, he'd go up to people and say, 'Do you want to see the love of my life?' and he'd produce a picture of Emily."

This was before Bob's grandson, Jack, was born, at which point Bob became obsessed with his grandson. I used to joke that he reminded me of how the movie *A Beautiful Mind* depicted mathematician John Nash, who battled schizophrenia and filled his back shed with newspaper clippings all over the walls. That's what Bob's office looked like—only it was plastered with giant pictures of Jack. Bob had discovered that grandchildren don't have politics and bullshit either.

Producer Harry Radliffe also loved wildlife stories. He and Bob traveled to Central Africa for a segment we called "The Secret Language of Elephants," which followed an American scientist, Andrea Turkalo, who for twenty years had been studying elephants and deciphering the sounds they made. Her goal was to create the world's first elephant dictionary. Bob interviewed Andrea at the edge of a clearing where more than fifty forest elephants were bathing in small ponds, drinking, and making noise. She told Bob what the noises meant—in other words, what the elephants were saying.

"Well, there's these low-frequency rumbles. It sounds like a big cat purring. And those are the vocalizations that help keep groups in contact with each other," she explained. "There are protest calls. In newborns, you have a particularly high cry. And when you hear it, you know it's a very, very young calf."

Bob Simon shows pictures of his grandson Jack to actor Mandy Patinkin in South Africa, on the set of Showtime's hit drama *Homeland*.

The archive of elephant behavior and sounds Andrea had compiled was fascinating and surprising. She was going through more of her research with Bob when they were interrupted by an elephant.

SIMON: Excuse me, we have a vocalization.

TURKALO: That's a protest.

SIMON: A protest?

TURKALO: That's somebody who's probably being refused by its mother.

SIMON: Baby elephants protest in a rather loud fashion, don't they?

TURKALO: Yeah, yeah, they're just like little bratty children.

Bob Simon and Harry Radliffe were mesmerized by forest elephants roaming the Dzanga Sangha clearing in the Central African Republic while shooting "The Secret Language of Elephants."

You could tell Bob was having fun. So was Harry, who had been working on the story for years. The trip was like heaven for a man who treated everything in his life as an adventure—but it was also difficult. Harry had been diagnosed with colon cancer less than a year earlier; he took the trip in between chemo treatments. He rarely complained, but it was hot, they were camping, and the days were long. Still, he never took for granted how lucky he was—and we all are—to be doing this for a living, especially then.

• • •

The stories that happen behind the scenes are often as interesting as those that find their way onto *60 Minutes*. They don't always show up on television, however, because they're often too much about us to make the final cut. But in the fall of 2010, we found a home for them. Pushed by our friend Joe Gillespie from the CBS Interactive Division, we came up with the idea for *60 Minutes Overtime*, a webcast filled with behind-the-scenes anecdotes and named by our clever producer Kara Vaccaro. We hired Annie Silvio, a digital maven from the *Boston Globe*, to host and produce it.

When we first announced the webcast and introduced Annie to the staff, Morley Safer approached her and said, "I don't get it. We report our stories and then we put them on *60 Minutes*. There's nothing else to say."

60 Minutes cameraman Ray Bribiesca put himself in the middle of the action with the 101st Airborne to capture what he called a "crazy shot" of a firefight that broke out in Afghanistan in 2010.

But when he came to see the webcast as a way for producers and cameramen, editors and correspondents, to tell their own stories, Morley became one of the most willing participants.

The very first *60 Minutes Overtime* in September 2010 featured one of our dedicated cameramen, Ray Bribiesca, a Native American marine veteran of two tours in Vietnam and a thirty-five-year employee of CBS News. He had been with Lara Logan on a treacherous mission at Afghanistan's border with Pakistan. They were with a unit of 101st Airborne soldiers, operating from one of more than fifty American combat outposts on the border, when they were ambushed by fighters from an Afghan guerrilla group called the Haqqani Network. Lara was rushed inside an armored vehicle when the intense firefight broke out, but Ray stayed outside with bullets flying all around him. He stood directly in the line of fire to get a frontal shot of the Americans firing back counting numbers using thousands, to make sure his shots were long enough.

Here's how Lara and Ray described the scene:

LOGAN: I remember at some point in the midst of the chaos in the
vehicle and everybody screaming, I looked out of the window.
Almost standing there, sort of like Moses when the waves parted,

Ray was just standing there, and he was calmly filming every-thing, getting all his shots.

BRIBIESCA: So I'm, like, "Okay . . . 1001 . . . 1002 . . . 1003 . . . 1004 . . . 1005 . . . 1006. . . Do I have it?"—the quote-unquote crazy shots. Those are the shots that when I see combat, I always say, "What does the face look like?" Instead of the point-of-view shot, which is the soldier from behind the shoulder, and you are seeing where he or she is shooting, how 'bout the face?

SILVIO: In order to get that, you have to be exposed.

BRIBIESCA: Sure.

SILVIO: You're no longer behind cover.

BRIBIESCA: Right. Yeah.

SILVIO: Why do you call them the crazy shots?

BRIBIESCA: I think, "Once my friends, my family, sees it, they'll say, 'Crazy shots!'" Yeah, they really will.

Ray was ready to retire after that, and even if he hadn't been, his wife, Linda, would have made him; that story did not make her happy.

·　·　·

Don Hewitt was still a presence at *60 Minutes* for several years after step-ping down. He would come to see us almost every day to talk and compare stories. He never lingered; he was conscious about taking up our time. But he seemed proud that we were still prospering.

I stood with him the summer of 2009 at Walter Cronkite's funeral. Don revered Walter, but he didn't say anything at the service. He was weak—suffering, he'd revealed only recently, from pancreatic cancer—and he had said everything that could be said about Walter over the half cen-tury he'd known and admired him. He did tell me this after the service, though: "It should have been half as long."

Don died less than a month later. We held his memorial service at the Frederick P. Rose Hall, the home of Jazz at Lincoln Center. Here's part of the tribute Les Moonves, the chairman and CEO of CBS, gave that day:

> When I joined the network, it was the early nineties. I remember how nervous I was to meet the legendary Don Hewitt . . . He made me feel really comfortable. I was now honored to be officially on the Don Hewitt pitch list to hear all of his new and exciting ideas. I would hear from him once, twice, three times a week. And it was very exciting. I was flattered. Until I realized that also on the Don Hewitt pitch list was the security guard at CBS and the woman who cleaned the office overnight. God, he was relentless . . . He'd say, "Kid, I got a great idea." . . . I still wait for the phone to ring and hear those words: "Kid, I've got a great idea for you." Thanks, Don.

We broadcast a special hour's tribute to Don. Though, really, every Sunday's broadcast is a tribute to Don.

· · ·

On many Monday mornings at *60 Minutes* the phone rings, and it is Hollywood calling. Producers see a story the night before and call seeking our help in chasing down the subject for a possible movie. There's no way of knowing how many *60 Minutes* stories have become films, but certainly a lot.

One of the first was a story we called "Genius," a 1983 profile of George Finn, who became the basis for the character played by Dustin Hoffman in *Rain Man*, an autistic savant whose brain possessed what Morley characterized as "an island of brilliance." Finn was obsessed with calendar calculation. If you gave him a date, as Morley did, he could tell you what day of the week it was.

SAFER: What day of the week was August 13, 1911?

FINN: Sunday.

SAFER: What day of the week was May 20, 1921?

FINN: Friday.

SAFER: Do you know how you do it?

FINN: I don't know, but it's just—that's fantastic, I can do that.

Morley did a few more stories about savants, including one from 2007 we called "Brain Man," about a twenty-seven-year-old named Daniel Tammet, who could memorize endless sequences of numbers and compute complicated math problems on command.

SAFER: Okay. So 31 by 31 by 31 by 31?

TAMMET: Yeah. Is 923,521.

SAFER: I dare say you're right. Or 17 times 17 times 17 times 17.

TAMMET: Eighty-three thousand, five hundred twenty-one.

What made Tammet fascinating was that, unlike most savants, he was able to describe his own thought process, which intrigued scientists who wanted to study his brain. So too could the five subjects of a 2010 story, "Endless Memory," who are not savants but are among a very small number of people known at the time to possess the extraordinary ability to remember exactly what happened on almost every single day of their lives: what they did and ate and wore and what had happened in the world. Neuroscientists were trying to figure out what might be going on inside their brains in an effort to better understand how memory works and, hopefully, to someday use this knowledge to help people with Alzheimer's disease and similar disorders.

The topic was original and fascinating, but Lesley Stahl didn't think it was either of those things when her longtime producer Shari Finkelstein pitched her the story. To Lesley, this supposedly rare ability—what scientists were calling "superior autobiographical memory"—sounded just like what her friend the actress Marilu Henner had. So, she thought, it couldn't be *that* unusual.

Lesley turned down the story. Normally, that would have been the end of it—correspondents here don't work on stories they don't want to do. But producers can also be strong-willed, and in this case, Shari wouldn't let it go. So Lesley arranged a lunch with Shari and Marilu in Beverly Hills, thinking this would shut down the story. But the meeting had the opposite effect, and, sure enough, Lesley was soon interviewing a group of five so-called memory wizards, including Marilu Henner, whom she put to the test.

STAHL: You and I have known each other—

HENNER: —twenty-five years. I can rattle off almost every time I've seen you. Do you remember the first time we went to Aureole, the restaurant? That was '93.

STAHL: Oh, my gosh.

HENNER: That was June 1, a Tuesday.

STAHL: And what did we eat?

HENNER: I had the salmon.

STAHL [*narration*]: She even remembers what day she first wore many of the shoes in her large and well-organized closet.

HENNER: Like these shoes, the first time I wore them was October 18, 2007. These I wore on April 21 of this year. So that was a Tuesday. Oh, these shoes I got a long time ago: 1982. I got them April the 9th, so that was a Friday.

STAHL: You really do remember your whole life.

HENNER: It's like putting in a DVD, and it cues up to a certain place. I'm there again. So I'm looking out from my eyes and seeing things visually as I would have that day.

They didn't make a movie out of that one, but it became a TV series called *Unforgettable* on CBS.

Many of the stories produced by the team of Stahl

Lesley Stahl interviewed a group of people with highly superior autobiographical memory, including her close friend, the actress Marilu Henner, seated in the center on the couch.

and Finkelstein have been unforgettable. Over the years they have covered a wide variety together, including profiles of fascinating people like Vy Higginsen, who guided Lesley and Shari through a remarkable inner-city music program called "Gospel For Teens." They recently covered the discovery of a town in Colombia, home to the largest concentration of people suffering early-onset Alzheimer's disease with implications for possibly preventing Alzheimer's some day.

It is their work involving the idiosyncrasies of the brain and behavior that have been some of the most interesting stories we have ever broadcast.

Lesley has always treated the people on her team with an equal measure of love and toughness. She can be very demanding, but also very funny. Producer Shachar Bar-On, who has worked with her for ten years, remembers once suggesting how they might fix part of a story they were working on, when Lesley said in exasperation, "Okay, but this time tell me in English, don't tell me in stupid!" *60 Minutes* correspondent teams are known to change often because of differences of personality and style. But Lesley's team has been remarkably stable, which is a reflection of the loyalty she inspires.

In all her years with *60 Minutes*, one of Lesley's favorite interviews was with Supreme Court Justice Antonin Scalia. It was one of my favorites too. Scalia didn't give many interviews, but this one, produced by Ruth Streeter, captured him well: he came across as the larger-than-life character that he was, blunt and scathing in his opinions about issues such as abortion, but also surprisingly charming and down-to-earth.

STAHL: So if we looked at your report card, it would never say you got in trouble.

SCALIA: No, no, absolutely not. Be straight A's too.

STAHL: Really?

SCALIA: Straight A's.

STAHL: The whole time? Come on.

SCALIA: Would I lie?

STAHL: No. No, you wouldn't lie.

SCALIA: If you can't trust me, who can you trust, right?

Still, Scalia was a polarizing figure who drew hostility from people who did not agree with him, along with deep admiration from his colleagues on the court. Justice Ruth Bader Ginsburg, one of his best friends despite being on the opposite end of the ideological spectrum, told Lesley what it was like to disagree with Scalia:

Supreme Court Justice Ruth Bader Ginsburg told Lesley Stahl what it was like to be an adversary of Justice Antonin Scalia's on the bench and his close friend off it.

STAHL: One of your opinions, he called "absurd." Another he called "implausible speculation"; another, "self-righteous," on and on.

GINSBURG: How about "This opinion is not to be taken seriously." He wrote that about Justice [Sandra Day] O'Connor.

STAHL: Justice O'Connor. Right.

GINSBURG: He's rather mild, I think, in the adjectives that he uses for me. But you can take every one of those words, run his opinions, and you'll see that all of us are implausible when we disagree with him.

STAHL: But do you ever, ever take it personally?

GINSBURG: No. I take is as a challenge: How am I going to answer this in a way that's a real put-down?

• • •

Another larger-than-life character with a reputation for being sharp and combative was Julian Assange, the elusive and somewhat eccentric founder of the website WikiLeaks who had started to make a name for himself by gathering leaked government documents and then sharing them with the mainstream press. He first caught our attention when he released a video showing a US Apache helicopter opening fire on a group of suspected insurgents in Baghdad, some of whom turned out not to be insurgents at all. Then there were classified military reports from Iraq and Afghanistan that showed civilian casualties were higher than the Pentagon had claimed, and classified State Department cables that exposed the inner workings of backroom diplomacy. Assange, an Australian, was accused of being out to damage the US government, and Steve Kroft wanted to interview him.

It took producers Howard Rosenberg and Tanya Simon six months to persuade Assange to come on *60 Minutes*, but the hardest part had been finding him. Assange was in hiding at the time, under attack on many different fronts. He was facing possible extradition to Sweden on rape charges and possible prosecution in the United States for his role in distributing classified information. So he was paranoid and always on the move. He insisted that all communication with *60 Minutes* take place over Skype because it was harder to trace than cell phones or email.

The interview was finally conducted in January 2011 on an estate in the English countryside, where Assange was holed up under house arrest while his extradition case played out in the courts.

The interview took place over two days, and things got heated when Steve asked about Attorney General Eric Holder's announcement that the Justice Department was considering prosecuting Assange under the Espionage Act of 1917.

ASSANGE: It's completely outrageous.

KROFT: Are you surprised?

ASSANGE: I am surprised, actually.

KROFT: But you're screwing with the forces of nature. You have made some of the most powerful people in the world your enemies. You had to expect that they might retaliate.

ASSANGE: Oh, no, I fully expected they'll retaliate.

KROFT: You—you've played outside the United States' rules.

ASSANGE: No. We've actually played inside the rules. We didn't go out to get—to get the material. Um, we operated just like any US publisher operates. We didn't play outside the rules. We played inside the rules.

KROFT: There's a special set of rules in the United States for disclosing classified information. There is—

ASSANGE: There's a special—

KROFT: —long-standing . . .

ASSANGE: —there's—there's a special set of rules for soldiers, for members of the State Department, who are disclosing classified information. There's not a special set of rules for publishers to disclose classified information. There is the First Amendment. It covers the case. And there's been no precedent that I'm aware of in the past fifty years of prosecuting a publisher for espionage. It is—it is just not done. Those are the rules. You do not do it.

By early 2011, popular uprisings in Egypt, Syria, Tunisia, and Libya were dominating the news. Bob Simon, with Draggan Mihailovich and producer Nathalie Sommer, went to Tunisia to cover the beginning of the Arab Spring in a story we called "The Spark," about a desperate young fruit vendor who set himself on fire to protest the government's confiscation of his measuring scale. Soon the protests grew larger and larger, eventually taking down the government and sparking a movement that spread through the region.

Lara Logan traveled to Egypt, where the Arab Spring had engulfed the country and surprised the world. This was the first time a dictator, entrenched president Hosni Mubarak, had faced—and proved unable to control—an uprising fueled by social media. Lara and producer Max Mc-Clellan planned to interview a Google employee who had led the movement on the internet. The two had run into trouble a few weeks earlier when they were taken by the Egyptian military and questioned for hours before being released, so we added more security for this trip: two drivers who could act as bodyguards, an Egyptian translator, and Ray Jackson, our CBS News security employee.

Upon their arrival in Cairo, the group headed straight to Tahrir Square, where crowds had packed to celebrate the fall of President Mubarak after thirty years. It was a jubilant celebration and our team wanted to see it. But before they knew what was happening, a mob of men grabbed Lara. The drivers and the bodyguard tried as hard as they could to hold on to her, but the mob, which was made up of dozens and dozens of men, pulled Lara away and into the square, ripping her clothes off and sexually assaulting her.

Lara said she didn't expect to survive, but the mob inadvertently pushed her into a tent of elderly women who saved her. She was bruised and bloodied, but because of those women, she was eventually reunited with the rest of the team—although she would be forever shaken by the horror she had experienced.

A few months later, when she had recovered from her physical wounds, Scott Pelley interviewed Lara for a *60 Minutes* story in which she described the assault.

LOGAN: I have one arm on Ray. I've lost the fixer, I've lost the drivers. I've lost everybody except him. And I feel them tearing at my clothing. I think my sweater was torn off completely. My shirt was around my neck. They tore the metal clips of my bra. They tore those open, and I felt that because the air; I felt the air on my chest, on my skin. They literally just tore my pants to shreds. And then I felt my underwear go. And I remember looking up and seeing them taking pictures with their cell phones.

PELLEY: Ray reported that he found himself with the sleeve of your jacket in his hand. It had been completely ripped from the rest of the jacket.

LOGAN: I felt at that moment that Ray was my only hope of survival. You know, he was looking at me, and I could see his face, and we had a sea of people

Lara Logan on camera in Cairo's Tahrir Square on the night of February 11, 2011, not long before she was attacked.

between us, obviously, tearing at both of us, beating us. I didn't even know that they were beating me with flagpoles and sticks and things, because I couldn't even feel that. Because I think the sexual assault was all I could feel . . . It was their hands raping me over and over and over again.

The forty-third season ended with the killing of Osama bin Laden, who met his end in Pakistan at the hands of a Navy SEAL unit known as SEAL Team Six on Monday, May 2, 2011. That week, Steve Kroft interviewed President Obama about the mission:

KROFT: Is this the first time that you've ever ordered someone killed?

PRESIDENT OBAMA: Well, keep in mind that every time I make a decision about launching a missile, every time I make a decision about sending troops into battle, I understand that this will result in people being killed. And that is a sobering fact. But it is one that comes with the job.

KROFT: This was one man. This is somebody who's cast a shadow in this place—in the White House for almost a decade.

PRESIDENT OBAMA: As nervous as I was about this whole process, the one thing I didn't lose sleep over was the possibility of taking bin Laden out. Justice was done. And I think that anyone who would question that the perpetrator of mass murder on American soil didn't deserve what he got needs to have their head examined.

Andy Rooney also weighed in that night on the killing of bin Laden:

There have only been a few times in my life when someone's death has been the occasion for rejoicing. The demise of Adolf Hitler was a good day for the world and a good day for me. The death of Osama bin Laden this week was that kind of a day for the world. They were both power-hungry men who would stop at nothing to get the power they lived for. It is hard to believe that such men existed. They didn't do it for their countrymen, either. They did it for themselves.

1 General Ray Odierno's 2008 interview with Lesley Stahl was his first since taking over command of US forces in Iraq.

2 Jeff Fager and Bill Owens in an edit room with associate producers Jennifer MacDonald and Anya Bourg screening Steve Kroft's March 2009 interview with President Obama.

3 Morley Safer visited painter and film director Julian Schnabel in his Long Island studio for a profile that aired in December 2008.

4 Scott Pelley caught a little shut-eye during his 2009 shoot with Company G, known as Golf Company, a marine battalion in Afghanistan.

5 Executive editor Bill Owens at a computer, getting the March 2009 interview with President Obama ready for air.

6 In November 2009, Scott Pelley reported on the restoration of Iraq's marshlands, believed to be the site of the Garden of Eden, which were all but destroyed by Saddam Hussein after the 1991 Gulf War.

7 Charlie Rose profiled Spanish actress Penelope Cruz in January 2010.

8 When Scott Pelley paid a visit to a group of Haitian orphans after the earthquake, some of them started calling him Papa Soft Hair.

9 Conan O'Brien, who had a short-lived stint as host of NBC's *The Tonight Show*, gave the thumbs-up to Steve Kroft in an interview that aired in May 2010.

10 Lesley Stahl spoke to Jimmy Carter about his memoirs, which were based on excerpts from a diary he dictated into a tape recorder almost every day of his presidency.

11 Lesley Stahl profiled John Boehner in December 2010, one month before he became Speaker of the House.

12 Steve Kroft tried to get a word out of the Stig, the always-masked and always-silent test driver on the BBC's hit car show *Top Gear*.

13 Steve Kroft met Julian Assange, the founder of WikiLeaks, on an estate in the English countryside, where he was under house arrest.

14 Morley Safer and producer David Browning traveled to London with trumpeter Wynton Marsalis.

15 Bob Simon and producers Michael Karzis and Harry Radliffe were the first American television journalists to visit Mount Athos, a vast complex of monasteries in Greece that have been home to Orthodox Christian monks for over a thousand years.

SEASONS

44-46

2011 to 2014

This is a moment I have dreaded. I wish I could do this forever. I can't, though.

—Andy Rooney in his final commentary, October 2, 2011

Andy Rooney was ninety-two years old when we started the new season in the fall of 2011. It was way past time for him to retire, but getting him to do so turned out to be more difficult than I expected. Not because he was a difficult person. He wasn't at all. He was a wonderful man who succeeded because he was an American original, a good writer with a keen eye for the absurdities in daily life. No, the process was difficult because every time we had the conversation about retirement he would agree it was time but five minutes later he would forget we'd had the conversation. He was suffering from dementia and his short-term memory was gone.

At one point, I met with Andy in his office with his agent (and mine), Richard Leibner, and the two of us did our best to persuade him to do one final commentary for that coming Sunday. But again, afterward he didn't remember the conversation.

The situation was impossible, and, in the end, his last appearance on *60 Minutes* would never have happened if not for his son, Brian, who came to New York to help Andy write his farewell piece. Brian, a longtime ABC News correspondent and a very good writer himself, actually wrote most of it. He knew his dad's voice well enough to pull it off. Here's some of what he said on *60 Minutes* that October night:

Andy Rooney bid farewell to viewers on October 2, 2011.

I've done a lot of complaining here, but of all the things I've complained about, I can't complain about my life. My wife, Margie, and I had four good kids. Now there are grandchildren. I have two great grandchildren, although they're a little young for me to know how great they are. And all this time, I've been paid to say what is on my mind on television. You don't get any luckier in life than that. This is a moment I have dreaded. I wish I could do this forever. I can't, though. But I'm not retiring. Writers don't retire, and I'll always be a writer. A lot of you have sent me wonderful letters and said good things to me when you met me in the street. I wasn't always gracious about it. It's hard to accept being liked. I don't say this often, but thank you. Although if you do see me in a restaurant, please, just let me eat my dinner.

Andy got hundreds, probably thousands, of cards, letters, emails, and phone calls after he signed off. He didn't understand why, because he didn't remember that he had retired on the air. Two weeks after his retirement, he had a stroke.

He died that same month.

• • •

Here we were in the fall of 2011, still reporting stories about the Great Recession. Perhaps the most sensational was the story of Bernie Madoff and the Ponzi scheme he had built from what appeared to be a legitimate business. When his multibillion-dollar scheme was discovered in December 2008, it became apparent that he had ruined a great many people who'd trusted him to invest their money because of his record of continuous profits—a record that, of course, turned out to be phony. Madoff ended up in prison for life.

Madoff's wife, Ruth, and son, Andrew, agreed to come on *60 Minutes*. Ruth had recently lost her other son, Mark, to suicide, and the family was keen on proving to the world that none of them had been aware of the scheme. But the interview with Ruth, produced by Deirdre Naphin, did not get off to a good start. She gave Morley Safer a hard time about a story he had done on Irving Picard, the man nicknamed the Liquidator because he was in charge of distributing what was left of Madoff's assets. Ruth was most upset about a jab Morley had taken at a sculpture that once sat behind Madoff's desk:

Ruth Madoff told Morley Safer that her last name was a burden in a profile that aired October 2, 2011.

PICARD: His desk was here.

SAFER [*narration*]: And close by, perhaps a work of art that sums up the entire story.

PICARD: And it was called *The Soft Screw* . . . And it was about four to six feet high. And it was sitting right here.

The interview with Ruth turned out to be both fascinating and sad—beginning with how she carries on as Mrs. Madoff.

SAFER: It's a tough name to live with.

MADOFF: It sure is.

SAFER: Do you feel the shame?

MADOFF: Of course I feel the shame. I can

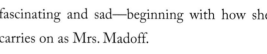

barely walk down the street without worrying about people recognizing me.

Ruth also admitted for the first time that she and Bernie had tried to kill themselves by overdosing on prescription drugs when he was under house arrest.

Producer Katy Textor, who also worked on the story, remembers coming away with a sense that the Madoffs had a marriage in which Ruth didn't ask any questions; she probably didn't know what was going on but also didn't *want* to know. None of the immediate family—Ruth, Mark, or Andrew, who died of cancer in 2014—was ever charged with anything.

The week after we broadcast the Madoff story, Lesley Stahl and veteran producer Ira Rosen reported on Washington's personification of greed and corruption, Jack Abramoff, in a piece called "The Lobbyist's Playbook." At a time when there was real anger about greed and recklessness on Wall Street, the lobbyist Jack Abramoff showed viewers how corrupt and money-driven Washington had become. Abramoff was a master at buying influence in the capital. He had pled guilty to fraud, tax evasion, and conspiracy to bribe public officials, and served three and a half years in prison before coming on *60 Minutes* to talk about how he bought and paid for influence on behalf of his clients.

Convicted influence-peddler Jack Abramoff sat down with Lesley Stahl in 2011 for his first television interview after being released from federal prison.

ABRAMOFF: At the end of the day, most of the people that I encountered who worked on Capitol Hill wanted to come work on K Street; wanted to be lobbyists.

STAHL: You're telling me this, the genius of figuring out you could own the office by offering a job to the chief of staff, say. I'm having two reactions: one is "Brilliant"; and the other is "I'm sick to my stomach."

ABRAMOFF: Right. Evil. Yeah. Terrible.

STAHL: Because it's—

ABRAMOFF: Shameful.

STAHL: —it's hurting our country.

ABRAMOFF: Absolutely. It's the worst thing that could happen. All parts of the system.

STAHL: I'm mad at you.

ABRAMOFF: I was mad at me.

STAHL: [*overlapping*] I'm not kidding. I'm not kidding.

ABRAMOFF: I was mad at me. Lesley, look, I did things and I was involved in the system I should not have been in. I'm ashamed of the fact I was there. The very reason why now I'm speaking about it and now I'm trying to do something, in recompense, is the fact that I thought it was . . . it was wrong of me to do it.

STAHL [*narration*]: One of the offices he keyed on was that of his good friend the majority leader Tom DeLay, eventually hiring his deputy chief of staff and his press secretary, and going into business with DeLay's chief of staff.

STAHL: Did you own his staff?

ABRAMOFF: I was . . . I was as close to his staff as to any staff. I had a very strong personal relationship with a lot of his staff.

STAHL: How many congressional offices did you actually own?

ABRAMOFF: We probably had very strong influence in a hundred offices at the time [*laughing*].

STAHL: Come on.

It was a Mike Wallace moment for Lesley, and she could do it as well as anyone.

Mike was now ninety-three years old, and the man we thought would live forever was struggling with Alzheimer's disease. When he died in the spring

of 2012, we were sad, but we did our best to celebrate a great life. Steve Kroft summed up Mike nicely at the memorial service we held a few months later:

Meryl Streep granted a rare interview to Morley Safer, which aired December 18, 2011.

Mike Wallace, photographed in the *60 Minutes* control room in 2001, died on April 7, 2012, at the age of ninety-three.

> He was audacious, impetuous, irrepressible, incorrigible, indefatigable, and egocentric, both on and off the air—a mixture of guile and gall . . . There was no professional persona. Mike was on all the time. I was stopped in the street last week by a woman who claimed that she was seated next to Mike at a dinner party about twenty years ago, and [she] said that he immediately began interrogating her. And by the time she'd finished the first course, she'd told Mike more about herself than she'd ever told her husband.

Steve also told of the time right before he came to work at *60 Minutes* when Dan Rather pulled him aside to say, "I just wanted to tell you, it's a jungle over there. It's filled with big cats. And all it takes is for one of them to give you a flick of the paw, and you'll be limping for six months."

Steve called Mike the biggest cat of all.

• • •

It was in this period that we started doing more stories with two of the best broadcast journalists in America: Charlie Rose and Anderson Cooper.

Charlie Rose, interviewing the actor and activist Sean Penn, has become a regular contributor to *60 Minutes*.

Anderson Cooper and Adele strolled the grounds of the estate the singer rented outside London for a profile that aired on February 12, 2012.

Charlie had been with CBS News since the early 1980s, starting out as the anchor of the overnight broadcast *CBS News Nightwatch*. I had hired him in 1999 to become a correspondent for *60 Minutes II*. He was perfect for *60 Minutes*: a unique voice and presence who studied his subjects carefully. I think that of all contemporary journalists, Charlie comes the closest to Mike Wallace in his ability to get people to tell him things. Part of why he succeeds is he comes across as genuine, sincere, and well-read; he is all of that and more. He is also a good friend and more people can say that about Charlie than anybody I know, because he has so many friends. Charlie's body of work on his own *Charlie Rose* program is the most significant collection of interviews anywhere.

Anderson had already contributed a few stories for *60 Minutes II* as well. He was just over forty but already admired for his intrepid reporting from around the world. Because of his worldwide CNN presence, he had also become an international star, which helped us get the kind of big celebrity interviews Mike and Ed had been so good at landing, although Anderson's subjects tended to be younger. That spring, he and producer John Hamlin profiled one such rising star: a twenty-three-year-old British singer named Adele, who had suddenly found herself up for six Grammy Awards. She was funny and down-to-earth about trying to adjust to her new circumstances.

ADELE: The kind of level of fame that I'm dealing with now, it's obviously got bigger over the year. But it was overnight, literally, on a flight to New York, I landed, and I seemed to be the most talked-about artist in the world that day. I wanted to be a singer forever. But it's not really my cup of tea, having the whole world know who you are.

COOPER: It's not your cup of tea?

ADELE: No. I find it quite difficult to think that there's, you know, about twenty million people listening to my album that I wrote very selfishly to get over a breakup. I didn't write it being that it's going to be a hit.

Anderson got Adele to play and sing for him, and to admit that she gets sick to her stomach from nerves before she performs.

COOPER: So what's that fear?

ADELE: That I'm not going to deliver. I'm not going to deliver. That . . . people aren't going to enjoy it. That I'll ruin their love for my songs by doing them live. I feel sick. I get a bit panicky.

COOPER: Have you ever thrown up?

ADELE: Yeah. Oh yeah. Yeah. A few times.

COOPER: Really?

ADELE: Yeah. Projectile. Yeah. Because it just comes, *waaahhh*. It just comes out. It does.

Anderson Cooper went deep underwater in search of the deadly Nile crocodile in Botswana's Okavango Delta.

One of Anderson's most interesting profiles was of Eminem. It was a rare interview for the rapper—and difficult to get—but the trouble paid off with a fascinating tale of a white kid who grew up in a mostly black public school in Detroit, who was bullied, and who rose to become one of the

Anderson Cooper and Eminem posing outside the rapper's childhood home in Detroit for a profile that aired October 10, 2010.

best rappers the music world had ever seen. But Anderson, a gay man, also challenged Eminem on some of the rough language in his work:

COOPER: I mean, some of the lyrics; like, in the song "Kill You," you say, "Bitch, I'm going to kill you, you don't want to F with me." You say, "My words like a dagger with a jagged edge that'll stab you in the head, whether you're a fag or a lez. Hate fags? The answer's yes."

EMINEM: Yeah, the scene that I came up in, that word was thrown around so much, you know? Faggot was, like, it was thrown around constantly, to each other, like embattling, that was just my—

COOPER: But . . . I mean, do you not like gay people?

EMINEM: No, I don't have any problem with nobody, you know what I mean? Like, I'm just "Whatever."

COOPER: And for, you know, some parent who's listening to this, and says, "Well, you know, my kid hears this, hears you calling somebody a bitch, or using the F-word, and starts to use it themselves." Do you feel a sense of responsibility?

EMINEM: I feel like it's your job to parent them. If you're the parent, be a parent. You know what I mean? I'm a parent. I have daughters. I mean, how would I really sound, as a person, like, walking around my house, you know, "Bitch, pick this up"? You know what I mean? Like, I don't—I don't cuss.

COOPER: That's not how you are in your real life?

EMINEM: Profanity around my house, no. But this is music, this is my art, this is what I do.

In the fall of 2012, Anderson reported on the fiftieth anniversary of the James Bond movie franchise. Anderson had already earned a reputation

as being up for just about anything that came his way during a shoot. So producer Tanya Simon requested access to Bond's famous Aston Martin sports car in order to film Anderson driving it. She managed to talk the studio into it, only to learn that Anderson didn't know how to drive a stick shift. He ended up doing that part of the story leaning against the car.

Otherwise Anderson usually said yes, no matter how risky or wild the assignment. When we asked him to go diving with great white sharks and then with the even more dangerous Nile crocodile—with no protection—he jumped right in. The only time he might have been fazed was when Lady Gaga showed up to an interview wearing almost nothing.

Anderson Cooper wasn't able to drive 007's Aston Martin, so he did a stand-up next to it instead, for a story about the James Bond franchise that aired in October 2012.

Lady Gaga wore little more than her Alexander McQueen boots to her interview with Anderson Cooper that aired in February 2011.

> COOPER: What—what are you wearing today?
>
> LADY GAGA: I just didn't want to wear clothes today. For whatever reason, I just didn't. I actually don't even have any foundation on my face. I just wanted eyeliner and my McQueen boots. That's it.

Our forty-fifth season started in the fall of 2012 with a segment on the two presidential candidates. Like most recent presidential campaigns, this one had been filled with nonsense and devoid of much talk about serious issues. Our broadcast was planned, as had been its predecessor four years earlier, as a public service. We would stick to the issues and the candidates' qualifications to give viewers a better sense of whom they might prefer.

It just so happened that we were also working on a story about historian and author of three presidential biographies David McCullough. So we decided to get him on the phone to find out what one of our finest historians might want to ask President Obama and Governor Mitt Romney just six weeks before the vote. Then we asked the candidates his question.

SCOTT PELLEY: The historian David McCullough says that great presidents learn from the history of the office. And I wonder what you've learned from the history of presidents in the White House.

GOVERNOR ROMNEY: You know, I enjoy reading David McCullough's writings. My favorite book is perhaps of a biographical nature: his book on John Adams, a person who had extraordinary character, a relationship with his spouse who may have been even brighter than he. We don't know as much about her as we do about him. But a man who had a very clear sense of direction, who helped guide the process of writing the Declaration of Independence and the Constitution. He wrote the constitution of my state of Massachusetts. And we saw in him an individual who was less concerned about public opinion than he was about doing what he thought was right for the country. And even though he was defeated in his run for reelection, he did what he thought was right for America. And I respect that kind of character.

Steve Kroft asked the same question of the president. It was the third week in September, and the race was a dead heat in most polls.

KROFT: David McCullough, the noted presidential historian, said all the great presidents have had a number of common traits. And one of them is an understanding of history and an understanding of the history of the presidency. Is there anything that you've read or learned from your study of this area that has helped you? Any examples you can give me?

PRESIDENT OBAMA: Well, whenever I look at the history of presidents I deeply admire, the one thing that I'm always struck by is persistence. It's a quality that's underrated. Being able to plow through, being able to stay buoyant in the face of challenges. And, you know, I think that's a characteristic of the American people. And I think our best presidents are able to tap into that resilience and that strength and that grit. And be inspired by it.

Arnold Schwarzenegger took Lesley Stahl to his childhood home in Austria and spoke to her about his careers in bodybuilding, movies, and politics, as well as his marriage to Maria Shriver, for a profile that aired in September 2012.

David McCullough explained the history of the Brooklyn Bridge to Morley Safer from a boat in New York City's East River, for a profile of the historian that aired in November 2012.

I don't know if our interviews changed anyone's opinion, but both candidates gave our viewers fascinating insight into their characters.

The Sunday before the election, we broadcast Morley's story about David McCullough, produced by David Browning, one of Morley's soul mates. It was the perfect preelection story.

"Every candidate running for any office ought to study the Harry Truman 1948 campaign," McCullough said. I think what's important about it, he ran by being himself. And he said, 'I'm going to go out there and say what I mean.' Can you imagine? A politician taking that as his approach? And people loved it."

McCullough was critical of both presidential campaigns and suggested we should demand more of our candidates. Morley asked whom he considered our greatest president.

"George Washington was our greatest president," he replied without hesitation, "in that he set the standard. He had no example to go by. If he had been a fool or a self-indulgent, lazy glory hound, it could've been disastrous. He did everything right."

By 2012, the war in Afghanistan had lasted more than a decade, making it the longest war in US history. "The Longest War" was the title of Lara Logan's latest story from the war zone, an interview with top US general John Allen. The war had started as an attack on the organization that had attacked the United States on 9/11, Al Qaeda, and the Taliban government of Afghanistan, which harbored the terrorist group. Eleven years later, Al Qaeda was back in Afghanistan, having found safe passage through neighboring Pakistan, and was killing American soldiers, mostly with roadside bombs. In speaking about this openly, General Allen seemed to be going against the White House party line that Al Qaeda was waning in strength.

General John Allen, commander of US forces in Afghanistan, spoke with Lara Logan about deadly attacks being waged against American troops by the very Afghan soldiers they were training, for a report that aired in September 2012.

GENERAL ALLEN: Al Qaeda has come back. Al Qaeda is a resilient organization. But they're not here in large numbers. But Al Qaeda doesn't have to be anywhere in large numbers.

LOGAN: And the effect on the battlefield remains exactly the same: American soldiers continue to die because of the support Pakistan gives to America's enemies.

GENERAL ALLEN: You've just stated the truth.

• • •

Bob Simon, who had covered his share of war stories, knew very little about sports. That's probably why he was so good at telling sports stories: he looked for the elements in a sports story that we could all appreciate. In the winter of 2013, he reported on one of the most successful sports franchises ever: the Barcelona Football Club, known as Barca. Right before he left for Spain, Bob asked his son-in-law if he had ever heard of an Argentine soccer player there named Messi. Evan, like most people even partly aware of sports, had heard of Lionel Messi—one of a handful of soccer players considered the greatest to ever play the game. But in telling the story, Bob put on full display his talents as a writer and an interviewer. Here's how he described Barcelona's iconic stadium, Camp Nou, on the biggest day of the year: a match between archrivals Barca and Real Madrid.

SIMON [*narration*]: Walking into Camp Nou on a night like this is entering the cathedral of football. Moments before the teams come onto the pitch, the crowd rises like a tidal wave. Some ninety thousand fans sing the Barca anthem, "Som I Serem." "We are, and we will be." The guy walking in last is Lionel Messi. He is the best player in the world. Many say the best ever . . . The ball often seems magically attached to his foot.

Lionel Messi took Bob Simon around Barca's training facility for a story about the football club that aired in January 2013.

SIMON: Now, when you score a goal today, are you just as happy as when you scored a goal when you were eleven years old?

MESSI: In the same way. I enjoy football in the same way I did when I was a little kid. And I love playing. I love winning the games. I love scoring. And I keep loving it all.

A year earlier, Bob had profiled tennis champion Novak Djokovic, who had escaped war-torn

Serbia and fulfilled his childhood dream of winning the Wimbledon tennis tournament and becoming the number one player in the world. Djokovic had a reputation for being something of a jokester—he famously did spot-on impersonations of other players—which is probably why he and Bob got along so well. It also helped that Bob was an avid tennis player himself. (This was the one sport he *did* know something about.) More than anything, Bob wanted to know what it was like to be on the receiving end of a Djokovic serve. Their time on the court ranks among the more memorable —and funniest—scenes to play out on *60 Minutes* because much to everyone's surprise, especially Djokovic's, Bob returned his serve.

SIMON: Hey! I—[*laughter*].

DJOKOVIC: Are you kidding me?

SIMON: What'd you think?

Bob Simon was genuinely surprised when he returned one of tennis champion Novak Djokovic's serves as part of a profile that aired in March 2012.

Snowboarding champion Shaun White, also known as the Flying Tomato, flew over Bob Simon's head while training in Silverton, Colorado, for the 2010 Winter Olympics.

Athletes and coaches have always been a regular part of *60 Minutes*. Their stories raise themes we love covering: human excellence and the ability to motivate individuals or a team toward the limits of human potential. Tom Brady had reached great heights winning three Super Bowls by 2005 as quarterback for the New England Patriots when Steve Kroft interviewed him, and Brady asked "why do I have three Super Bowl rings and still think there is something greater out there for me . . . I think God, it's got to be more than this."

But we have also done stories on the darker side of sports: Baseball player

José Canseco admitted to Mike Wallace that he had used steroids throughout his career, one of the first baseball players ever to make such a public admission. He also named five other prominent players he said had used steroids as well, breaking open a scandal that enveloped Major League Baseball for years.

Lance Armstrong gave us plenty to cover on the dark side of sports as well. We reported several stories on Armstrong over the years, beginning with his miraculous rise in the late 1990s to win more Tour de France races than anybody else in cycling—and doing so after having beaten testicular cancer. Then our investigations turned devastating for Armstrong. In January 2013 Scott Pelley, with producers Michael Radutzky, Oriana Zill, and Michael Rey, reported our second story on Armstrong in two years, exposing his use of performance-enhancing drugs. At the heart of the story was Travis Tygart, the director of the US Anti-Doping Agency (USADA), who had relentlessly pursued the truth even after others had given up. Tygart found that Armstrong ran a systematic and sophisticated doping program for the US Postal Service cycling team. He gathered so much evidence to prove this that Armstrong had to surrender his titles, lose his sponsors, and quit his own charity.

Scott Pelley interviewed Tygart for *60 Minutes* a week after Armstrong admitted, in an interview with Oprah Winfrey, to doping for the first time:

> PELLEY: Armstrong described doping as so routine it was, quote, "Like the air in our tires and the water in our bottles."

Anderson Cooper went up against Michael Phelps in a simulated swimming competition on Xbox for a profile of the Olympic gold medalist that aired in May 2012.

Former Houston Rockets star Yao Ming, who is seven feet six inches tall, towered over Lesley Stahl in Shanghai during a shoot for a profile of the retired NBA player from China.

TYGART: It's just simply not true. And I think it's a pretty cowardly self-interested justification or rationalization for his decision to defraud millions of people.

PELLEY: He suggested that cycling in those years was a level playing field because everyone did it. He wasn't doing anything special.

TYGART: It's—it's just simply not true. The access they had to inside information on how the tests work, what tests went in place at what time, special access to the laboratory, he was on an entirely different playing field than all other athletes, even if you assume all the other athletes had access to some doping products.

PELLEY: Armstrong admitted in the interview to doping throughout his seven Tour de France victories. He tried to make a comeback in 2009. He admitted to the first seven, but those last two races in '09 and 2010, he said he did not dope, he was racing clean.

TYGART: Just contrary to the evidence. The evidence is clear. His blood tests in 2009, 2010, expert reports based on the variation of his blood values from those tests, one to a million chance that it was due to something other than doping.

The big break in Tygart's case against Armstrong had come in the spring of 2010, when a number of Armstrong's former teammates broke their silence. Among them was Tyler Hamilton, who testified before a grand jury that he and Armstrong had taken performance-enhancing drugs during their time on the US Postal team. Hamilton's testimony was secret until he came on *60 Minutes* in May 2011. Three weeks after that story aired, he ran into Armstrong in a crowded bar in Aspen, Colorado. Here's how Hamilton described the encounter to Scott in January 2013:

HAMILTON: Turned to my right, and it was Lance Armstrong.

PELLEY: So he stops you cold.

HAMILTON: Stops me cold, yeah.

PELLEY: And says what?

HAMILTON: Well, first he asked how much *60 Minutes* had paid me to do that interview.

PELLEY: Answer, nothing.

HAMILTON: Obviously, nothing. Yeah. The biggest thing he said is, "You know, we're going to make your life a living, f---ing hell," both in the courtroom and out.

PELLEY: He was, at that moment, the target of a federal investigation. And you were a witness in that federal investigation.

HAMILTON: Yeah.

PELLEY: Intimidating a witness is a federal crime.

HAMILTON: Yeah.

PELLEY: Did you feel intimidated?

HAMILTON: I did. I did. I did.

Tyler Hamilton, the former professional cyclist who testified against Lance Armstrong in a 2010 federal doping investigation, told Scott Pelley what it felt like to come clean about the use of performance-enhancing drugs in the sport.

It wasn't just riders who felt threatened. Travis Tygart told Scott that he'd received anonymous death threats and that the agency where he worked, the US Anti-Doping Agency, came under attack after friends of Armstrong's cancer charity lobbied Congress to shut it down. I remember thinking that Tygart was a real American hero, and we were proud to have him on *60 Minutes*.

PELLEY: And yet you chose to go ahead. You were gambling [the] fate of [the] USADA itself on this one case.

TYGART: If we're unwilling to take this one case and help this sport move forward, then we're here for naught. We should shut down. And if they want to shut us down for doing our job on behalf of clean athletes and the integrity of competition, then shut us down.

PELLEY: If Lance Armstrong had prevailed in this case and you had failed, what would the effect on the sport have been?

TYGART: It would have been huge because atheletes would have known that some are too big to fail.

PELLEY: And the message that sends is what?

TYGART: Cheat your way to the top. And if you get too big and too popular and too powerful, if you do it that well, you'll never be held accountable.

The Armstrong story had many important dimensions that we look for at *60 Minutes*. Somebody who had something significant to hide (news, by some definitions, is anything somebody doesn't want reported) and was able to persuade several prominent and powerful people to unknowingly assist him in his deception by helping him undermine the very government agency set up to protect clean athletes. It was gratifying that we could expose the truth with the help of Travis Tygart.

We will also remember our Lance Armstrong stories because of Tom McEneny, our good friend and talented videotape editor who worked through the weekend on the first of the two stories and died of a massive heart attack just after he finished working on it, the very day it aired.

. . .

By September 2013, the war in Syria, already two years old, was front-page news again because of a sarin gas attack on civilians that seemed certain to be the work of the Syrian government of President Bashar al-Assad. Two years of a brutal and relentless crackdown had already caused two hundred thousand deaths. But this attack crossed a red line set by President Obama just that summer when he stated that the use of chemical weapons would prompt American military intervention. With the threat of a US military strike looming, Charlie Rose landed a rare interview with Assad.

Charlie and I went to Damascus together via Beirut, taking the same road we had traveled when we covered the civil war in Lebanon, only in the opposite direction. Back then, Damascus was the city safe from the war zone.

It was an odd adventure into the heart of the Syrian dictator's palace. We weren't allowed to bring our own cameramen or equipment; Syrian TV would shoot the interview. Assad requested a private meeting in advance of the interview, which proved an opportunity for us to remind him that the interview would be blunt and wide ranging. We also asked about an American journalist, Austin Tice, who had gone missing in Syria a year earlier. (We didn't get an answer.)

In the interview Assad was relaxed and spoke perfect English. Charlie asked him what he had learned from his father, who had gassed the Syrian village of Hama in 1982 during an uprising led by the Muslim Brotherhood, killing his own people. Assad's answer was more revealing than we expected:

ROSE: We remember Hama and your father, Hafez al-Assad. He ruthlessly set out to eliminate the Muslim Brotherhood. Are you simply being your father's son here?

PRESIDENT ASSAD: I don't know what you mean by ruthlessly, because—

Charlie Rose and Jeff Fager with Syrian president Bashar al-Assad before interviewing him at his Damascus compound in 2013.

ROSE: You know what happened at Hama.

PRESIDENT ASSAD: Have you heard about soft war? There is no soft war. War is a war. Any war is ruthless. And when you fight terrorists, you fight them like any other war.

ROSE: But now they say, their words, a butcher. Comparisons to the worst dictators ever to walk on the face of the earth.

PRESIDENT ASSAD: Mmm-hmm.

ROSE: Comparing you to them. Using weapons that go beyond warfare. Everything they could say bad about a dictator, they're now saying about you.

PRESIDENT ASSAD: First of all, when you have a doctor who cut the leg to prevent the patient from the gangrene, if you have to, we don't call him butcher, we call him doctor. And thank you for saving the lives. When you have terrorism, you have a war. When you have a war, you always have innocent lives that could be the victim.

Assad warned the United States against attacking him, saying this would lead to more 9/11-style attacks against the United States. A few days later, Scott Pelley was at the White House interviewing President Obama. He brought that up with the President.

PELLEY: Assad essentially put you on notice. In the interview with Charlie Rose, he said of the United States, "If you strike somewhere, you have to expect the repercussions somewhere else in a different form, in a way that you don't expect." He brought up 9/11 as an example of the kind of thing America did not expect. Do you take that as a threat?

PRESIDENT OBAMA: Well, I mean, I think it was intended as a threat. I don't take it as a credible threat in the sense that Mr. Assad doesn't have the capacity to strike us in a significant way. Some of his allies, like Iran and Hezbollah, do have the capacity to engage in asymmetrical strikes against us.

Syria was vexing for President Obama, and his red-line threat haunted him. It would be hard to find a military leader who didn't consider that about-face a low point of his presidency.

A few months later, *60 Minutes* hit a low point of our own with our worst mistake on my ten-year watch. It came in Lara Logan's report about the September 11, 2012, attack on the American embassy in Benghazi, Libya, that killed four Americans, including Ambassador Chris Stevens.

The story had serious flaws, the most significant being that even though they had interviewed important and credible sources with knowledge of the event, Lara and producer Max McClellan had wrapped a lot of their reporting around a British security specialist named Dylan Davies. He had been hired to train the unarmed guards who surrounded the American embassy and had written a book about what he said were his experiences. He told Lara that he had warned the Americans not to rely on local guards to protect the compound.

> DAVIES: I was saying, "These guys are no good. You need to get 'em out of here."
> LOGAN: You also kept saying, "If this place is attacked, these guys are not gonna stand and fight"?
> DAVIES: Yeah. I used to say it all the time. Yeah, in the end, I got quite bored of hearing my own voice saying it.

Davies told Lara he had seen Ambassador Stevens lying dead at the hospital that night. He told her many elaborate details about what he'd witnessed and done, including that he had jumped the embassy wall during the attack and fought at least one member of the attacking Libyan militia. Ten days after we broadcast the story, however, the *New York Times* reported that Davies had told a completely different story to FBI agents investigating the incident. He didn't even go to the embassy the night of the attack, he'd told them.

Our mistake was covered everywhere, sometimes on the front page. The timing made the story particularly explosive, as the Obama administration was fighting off accusations that it had mishandled the attack. We were criticized for drawing on the story of a liar to help make the case against the State Department. And among the many questions raised was this: Why had our reporting not uncovered the discrepancies the *Times* had?

We apologized for the mistakes two Sundays after the broadcast had aired. After a monthlong internal investigation, we suspended Lara and Max indefinitely. This was not an easy decision to make—many *60 Minutes* staffers thought they should have been fired. Among our most serious concerns was that Lara and Max had continued to fight for their story even though questions about Davies's credibility had surfaced almost immediately after the piece aired.

The internal investigation discovered nothing suggesting they had intended to deceive. Their worst journalistic crime was the one most often committed when news organizations get things wrong: they appeared to have gone into the story with a preconceived notion of what had happened and did not adequately question evidence that failed to support this belief. They also treated Davies's story like many firsthand accounts from conflict zones that are hard to corroborate—with inadequate skepticism and scrutiny.

All *60 Minutes* stories go through a thorough vetting process that typically catches mistakes like this one. We pride ourselves on a system of checks and double checks—and yet this time that system failed. Ultimately the executive producer is responsible for everything that goes on the air, and I took responsibility for the error. Had I asked more questions during the screening, we might have exposed the story's weaknesses. That's another way we keep mistakes from getting on the air.

Our credibility was damaged for a time. But I do believe that after you admit mistakes in journalism—and we have had our share of them over the years—you do your best to understand how the mistakes were made and start to earn back your reputation, one story at a time.

. . .

David Martin is one of the most knowledgeable and experienced reporters ever to work the Pentagon beat, and we have been fortunate to have him at CBS News since the 1980s. In early 2014 he and producer Mary Walsh reported a story about the F-35, America's next-generation fighter plane. The country's most expensive weapons program—costs had been estimated at $400 billion—was also $68 billion over budget and nearly seven years behind schedule.

David took viewers behind the scenes of the building of the F-35s, with Lieutenant General Chris Bogdan as our guide. The general had been appointed a year earlier to get costs under control, fix mistakes, and improve the military's relationship with the plane's manufacturer, Lockheed Martin.

> MARTIN: How would you characterize the relationship between the
>   Pentagon and Lockheed Martin?
> LIEUTENANT GENERAL BOGDAN: I'm on record after being in the job
>   for only a month standing up and saying it was the worst rela-
>   tionship I had seen in my acquisition career.

That was because the plane had a number of surprisingly basic defects. The F-35 couldn't fly at night, for example, because the wingtip lights didn't meet FAA standards.

> LIEUTENANT GENERAL BOGDAN: When you hear something like that,
>   you just kind of want to hit your head like this and go "Multi-
>   billion-dollar wingtip lights? Come on."

MARTIN: We found out that the tires were wearing out two, three, four times faster than expected. Tires.

LIEUTENANT GENERAL BOGDAN: Tires aren't rocket science. We ought to be able to figure out how to do tires on a multibillion-dollar, highly advanced fighter.

Still more surprising was that the plane was given top dollar and priority even though the wars being fought today wouldn't need it: for almost two decades, we've been fighting guys in pickup trucks firing Kalashnikov automatic rifles. But David Martin was told that this was an opportunity to go way beyond the capabilities of the Chinese and the Russians. No aircraft would survive a fight with the F-35, the most technically sophisticated weapon on earth.

In contrast, Lesley Stahl took viewers to the surprisingly decrepit weapons system that still stands ready to wipe out entire cities: the land-based American Minuteman III nuclear missiles, tucked away and ready to launch from underground silos spread across the American West. Lesley and producer Andy Court were allowed to go down into one of the silos, designed in the 1960s to withstand a nuclear attack. There they met a pair of missileers, so called because they watch over and control the missiles. It was striking how young the missileers were, though the equipment they used was ancient. The phones didn't always work, and one of the computers that might receive a launch order from the president still used floppy disks, as Lesley was shown.

STAHL: Before you got down here, you probably had never seen one of these?

DANA MEYERS: I had never seen one of these until I got down in missiles.

Lesley reported that the ancient equipment had its benefits, though: it can't be hacked or compromised because it isn't online.

In February 2017, soon after his inauguration, President Donald Trump told Scott Pelley and a group of journalists about the country's aging nuclear weapons equipment. He remembered seeing the story on *60 Minutes* and said he planned to do something about it.

Few people in the United States are more associated with wondrous, new technology and a bold vision for the future than Elon Musk. He's a dreamer, an inventive and creative individual who saw something nobody else did—very much like Steve Jobs—and tried to change the world. Musk told Scott Pelley for a story in March 2014 that he launched his company Space Exploration Technologies Corporation, or SpaceX, so that humans could colonize Mars, and he started Tesla, which makes electric cars, to save the Earth by reducing greenhouse gases. They were impossible businesses, to say the least—and they got off to very bad starts.

PELLEY: In 2008 the rocket company is not going well; you've had three failures.

MUSK: Yeah.

PELLEY: The car company is hemorrhaging money.

MUSK: Yeah.

Associate producer Vanessa Fica, producer Harry Radliffe, and Scott Pelley pose for a picture with entrepreneur Elon Musk for a story that aired in March 2014.

PELLEY: And the American economy has tanked in the worst recession since the Great Depression.

MUSK: Right.

PELLEY: What was that year like for you?

MUSK: And I'm getting divorced, by the way—[to] add to that. That was definitely the worst year of my life . . . I remember waking up the Sunday before Christmas in 2008 and thinking to myself, "Man, I never thought I was someone who could ever be capable of a nervous breakdown, but . . ." I felt this is the closest I'd ever come. It seemed pretty dark.

PELLEY [*narration*]: Toward the end of 2008, SpaceX prepared its fourth attempt.

MUSK: We were running on fumes at this point; we had virtually no money.

PELLEY: So a fourth failure?

MUSK: A fourth failure would have absolutely been game over.

PELLEY: Done.

MUSK: Done.

PELLEY: SpaceX bankrupt.

MUSK: Yeah. It's bad enough to have three strikes; having four strikes is really kaput.

The fourth launch was flawless. Soon after, NASA awarded Musk a $1.5 billion contract. And two days later, Tesla's investors decided to pour more money into the electric car.

• • •

In the spring of 2014, we lost Clem Taylor, a producer who died at just age sixty from pancreatic cancer. Clem had been at *60 Minutes* for only a few years, but in that short time he made a significant mark on all of us. He was a wonderful person with a great spirit and a generous soul. And his stories were excellent.

1 Amazon's Jeff Bezos unveiled for Charlie Rose the prototype of his company's newest venture, the octocopter, a type of drone designed to one day deliver packages autonomously.

2 Bob Simon paid a visit to Don "Cola" Gomez, a carpenter who creates musical instruments for a children's orchestra using recycled garbage from the landfill in Paraguay, where he lives.

3 Bob Simon, with producer Tanya Simon, interviewed Detroit firefighters who were unable to do their job because their truck had no water, for a report about the bankrupt city that aired in October 2013.

4 Producer Clem Taylor, pictured in the Democratic Republic of Congo, died in March 2014.

5 Jay Leno talked to Steve Kroft about his impending departure from *The Tonight Show*, for a profile of the late-night host that aired in January 2014.

6 Scott Pelley and volcanologist Haraldur Sigurdsson hiked to the summit of the Eyjafjallajökull volcano in Iceland not long after it erupted, for a report that aired in January 2014.

7 Cate Blanchett took Lesley Stahl on a tour of the Sydney Theater Company, where she got her start, for a profile of the Australian actress that aired in February 2014.

Just a few years earlier, Clem won a Peabody Award for a story he produced with Magalie Laguerre-Wilkinson called "Joy in the Congo," a beautiful Bob Simon story about the only symphony orchestra in Central Africa and the only all-black orchestra in the world. The conductor and the musicians had created something beautiful from almost nothing in one of the poorest countries in the world, purely because of the joy it brought them.

The story began with this line from Bob:

"Beauty has a way of turning up in places where you would least expect it."

This is how it ended:

"Finally, it all came together, and on the night of the performance, in this rented warehouse, Beethoven came alive. It's called the 'Ode to Joy,' the last movement of Beethoven's last symphony. It has been played with more expertise before. But with more joy? Hard to imagine."

SEASONS

47-49

2014 to 2017

Bill Whitaker joined us as a new correspondent when we started our forty-seventh season, and he was apprehensive. "Try walking onto the ninth floor, with all those pictures on the walls and all that history in the air, and not feel the weight," he said. "You'd be delusional if you didn't."

And if the history was daunting, so was the workload, as Bill discovered soon after his arrival when he asked Lesley Stahl to lunch. "We'd make a date, we'd have to break it, because one or both of us would be out of town," he remembers. "She'd come to my office to ask if I were free, I'd shake my head no."

It took them two years to find a date that worked.

Bill had been at CBS News for more than twenty-five years when he joined *60 Minutes*. He was an outstanding broadcast journalist who had covered just about every kind of story based out of our Los Angeles bureau

60 Minutes isn't known for having welcoming parties, but Bill Whitaker, pictured with Jeff Fager, got one in August 2014 when he joined the program as its new correspondent.

Bill Whitaker went fly-fishing in British Columbia with April Vokey for a story that aired in November 2013.

and before that from China, Japan, Atlanta, and all points in between. But I had not considered him for *60 Minutes* until he reported a story for us about a fly fisher from the Pacific Northwest, a woman named April Vokey. It was a good story, thoughtfully told with solid interviews in which Bill was spontaneous, natural, and very likeable. He is a wonderful human being—and that comes across on the air.

Bill's maiden voyage, produced by Howard Rosenberg, had the potential to be a *60 Minutes* classic—unless, Bill worried, he screwed it up. It profiled Joaquin Guzman, the billionaire drug kingpin from Mexico known as El Chapo—Spanish for "Shorty"—who had managed to evade capture for thirteen years. We called the story "Public Enemy Number One" because El Chapo's Sinaloa drug cartel had manufactured and moved more drugs into American cities than any previous drug syndicate.

The calling card of the cartel was its distribution methods: packing drugs into fake fruit and shipping them alongside real produce; digging elaborate tunnels to transport drugs under the US-Mexico border; and building underground escape routes from El Chapo's many hideouts to ensure he could always get away.

When they thought they finally had him cornered, the Mexican marines, a highly respected group, battered down the front door of the house where El Chapo was hiding and stormed the place—only nobody was home. But upon further inspection, they found a bathtub equipped with a hydraulic lift and, underneath it, a steep staircase leading down to a dark tunnel.

With a flashlight to guide him, Bill Whitaker took us down those stairs and into the tunnel El Chapo had used to escape. Here's what he reported:

"This was part of a maze of tunnels connected to the city sewers of Culiacan and, it turns out, to six other safe houses, all equipped with hydraulically controlled bathtub escape hatches. Our guide told us that even though they had a ten-minute head start, he could hear the fugitives splashing through the water. But they were too far ahead to catch. When the marines emerged from this spillway by the river, El Chapo had vanished."

Bill Whitaker explored one of the tunnels El Chapo used to escape Mexican law enforcement for a story about the drug kingpin that aired in October 2014.

Five days later, American law enforcement agents had traced El Chapo to a resort town 136 miles way. Not long after, the Mexican marines burst into a beachside apartment building and found El Chapo hiding in a bathroom. He surrendered without a fight, with no shots fired. It was an anticlimactic end for a once-mighty drug lord, but a terrific beginning for a veteran CBS correspondent.

If you have earned the title "Most Wanted Man," as El Chapo had, chances are good that you'll end up on *60 Minutes*—and probably more than once. And the Most Wanted Man with the most stories on *60 Minutes* is James "Whitey" Bulger, the notorious Boston Irish mobster and head of the Winter Hill Gang, whose first mention on the broadcast came in the 1992 profile Morley and I did of his brother Billy, then the president of the Massachusetts State Senate.

Whitey was the subject of endless fascination. He was a ruthless killer who had infiltrated the local FBI office and bought off agents who

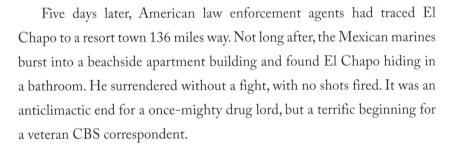

supplied him with information, including a tip in 1994 that he was about to be arrested. Whitey went on the run—and vanished. His disappearance set off the biggest manhunt in FBI history. In the decade and a half that he was in hiding, we did story after story about him and his organization, investigating his relationship with the FBI and interviewing his associates—including one of his hit men—as well as the federal agents who eventually arrested him in 2011.

It had always been assumed that Whitey was living a lavish lifestyle on the lam in Ireland, Italy, or Mexico. But it turned out that he'd been hiding in plain sight, living with his girlfriend in a modest Santa Monica, California, apartment under the pseudonym Charlie Gasko. He'd convinced his neighbors he was a retiree in the early stages of dementia.

The story of how he managed to elude the authorities for so long was interesting, but the story of how he was captured was hilarious—at least the way Steve told it in his 2013 report. It happened, as only Steve could write, "with the help of a boob job and an alley cat." (There was a lot of debate at the screening about whether Steve should say "breast implants" instead of "boob job.")

Whatever you called it, it was important because someone had told the FBI that Whitey's longtime girlfriend, Catherine, had undergone plastic surgery before fleeing Boston. Agents found medical records that contained photographs of her face. They created a public service announcement using the pictures, and the very next morning, a former beauty queen from Iceland who'd been living in Santa Monica called the FBI's tip line to say she knew the woman in the PSA. They'd taken turns caring for a stray cat that used to wander up and down their street.

The FBI agent who arrested Whitey Bulger was named Scott Garriola. Tanya Simon and coproducer Nichole Marks got him to sign a picture for me of the moment he took the eighty-one-year-old former gangster into custody. The exchange that took place just before the picture was captured is one for the ages:

GARRIOLA: Gave the words, "Hey, FBI, you know, get your hands up!" And hands went up right away. And then at that moment, we told him get down on his knees, and he gave us a "I ain't getting down on my f---ing knees."

KROFT: Didn't want to get his pants dirty?

GARRIOLA: Didn't want to get his pants dirty . . . I asked him to identify himself, and that didn't go over well. He asked me to f---ing identify myself, and then he said, "Well, you know who I am." And I asked him, "Are you Whitey Bulger?" He said, "Yes."

But the punch line came when one of Whitey's neighbors walked by on the way to do her laundry. She told Garriola that the man he was arresting had dementia, which might explain his odd behavior.

GARRIOLA: Immediately, what flashed through my mind is, "Oh, my God, I just arrested an eighty-one-year-old man with Alzheimer's who thinks he's Whitey Bulger! What is he going to tell me next, he's Elvis?" So I said, "Do me a favor." I said, "This woman over here says you have a touch of Alzheimer's." He said, "Don't listen to her. She's f---ing nuts." He says, "I'm James Bulger."

FBI Special Agent Scott Garriola arrested Whitey Bulger in the garage of the mobster's Santa Monica apartment building in June 2011.

Steve Kroft interviewed Whitey Bulger's hit man, John Martorano, in an Italian restaurant in Boston.

• • •

By the fall of 2014, it became apparent that the withdrawal of all US forces from Iraq had allowed a resurgence of the organization that called itself the Islamic State. We had reported on ISIS many times using the name Al Qaeda in Iraq: in 2004, with our story about the founder of the organization, Abu Musab al-Zarqawi, and in 2006, when the US Infantry, led by then Colonel H. R. McMaster, liberated the small city of Tal Afar from the group's control.

This time Scott Pelley went right to the front lines in Iraq, as ISIS was taking one town after another. We knew the group was getting strong, but we didn't know how strong until Masrour Barzani, the head of Kurdish intelligence, explained ISIS's dominance to Scott in disturbing detail:

BARZANI: I think everybody underestimated the strength of ISIS, especially with all the weapons they seized from the Syrian army and the Iraqi army. Five Iraqi divisions melted away, and, you know, they just left their weapons, which fell into the hands of ISIS. Weapons, bought by American taxpayers, were captured by ISIS as it paraded into cities that had been won by American troops.

Scott Pelley on the Al Rashad Bridge southwest of Kirkuk in Iraq, with the black flag of ISIS flying in the distance over his right shoulder.

PELLEY: How many ISIS fighters are there?

BARZANI: There are perhaps forty thousand ISIS fighters who are carrying guns, fighting both in Iraq and Syria; maybe equally divided in two countries.

PELLEY: And how many people collaborating with them?

BARZANI: Well, collaborating whether they believe in helping them or not or out of fear, I would say over one hundred thousand.

In our coverage of Syria that same year, Scott reported a frightening story we called "A Crime Against Humanity," produced by Nicole Young and Katie Kerbstat. They had been investigating the sarin gas attack on civilians in the suburbs of Damascus in August 2013 and used footage taken by a local cameraman named Kassem Eid, who lived in the town of Moadamiyeh and had witnessed strange rockets landing nearby.

> KASSEM: When they crashed, they didn't make the same old-fashioned bombing sound. It was, in a way, silent.
>
> PELLEY: The rockets hit the ground, but it didn't sound to you like they were exploding?
>
> KASSEM: Yes. The closest rocket hit almost a hundred meters away from the place that I was staying in. and within seconds, I lost my ability to breathe. I felt like my chest was on fire.

Kassem was lucky. He survived, while hundreds of others did not. His pictures captured the horror of the attack: the gas taking the breath out of so many children and their parents, choking them to death.

The Ebola outbreak was another major international story that was, like the war in Syria, difficult to cover. The Ebola virus was so lethal that most reporters didn't want to go near it, and there were rules about coming back into the United States after having been in a high-exposure zone.

Lara Logan and Max McClellan flew to Liberia for a story we called "The Ebola Hot Zone," about a treatment center run by an American relief organization in what used to be a leper colony. When Lara and Max left the African country, they had to stay in quarantine for three weeks while writing and editing. The story captured the difficulty of containing the virus in a rural hospital encampment. In the time it took to shoot, twenty-six people had died, including a five-year-old boy named William.

Lara Logan, on the road to an Ebola treatment center outside Monrovia in Liberia, had to stop at a government checkpoint to have her temperature taken and her clothes and shoes sprayed with chlorine to prevent the spread of infection.

Bob Simon with his daughter, producer Tanya Simon, in December 2014 at a Winnipeg laboratory that developed an Ebola treatment, shooting what was to be his last story for *60 Minutes*.

LOGAN [*narration*]: There were thirty-four filled graves when we arrived. Two and a half weeks later, there were more than sixty. The patient, who came strapped inside the ambulance, is now lying here. For every death, a simple funeral. A patient's brother clutched a wooden grave marker on his way to the graveyard. For the boy, William, and his father, George, who survived Ebola with the help of the American doctors and nurses here, there was much hope as they fought for his son's life. But in that same graveyard a few days later, another small grave was added.

Bob Simon set his sights on another Ebola story, this one about a promising experimental treatment that was made from, of all things, tobacco.

It had been a good season for Bob. He had recently come out of a very bad period of depression; when he came to understand that a big part of what had triggered the depressive episode was his captivity in Iraq in 1991, he started to recover. In the fall of 2014 and winter of 2015, he was happier than any of us had seen him in years. At seventy-three, he was wandering the halls of *60 Minutes*, laughing and gossiping and telling jokes.

His story about the Ebola drug wasn't the first *60 Minutes* story he had done with his daughter, Tanya, producing, but this one, like the others, was so good that I wanted to air it immediately that coming Sunday. Bob was thrilled. He walked the halls telling everyone who would listen that his story had bumped someone else's. On his way out that evening, he stopped in Bill Owens's office to lay claim to a forthcoming story about *Daily Show* host Jon Stewart and then got into a town car to head to an appointment downtown. About twenty minutes later, his driver barreled into a barricade divider between lanes. Bob was killed.

The news was devastating. I learned of Bob's death from my friend Chris Licht, who was running *CBS This Morning*. I immediately called John Miller, who had left CBS News to become deputy commissioner of intelligence and counterterrorism with the New York City Police Department. He confirmed that he had been to the scene of the accident and had seen Bob's body.

What I did next was among the hardest things I have ever done. I called Tanya to tell her about her dad. It was around eight o'clock, and I found her on her cell at her desk, waiting for Bob to come back to the office so they could finalize the story for airing. When I told Tanya I had bad news, she thought it was about the story. Maybe it was being postponed. If only.

Bob's funeral was held a few days later at his favorite place in New York: the Metropolitan Opera at Lincoln Center. Bob loved the opera; he had managed to talk us into doing two opera stories in just the past two years. The Met's opera company, led by Peter Gelb, was in grief just as we were and was honored to hold the service in the elegant foyer of the building.

During Bob's captivity in Iraq, he would dream of watching a performance of *Tosca* and then walking down the Met's grand staircase in his tuxedo, beneath the two Marc Chagall paintings hanging in spectacular display on either side of the foyer. There he lay now in a coffin, beneath one of them.

It was a cold winter day, with sparkling snowflakes drifting outside the giant glass windows. I will never forget listening to Tanya eulogize her dad:

Bob Simon soaked up the sun aboard *The Moken Queen*, in the Andaman Sea, during a shoot in 2005.

As long as I can remember, my dad had a framed quote on his desk. It was written on an index card in his chicken scrawl, and it was in French, and it said, "*Il vaut mieux mourir sous le soleil que vivre sous la pluie*": "It's better to die under the sun than live under the rain." We're not sure whose quote that is, but that's how he lived his life, braving the elements, navigating the choppy weather, but I think he finally found his break in the clouds. Dad, I know you're up there, in your very own patch of sun. Please, save a spot for me.

There were about two hundred people invited to the funeral, and many of them came from overseas. Our CBS family extends to every continent, and that so many people traveled from so far says a lot about our sense of kinship—and about Bob. The funeral spilled over into the lower-floor bar at a nearby restaurant, P. J. Clarke's, where about fifty of us drank beer and retold Bob's favorite stories and jokes for the next several hours.

The following Sunday, we broadcast the story he had just finished on Ebola. Here's how Scott Pelley set it up:

We begin tonight with a story by Bob Simon, our colleague and friend, whom we lost this past Wednesday in a tragic car accident. In a forty-seven-year career, reporting from every corner of the globe, Bob set the standard for CBS News. On Wednesday evening, Bob finished a story intended for this broadcast tonight. It's especially fitting that the producer was his daughter, Tanya, a veteran producer at *60 Minutes*, who from time to time worked with her dad.

We thought the best way to pay tribute—and what Bob would have wanted—would be to put his story on the air in his own words, beginning right here.

SIMON [*narration*]: This is the front line in the war against Ebola— Canada's national microbiology lab on the desolate prairie in

Manitoba. It's a good place to experiment with viruses because inside are some of the most dangerous in the world, which is why Dr. Gary Kobinger—who has spent a decade here trying to find the cure for Ebola—has to seal himself inside layers of protection before getting to work. One pair of gloves isn't enough.

The following Sunday, we dedicated the entire broadcast to Bob and his remarkable work over so many years.

But Bob's work was not over. Shortly before he died, he had completed shooting for a story with Harry Radliffe about the Scottish island of Islay, home to some of the finest single malt whiskeys. Harry was fighting colon cancer, so he had not been able to work on the story much since—and now Bob was gone. We felt a need to finish the segment, so I asked Steve Kroft if he would step in and write the story using Bob's interviews, working with Harry and associate producer Vanessa Fica. It was a great opportunity to bring Bob back to life for thirteen memorable minutes.

KROFT [*narration*]: *60 Minutes* is constantly on the lookout for places we've never been before. So when our late colleague Bob Simon heard about a magical place in the Hebrides islands off the coast

Bob Simon tasted a single malt whiskey with Jim McEwan, master distiller at Bruichladdich, on Scotland's Isle of Islay.

of Scotland, known for making some of the great whiskeys in the world, well, the story spoke to him.

Bob liked good scotch and beautiful places. So he went off to Scotland. He died before he could finish the piece, leaving behind a stack of videotapes and some random notes. We decided to finish it for him and raise a glass in his memory.

The story ended with Bob having one more scotch with the master distiller, who had plied him with glass after glass of his finest stuff.

JIM McEWAN: Cheers, Bob. Hope you've enjoyed this little visit here.

SIMON: You're speaking in the past. It's not over.

JIM McEWAN: Yeah, I've gotta get you outta here, man [*laughter*]. You're costing me a fortune.

· · ·

People often ask me, "What's your favorite *60 Minutes* story?" It's a difficult question. But for a time, I had an answer. It was a story about a remarkable discovery in the fight against cancer that we broadcast in March 2015. Newspeople tend to use the word "breakthrough" a lot. It's so overused that it has little meaning. But this story *was* a breakthrough as defined by the US Food and Drug Administration (FDA). After years of research, doctors at Duke University believed they had found a new way to treat patients with glioblastoma, a relentless brain cancer typically considered a death sentence. It was the kind of story you hope you come upon once in a lifetime of reporting: one of the worst forms of cancer might be curable. And it was how the doctors were doing it that made the story even more compelling. They were treating glioblastoma patients with the polio virus, genetically engineered to remove the effects that had crippled and killed people for centuries.

The Duke researchers had discovered that the polio virus has a receptor that locks onto the cancer cell and then multiplies, giving off a toxin that starts to kill the tumor. They believe the body also recognizes the intruding virus and attacks the tumor to get at the polio—helping to kill the tumor in the process. This is one of the most promising areas of immunotherapy, and we were there from the very beginning of the first clinical trials on people with glioblastoma.

Henry Friedman is cohead of the Preston Robert Tisch Brain Tumor Center at Duke, and it wasn't his first time on *60 Minutes*. He had been an invaluable source for producer Michael Radutzky over the years, and the doctor trusted Michael enough to let him and producer Denise Schrier Cetta follow patients through the first ten months of this experimental therapy in phase one of a three-phase trial (phase one is meant to determine the best dosage amount and positive results are not always expected). They were with an early patient named Nancy Justice when the polio virus was dripped directly into her massive brain tumor and went to work dissolving it.

SCOTT PELLEY: How surprised are you by that?

DR. FRIEDMAN: I'm surprised because you never expect on a phase one study in particular, which is what she is on, to have these kinds of results.

PELLEY: You're not expecting to cure people in a phase one trial.

DR. FRIEDMAN: You're not even necessarily expecting to help them. You hope so. But that's not the design of a phase one study. It's designed to get the right dose. When you get anything on top of that, it's a cake.

PELLEY: Quite a cake.

DR. FRIEDMAN: Quite a cake. Biggest cake we've seen in a long, long time.

Scott Pelley was with Nancy Justice at Duke University Cancer Center after she received an experimental cancer treatment using the polio virus, for a story that aired in March 2015.

Nancy was one of three patients we followed whose tumors disappeared over time. There were also several patients who did not see good results, but given how early it was in the trial, any good response was considered remarkable.

A year later, in our second report, we broke the story that the FDA was giving the polio treatment so-called breakthrough status, meaning that hundreds of new patients will have access to the treatment before it goes through the full scrutiny of the FDA approval process. For the government to bless the Duke program in this way confirmed that we were onto something very important. We remain on the story to this day and we continue to witness the potential and the difficulties of the polio virus experiment. Nancy Justice died in April 2016 from a recurrence of the cancer.

• • •

Before his run for president in 2015, Donald Trump had been on *60 Minutes* a total of eight times. In all of those appearances, one thing stands out: he is the same person Mike Wallace interviewed in 1985, when Mike called him a swashbuckling billionaire accused of driving up rents to evict tenants.

> WALLACE: And when they call you arrogant and cruel, those tenants over there, does that get under your skin?
>
> TRUMP: No, because, you see, I think I'm right; and when I think I'm right, nothing bothers me.

And he is the same person Morley Safer interviewed in 1996 about businessman Steve Wynn's plan to bring the Mirage casino to Atlantic City. Wynn was, and still is, considered one of the most successful casino developers in the world:

> TRUMP: I will beat Mirage as badly as I beat Steve Wynn individually in golf. I mean, I *want* Mirage to come in. I really want him to come in be—
>
> SAFER: You want to whip him.
>
> TRUMP: And I want to beat him, yeah. And I will.

In the year 2000, Dan Rather reported a story for *60 Minutes II* about Mr. Trump starting an exploratory campaign for president. Trump was very unhappy about that story because of what we've since recognized as a recurring issue for him: crowd size. He let us know he believed that when we showed him giving a press conference, we added false video of empty chairs; the venue was actually full, he claimed.

"Don Hewitt never would have done that to me," he told me when I ran into him. So we double-checked all of the tape and confirmed that the crowd size had been portrayed accurately. There were about twenty reporters present for the presser, a pretty good number for an exploratory campaign.

Over the years, I got to know Mr. Trump better. I saw him once at a New York Yankees game, where I told him I thought we were fair and would always be fair. He seemed to accept that. He had an appreciation for *60 Minutes*, and I don't think he liked being at odds with us.

By the summer of 2015, it was apparent that his run for president was having an enormous and unprecedented early impact, so we decided to interview him at the beginning of season forty-eight, well before the start of the primary campaign. Scott Pelley conducted the interview in the candidate's private home in Trump Tower, where he challenged Mr. Trump on all of his positions: China, a wall on the Mexican border, throwing illegal immigrants out of the country, taxes, and the economy. It was as tough and direct as any interview Trump had done to that point. But the interview itself didn't get as much attention as what Mr. Trump said after it aired, on the same broadcast with our Charlie Rose interview of Russian president Vladimir Putin:

"I got to know him [Putin] very well because we were both on *60 Minutes*. We were stablemates, and we did very well that night."

It was funny, considering the two were interviewed in their home cities, several days and half a world apart.

But the Putin interview also made news on its own merit; it was a

Scott Pelley pressed
presidential candidate Donald
Trump at Trump Tower on
a number of policy issues
including taxes, immigration,
and job creation, for
a profile that aired in
September 2015.

Producer Bob Anderson
jetted around the country
with Donald Trump on the
candidate's private plane
to prepare the September
2015 profile.

great example of Charlie at his finest. The interview took place at Russia's presidential headquarters just outside Moscow, a few days before Russia announced it would send military assets into Syria to bolster President Assad.

ROSE: But your pride in Russia means that you would like to see Russia play a bigger role in the world, and this is just one example.

PRESIDENT PUTIN *[through interpreter]*: Well, it's not the goal in itself. I'm proud of Russia, that's true. And we have something to be proud of, but we do not have any obsession with being a superpower in the international arena.

ROSE: But you are in part a major power because of the nuclear weapons you have. You are a force to be reckoned with.

PRESIDENT PUTIN: I hope so. I definitely hope so. Otherwise why do we have nuclear weapons at all?

ROSE: You're much talked about in America. There's much conversation.

PRESIDENT PUTIN: Maybe they have nothing else to do in America but to talk about me.

ROSE: No, no, or maybe they're curious people. Or maybe you're an interesting character. Maybe that's what it is. They know of a

former KGB agent who came back and got into politics in Saint Petersburg and became deputy mayor and then came to Moscow. And the interesting thing is, they see these images of you bare-chested on a horse, and they say there is a man who carefully cultivates his image of strength.

PRESIDENT PUTIN: You know, I'm convinced that a person in my position must provide a positive example to people. And those areas where he can do this, he must do this.

Charlie Rose asked Vladimir Putin if he intentionally tried to project an image of strength, in an interview with the Russian president that aired in September 2015.

Vladimir Putin, with a translator, sat down for a meal in September 2015 with *60 Minutes* associate producer Sarah Fitzpatrick, Jeff Fager, and Charlie Rose.

What made the experience even more interesting was what happened when the cameras stopped rolling. Putin invited us—Charlie and me, along with producers Andy Court and Sarah Fitzpatrick—into another room, where we thought we might be served some tea. But what followed developed into a multicourse meal of traditional Russian dishes and a long conversation. We asked Putin if he would take President Assad into asylum in Russia if he were forced to flee Syria. He rolled his eyes and said, "We already have Snowden," referring to Edward Snowden, the former NSA contractor who leaked thousands of classified US documents. We asked if he had a preference in the 2016 US presidential contest, and he told us it never matters to him because, once in office, all US presidents act the same, no matter which party they're from. We talked about how he stays in shape. Ice hockey, he said.

Charlie asked the Russian president if he liked to arm wrestle, and he said yes, so I challenged him. We arm-wrestled to a draw.

Looking back on the fall of 2015, it is remarkable how many other significant international figures we interviewed within less than two months. There was Iran's president, Hassan Rouhani, soon after the signing of the controversial nuclear weapons accord with the United States, Russia, China, the United Kingdom, and other world powers. Steve Kroft asked Rouhani if he thought America was still the "Great Satan"—as Ayatollah Khomeini had vilified us in his rhetoric. The president suggested that he did indeed believe that, based on past performance. Then came this exchange, which included one of my all-time favorite questions:

KROFT: "Death to America" is a very simple concept. Three words, not much room left for interpretation. Not very conciliatory. Do you see the day when that language will not be used?

PRESIDENT ROUHANI: If America puts the enmity aside, if it initiates goodwill, and if it compensates for the past, the future situation between the United States and Iran will change.

There was Pope Francis, who answered five questions from Scott Pelley during his massive weekly outdoor audience at St. Peter's Square in

Steve Kroft getting TV-ready for his interview with Iranian president Hassan Rouhani while talking through the questions with producer Michael Karzis at the presidential compound in Tehran.

Jeff Fager was caught on camera carrying a tripod in Vatican City in September 2015, during a shoot about Pope Francis.

Vatican City on the eve of his first visit to the United States. We didn't get much out of him, though he made one request before his visit, saying, "Pray for me, I need it." And then in English, as he left us: "God bless you."

There was Vice President Joe Biden, still grieving over the recent death of his son, Beau, and having just announced that he would not run for president. Biden told Norah O'Donnell, a *CBS This Morning* anchor now contributing stories to *60 Minutes*, that he had decided not to run because he didn't think he could win. Due to Beau's death, he hadn't started early enough to make a good run of it.

In the middle of all of this, Steve conducted a relatively contentious interview with President Obama about where things stood in the Syrian war and the strength of ISIS.

KROFT: You said that this would degrade and eventually destroy ISIS.

PRESIDENT OBAMA: Over time.

KROFT: Over time. It's been a year, and—

PRESIDENT OBAMA: I didn't say it was going to be done in a year.

KROFT: No. But you said—

PRESIDENT OBAMA: There's a question in here somewhere.

KROFT: There's a question in here. I mean, if you look at the situation, and you're looking for progress, it's not easy to find.

Pope Francis held a General Audience in St. Peter's Square and then stopped to answer a few of Scott Pelley's questions in September 2015.

Norah O'Donnell interviewed Vice President Joe Biden and his wife, Jill, at the Naval Observatory in the fall of 2015 about why he decided not to run for president.

The interview was intense, and Steve added to the heat when he questioned the president's call to train and equip five thousand moderate Syrians to fight there. By most accounts, the program ended up costing a fortune and trained only five people.

KROFT: I know you don't want to talk about this.

PRESIDENT OBAMA: No, I'm happy to talk about it.

KROFT: I want to talk about this program, because it would seem to show, I mean, if you expect five thousand, and you get five, it shows that somebody someplace along the line made some sort of a serious miscalculation.

PRESIDENT OBAMA: Steve, let me just say this.

KROFT: It's an embarrassment.

PRESIDENT OBAMA: Look, there's no doubt that it did not work.

Steve Kroft and President Barack Obama had a few light moments in the West Wing Colonnade during what was otherwise a relatively intense interview in October 2015.

60 Minutes producers Frank Devine, Maria Gavrilovic, and Michael Karzis, along with Jeff Fager, at the White House, watching Steve Kroft interview President Obama in October 2015.

After we took a break, the president started the second part of the interview by saying with some playful belligerence in his voice, "What else you got?"

A weekly broadcast like *60 Minutes* doesn't have much time to stop during the regular season. We finish one Sunday-evening broadcast—often

on Sunday—and move on to the next. One of the few times we do stop to reflect is when we lose someone important to us. In early December 2015 we lost Harry Radliffe to colon cancer. We remembered him at the end of the following Sunday's broadcast:

> STEVE KROFT: He was the ultimate world traveler on a broadcast of world travelers. He knew where to get the best bouillabaisse in Marseilles, and the best barbeque in Tennessee. He knew where to go to find a great story and who to talk to when he got there. He was kind and calm, and a great journalist.

Harry never lost his enthusiasm for exploring.

He made *60 Minutes*, and all of us here, better just by having the privilege of working with him.

Harry, knowing that he was on the verge of dying, had thrown a party at his home in Connecticut, inviting a collection of his friends to eat and drink and celebrate his life with him. He couldn't get out of bed. But he had a big smile on his face, particularly when our friend and *60 Minutes* contributor Wynton Marsalis showed up to serenade the gathering with his beautiful horn. Harry died a week later.

Longtime friends Harry Radliffe and Jeff Fager at a *60 Minutes* holiday party in 2011.

Wynton Marsalis serenaded Harry Radliffe at his home during a gathering of friends, a week before Harry died.

• • •

That spring came another crushing loss: Morley Safer passed away at the age of eighty-four. Morley had been sick for several months suffering complications from radiation treatments for a few cancer spots. We agreed in January that he should retire, and he helped us work on a tribute to his remarkable career. The team that put it together was Morley's dream: David Browning, Warren Lustig, Katy Textor, and Michelle St. John. We worked on the tribute all spring, and got it ready for an air date of May 15. It was to be a full hour of Morley's favorite stories and memories.

We broadcast "Morley Safer: A Reporter's Life" (the title was his idea) that Sunday, and Morley died later in the week. I believe he had been hanging on to life just to see the special on television.

The Sunday after he died, we had another opportunity to remember Morley by airing his 2008 story "All in the Family," about the Antinoris, a family that had been making wine in Tuscany for more than six hundred years. The story had everything Morley loved: Italy, beauty, fine food and wine, adventure, lovely people, and an opportunity to write some beautiful lines:

Morley Safer's last *60 Minutes* story, about Danish "starchitect" Bjarke Ingels, aired in March 2016.

Morley Safer signed graphic artist Bob Corujo's sketch of him "To Jeff with love."

SAFER [*narration*]: As anyone who's sat through a Thanksgiving dinner can tell you, families can drive you nuts. And if you're bold or crazy enough to go into business together, beware. A recent study found only fifteen percent of family businesses survive past

Produced By David Browning
Warren Lustig

Morley Safer:
A Reporter's Life

the second generation, meaning if the whims of the marketplace don't get you, familial rivalry or plain old-fashioned greed will, which makes the Antinori family of Italy all the more remarkable. They've been in the same line of work for six centuries now. The Antinoris make wine, and the family story reads like something a wine critic might write about their product: complex, stylish, sophisticated, with a bouquet both elegant and earthy.

The spring of 2016 brought one of the most unusual presidential contests in memory. By May, it was apparent that Hillary Clinton would be facing Donald Trump. That month, producers Ruth Streeter, Rich Bonin, Henry Schuster, and I met with the two campaign managers to discuss what we wanted from both: the first interview with the running mate and the candidate just before each convention in July; an interview with the two candidates wholly about issues, as we had done in the previous two general elections, come September; and the first interview with the president-elect.

By the end of July, our first requests were granted. Lesley Stahl did the first interview with Donald Trump and Mike Pence in Trump Tower; and Scott Pelley, the first interview with Hillary Clinton and Tim Kaine in Miami. The interviews didn't make much news, but it's always interesting to see the interactions between running mates. Mike Pence told Lesley he would walk to the president's office if he thought he was wrong about

Morley Safer in one of his favorite places, Italy, with some his favorite *60 Minutes* characters, the wine-making Antinori sisters.

Lesley Stahl and Jeff Fager talked off camera with Donald Trump and his running mate, Mike Pence, in their first joint interview, which aired in July 2016.

Scott Pelley had the first joint interview with Hillary Clinton and her running mate, Tim Kaine.

something and tell him so. He also did what a running mate is expected to do: he sucked up.

PENCE: This man is awed with the American people, and he is not intimidated by the world. And Donald Trump, this good man, I believe, will be a great president of the United States.

TRUMP: I love what he just said.

A week later, we were with the other team, getting ready for the interview with Clinton and Kaine. The Clinton team was obsessed with what pillow would be right for her back in the chair they had chosen. There were a half dozen people involved over several hours, changing the pillow and taking pictures of it over and over again. By the time Mrs. Clinton sat down, Scott Pelley said:

PELLEY: There's been an enormous amount of concern about the pillow you're sitting on.

CLINTON: Has there been?

PELLEY: And there've been many pillows that have been road-tested and rejected. That was deemed to be the perfect one, so . . .

CLINTON: Well, I don't know who your pillow expert is, but tell that person thank you.

But it wasn't our people, it was hers—and as hard as they'd tried to make her comfortable, she wasn't. In eight interviews with *60 Minutes* over twenty-five years, Hillary Clinton never seemed comfortable. I was there for many of them, and there was almost always concern about what we would ask, as if we were somehow out to "get" her. This one was no exception. All went reasonably well from our perspective, but the Clinton people were not happy with this question:

> PELLEY: Jimmy Carter said in 1976, "I'll never tell a lie." What can you tell the American people in this interview about your own honesty with them and the honesty of a Clinton White House?
>
> CLINTON: I think if you look at my public service, I have been as straightforward and honest as I could be. I haven't always been perfect, but I don't know anyone who is. And we're going to have a campaign and a White House that the American people will be able to look at and believe that Tim and I are working every day for them, that they can count on us, that they can trust us.
>
> PELLEY: Your critics are going to say, "See? She didn't say 'I will never tell a lie.'"
>
> CLINTON: Well, you've done this to me before, Scott. And I remember that very well.
>
> PELLEY: It was a question you didn't like.
>
> CLINTON: Well, no, but I guess my answer would be the same. I certainly never intend to, and I certainly don't believe I have.

Scott had asked a similar question of Hillary about a month earlier because most polls consistently showed that between 60 percent and 70 percent of Americans did not trust her. He expected she would be delighted to have an opportunity to change that perception. But her campaign managers were not delighted. They were very upset and told me they would never do another interview with Scott. This put the September hour we'd hoped to do with the two candidates in jeopardy, because we don't like when a politician tries to pick who'll ask the questions.

That September broadcast would have been a great opportunity to cut through all the nasty campaigning to focus on where the candidates stood on major issues. But Hillary wouldn't do it with Scott, and we wouldn't change correspondents. I think it was a mistake on her part, because the potential audience was as high as twenty million in prime time. Why wouldn't she take a question like Scott's and blow it right back at him with something like, "You're damn right I won't lie to the American people, Scott, and I doubt my opponent could say the same thing!"?

The day after the election, I called Hope Hicks, who handled all of Mr. Trump's press requests, to talk about the first interview with President-elect Trump. Within five minutes, we'd agreed to noon on Friday with Lesley Stahl. We had two days to prepare.

It was a difficult moment for journalists because the country was so divided: half of our viewers were sick about the Trump victory; the others elated and probably a bit surprised. It was not an easy situation for Lesley to be in, but we did our best to stick to what we knew would be important: questions about his campaign promises, and how much of what he had said would turn into real plans. Questions about the mood of the nation and what he planned to do about it—and what he planned to do about the fears of the millions of illegal immigrants living in America.

We started the interview in the early afternoon in the president-elect's home in Trump Tower. The atmosphere was subdued. Everyone seemed exhausted. Mr. Trump said he wanted to build a wall on the Mexican border but would accept a fence in parts. He said he wanted illegal immigrants with criminal records to be deported, but when Lesley suggested that some of his supporters had apparently been harassing Muslims and other immigrants, he looked straight into the camera, as if he were speaking directly to those people, and said, "Stop it!" He also talked about his meeting with President Obama in the White House two days after the election.

> STAHL: You looked pretty sober sitting there in the Oval Office. Did something wash over you?
>
> PRESIDENT-ELECT TRUMP: No, I think I am a pretty sober person. I think the press tries to make you into something a little bit different; in my case, a wild man. I am not.

Lesley asked if he planned to tweet as he had during the campaign.

> STAHL: You're going to do that as president?
>
> PRESIDENT-ELECT TRUMP: I'm going to do very restrained; if I use it at all, I'm going to do very restrained.

She asked if it was true that he had gone silent as he watched the results come in on election night.

Lesley Stahl sat down with President-elect Donald Trump in his Trump Tower apartment with his family—wife, Melania; daughters, Ivanka and Tiffany; and sons, Donald Jr. and Eric—for his first television interview since winning the White House.

STAHL: It kind of just took your breath away? You couldn't talk?

PRESIDENT-ELECT TRUMP: A little bit, a little bit. And I think I realized that this is a whole different life for me now.

Two months later, we were in the Oval Office with President Obama for his last big television interview as president. There were moving vans outside and people packing things up in crates. The staff was tired and seemed a bit numb. White House Communications Director Jen Psaki and White House Press Secretary Josh Earnest, both of whom had been very good to work with, were trying to find out if the First Lady would be joining us. Three hours before the interview, we learned that Michelle would not be participating. We all got the sense that she wanted to get out and move on. Steve asked the president about it as they walked toward the Oval Office.

PRESIDENT OBAMA: Michelle never fully took to the scrutiny. I mean, she's thrived as a First Lady, but it's not her preference. And so . . .

KROFT: She was the hardest sell.

PRESIDENT OBAMA: She was the hardest sell. And she never fully embraced being in the public spotlight, which is ironic, given how good she is.

KROFT: But you're still all right—I mean, everything's okay?

PRESIDENT OBAMA: As far as I know. I better check later.

The exit interview with a president can be a real opportunity to learn about life in the White House. Steve asked President Obama what he would write in a description for the job:

PRESIDENT OBAMA: Thick skin helps.

KROFT: Thick skin.

PRESIDENT OBAMA: Stamina. There is a greater physical element to this job than you would think, just being able to grind it out. And

President Obama joked with Jeff Fager and Steve Kroft after his January 2017 exit interview that they would stop taking his calls once he left the White House.

I think your ability to—not just mentally and emotionally but physically—be able to say, "We got this."

Steve asked if he was surprised by anything over his eight years, and the forty-fourth president said the "severity of the partisanship" continues to surprise him. He took some blame for not being able to make progress on that front. He did not, however, sound contrite when answering a question about whether he should have referred to a red line that would be crossed if Syria used chemical weapons. But he did say this:

"You know, there's no doubt that probably at least once a week, maybe once a day, I said, 'Ah, I should have done that better.' I bet at the end of this interview I'll say, 'Oh, that would have been a really good answer for that or this.' I think we've done the big stuff right. I think that there are some big, obvious fumbles."

After two of his final hours in the White House, the president looked at us as we shook hands and quipped, "You're not going to take my call next week, are you?"

We did our share of stories amid the chaos of the new Trump administration. We reported on the vetting process for immigrants coming to the

United States from places such as Syria—a well-established and arduous screening that takes at least two years. We reported stories about sanctuary cities here in the United States for illegal immigrants worried about getting deported. We reported on the president's travel ban, tensions with North Korea, and allegations that President Putin's government was poisoning adversaries. We reported on the proliferation of fake news stories in America and were surprised to learn that in Michigan alone, a state with a razor-thin presidential voting margin, more than half of the so-called news consumed by voters was fake—planted by people trying to make money or have a negative impact on one of the candidates.

It was, by most measures, a good season for *60 Minutes*: we were up

---

1 Charlie Rose interviewed Reese Witherspoon and her mother, Betty, for a profile of the actress that aired in December 2014.

2 Bill Whitaker sat down with violinist Itzhak Perlman for a December 2014 story about the medieval Italian city of Cremona, which gave the world the famed Stradivarius violin.

3 Anderson Cooper had to give up his cell phone for twenty-four hours and get hooked up to electrodes that measured his brain activity for a story he reported on mindfulness in December 2014.

4 Larry David was interrupted by a phone call from his agent when he was being interviewed by Charlie Rose, who took the writer-and-comedian back to his childhood home in Brooklyn for a profile that aired in March 2015.

5 Lesley Stahl profiled Michael Caine who, at the age of eighty-two, was starring as the leading man in a 2015 film called *Youth*.

6 Charlie Rose went on the set of the blockbuster Broadway musical *Hamilton* with its creator and star, Lin-Manuel Miranda, for a profile that aired in November 2015.

7 Bill Whitaker sat in on a sound-editing session for the 2015 *Star Wars* installment, *The Force Awakens*, while J. J. Abrams, the film's director and cowriter, worked with Lindsey

Alvarez, the film's sound editor, to create the voice for a new droid, BB-8.

8 Bill Whitaker tasted extra virgin olive oil in Sicily with Nicola Clemenza, an olive farmer who was trying to break the Mafia's stranglehold on the olive oil industry in Italy, for a report that aired in January 2016.

9 Steve Kroft, with producer Michael Karzis, profiled architect Peter Marino, who attracts as much attention for his look as he does for his work.

10 Anderson Cooper got close to one of his subjects, a type of endangered ape called a bonobo, in the Congo in 2015.

11 Bill Whitaker interviewed Denzel Washington in Los Angeles on the set of his 2016 movie *Fences*.

12 Lesley Stahl had never shot a rifle until she reported a story on smart guns that are specially designed so only their owners can fire them.

13 Lesley Stahl reported a story about *Sesame Street* when the television program introduced a new muppet with autism named Julia.

14 Former New York City mayor Michael Bloomberg took Steve Kroft on a tour of the Bloomberg L.P. headquarters for a story about his work after government that aired in April 2017.

slightly in total viewers compared with the year before and finished in the top ten broadcasts almost every week. Our cumulative number—the Nielsen measurement of how many people tune in at least once during the season—put us again at number one of all television programs.

By March 2017, we were already well into one of our annual rituals: starting work on stories for the next television season, our fiftieth anniversary. We look ahead to every season as best we can, trying to predict what the big stories might be. There will be some hoopla spread through this anniversary season, and a new face joining us as we reach that milestone: Oprah Winfrey, who will be a special contributing correspondent. But at the same time, our fiftieth season will be a lot like the forty-nine that preceded it. We will be taking things as we usually do, one Sunday at a time.

This has been part of the character of our broadcast for fifty years, drawn from the character of the original CBS News. We're an ensemble of reporters doing our best to shed some light where it is needed, producing consequential reporting to help people get a better understanding of this crazy world. We carry on, without many of the people who started *60 Minutes*, but with them always in mind. In that spirit, the last words in this book belong to Morley Safer, from his 2011 eulogy of the great producer Joe Wershba:

And though I doubt it, if he is somehow listening to this,
I just want to assure him that our merry ship sails on.
That his example is still the order of the day.
Some of the older timbers may be getting a little creaky,
But the course remains true and the weather fair.

ACKNOWLEDGMENTS

Almost everything at *60 Minutes* involves some kind of collaboration, and this book was no exception.

It would not have happened without Tanya Simon. She was my partner in this venture, beginning with the difficult job of going through five thousand stories to help decide what ended up in the book. Her skills organizing, reporting, writing, and editing were essential every step of the way.

Tanya now knows more about *60 Minutes* than she would ever want to know. Unless she is already too sick of it by now, she will be an important part of this broadcast for many years to come.

I didn't ever think of writing this book until Priscilla Painton suggested it and then edited it. Her judgment and her guidance have been steady and superb. I am also grateful for Jonathan Karp's insights and observations. He runs a well-oiled operation at Simon & Schuster, and my thanks goes to that collection of talented people, including Cary Goldstein, Richard Rhorer, Cat Boyd, Jessica Breen, Jonathan Evans, and Elisa Rivlin.

Thanks to Ruth Lee-Mui for designing the book and Jackie Seow for the cover. Thanks to Megan Hogan for her fine editing work and Phillip Bashe who, with his grasp of journalism and history, was an excellent copy editor.

In addition to being a great friend, partner, and constant resource, Bill Owens, as always, made sure our broadcast kept going strong while I was distracted.

Alison Pepper is a significant part of everything we do at *60 Minutes*; not much happens without her insightful input. I am grateful for her advice and support from beginning to end.

Thanks to Steve Kroft and Lesley Stahl for their help and suggestions and also to Debbie De Luca Sheh, Claudia Weinstein, Frank Devine, and Kevin Tedesco, who helped with the book and who make *60 Minutes* better every Sunday night.

Among many other things, Chrissy Jones chased down every detail before I even asked for it. Thanks also to Kara Vaccaro and Jaime Woods for their invaluable support.

So many people have contributed to this book and the broadcast who deserve mention. The fine people who do the camerawork at *60 Minutes* venture into difficult and dangerous situations on a regular basis to make the broadcast better. My thanks to Chris Albert, Greg Andracke, Ray Bribiesca, Richard Butler, Dan Bussell, Billy Cassara, Ron Dean, Wim de Vos, Dennis Dillon, Chris Everson, Tom Fahey, Rob Fortunato, Ken Fuhr, Bob Goldsborough, Blake Hottle, Mark Laganga, Don Lee, Massimo Mariani, Scott Munro, Sam Painter, Jonathan Partridge, Ian Robbie, and Aaron Tomlinson, who also took many of the photographs that illustrate this book. Thanks to Tom Honeysett, Warren Lustig, and Matt Richman for running the best shop of tape editors ever assembled; Roy Halee for making all of our sound so sharp; Ann Marie Kross for staffing all of our shoots with the very best people; and Rob Klug, Alicia Tanz Flaum, and the entire crew of Control Room 33 for their friendship and dedication in making *60 Minutes* work as well as it does every single week.

We will always be indebted to Don Hewitt, but I am particularly grateful to have had his book *Tell Me a Story* as a resource, as well as the only detailed book about *60 Minutes*, *Tick . . . Tick . . . Tick* by David Blum.

I can't imagine taking on this project without my wife, Melinda, at my side. Her encouragement and advice have made everything I have attempted possible.

IMAGE CREDITS

290 John Filo/CBS

293 John Filo/CBS

294 CBS News/60 Minutes

296 CBS News/60 Minutes

297 Aaron E. Tomlinson

299 Aaron E. Tomlinson

301 CBS News/60 Minutes

303 Sam Painter

304 Toby Strong

305 Graham Messick

306 Magalie Laguerre-Wilkinson

307 CBS News/60 Minutes

311 CBS News/60 Minutes

313 Aaron E. Tomlinson

316 CBS News/60 Minutes

319 (1) CBS News/60 Minutes, (2) Matt Richman, (3) Aaron E. Tomlinson, (4) Chris Everson, (5) Matt Richman, (6) Chris Everson, (7) Aaron E. Tomlinson, (8) Nicole Young, (9) Aaron E. Tomlinson, (10) CBS News/60 Minutes, (11) Aaron E. Tomlinson, (12) Graham Messick, (13) Aaron E. Tomlinson, (14) Aaron E. Tomlinson, (15) Aggelos Petropoulos

321 Brian Rooney

322 CBS News/60 Minutes

323 CBS News/60 Minutes

325 (left) Aaron E. Tomlinson, (right) Peter Freed/CBS

326 (left) CBS News/60 Minutes, (right) John Hamlin

327 CBS News/60 Minutes

328 CBS News/60 Minutes

329 (left) CBS News/60 Minutes, (right) Aaron E. Tomlinson

331 (left) Billy Cassara, (right) CBS News/60 Minutes

332 CBS News/60 Minutes

333 CBS News/60 Minutes

334 (left) CBS News/60 Minutes, (right) CBS News/60 Minutes

335 (left) CBS News/60 Minutes, (right) Dan Bussell

337 CBS News/60 Minutes

339 Jeff Fager personal collection

345 Vanessa Fica personal collection

347 (1) CBS News/60 Minutes, (2) Scott Munro, (3) Aaron E. Tomlinson, (4) Magalie Laguerre-Wilkinson, (5) CBS News/60 Minutes, (6) Aaron E. Tomlinson, (7) CBS News/60 Minutes

350 (left) Harold Gold, (right) Eric Kerchner

351 Eric Kerchner

353 (left) FBI, (right) Aaron E. Tomlinson

354 Eric Kerchner

356 (left) CBS News/60 Minutes, (right) Aaron E. Tomlinson

357 Derek Williams

359 CBS News/60 Minutes

361 Aaron E. Tomlinson

364 (left) CBS News/60 Minutes, (right) Eric Kerchner

365 (left) Aaron E. Tomlinson, (right) Jeff Fager personal collection

366 (let) Aaron E. Tomlinson, (right) Nicole Young

367 (left) Vatican Secretariat for Communication, (right) David Lienemann, White House Photo Office

368 (left) Aaron E. Tomlinson, (right) Aaron E. Tomlinson

369 (left) Harold Gold, (right) Jackson Fager

370 (left) Aaron E. Tomlinson

371 Gregory Andracke

372 (Left) Aaron E. Tomlinson, (right) Stan Wilkins

375 Chris Albert

377 Aaron E. Tomlinson

378 (1) Ruth Streeter, (2) Aaron E. Tomlinson, (3) CBS News/60 Minutes, (4) CBS News/60 Minutes, (5) CBS News/60 Minutes, (6) Graham Messick, (7) Aaron E. Tomlinson, (8) CBS News/60 Minutes, (9) Aaron E. Tomlinson, (10) CBS News/60 Minutes, (11) Ruth Streeter, (12) Don Lee, (13) Jim Farrell, (14) CBS News/60 Minutes

INDEX

Italicized page numbers indicate illustrations

CBS News employees' criticisms of, 204–5

Christmas parties of, 259

claims of unfairness and shoddy journalism against, 195–96

clashes between *60 Minutes II* and, 231–32

clichés avoided by, 15–16

collaborations between *60 Minutes II* and, 251

as collegial and collaborative place, 15, 23

comparisons between *60 Minutes II* and, 231, 246, 264

competition and rivals of, 17, 26, 33, 47–48, 94–96, 114–15, 136, 178, 220, 231

competition within, 102, 155–56

in controversies, 30–34, 220–24

crash unit of, 115

damaged credibility of, 343

Fager's favorite story on, 360–62

fairness and standards editors of, 220

finances of, 150, 152–53, 171

goals, focus, format, and concept of, 1, 8–9, 14–15, 100, 103, 133, 136, 158, 164, 166, 202, 224

growth of, 202

job of producers at, 79–80

and launch of *60 Minutes II,* 217–19, 227

live interviews on broadcasts of, 252

longevity of, 1–2, 17, 21, 93–94

offices of, 275

origins of, 5–7, *6,* 21, *132,* 133–35, 137, *293*

popularity and success of, 1, 7–14, 17, 22, 26, 42–43, 78, 95, 102, 114–15, 130, 158, 160, 169–71, 191, 205, 207, 380

practical jokes at, 206

pursuing stories and, 26

questionable or criminal characters on, 188–95

rules and lessons learned at, 26, 37

set of, *132,* 219–20

stopwatch logo of, *19, 131,* 134, *173, 182, 200, 215,* 219, 226, 285, *289*

story vetting process of, 342

time slots and scheduling of, 136, 148, 153, 159–61

twentieth anniversary of, 21

twenty-fifth anniversary of, 93–94

thirtieth anniversary of, 130

workload and schedule of, 26, 43, 349, 368–69

60 Minutes II, 51, 302, 326, 363

Afghanistan War reporting and, 246–47

audience sizes of, 226

big interviews landed by, 236–37

canceling of, 279–80

clashes between *60 Minutes* and, 231–32

collaborations between *60 Minutes* and, 251

comparisons between *60 Minutes* and, 231, 246, 264

competition of, 255

crisis at, 262–64

Fager as executive producer of, 218–20, *219,* 231–32, 237, 240–41, 246, 250, 253, 255–56

fairness and standards editors of, 220

finances of, 220

Hewitt's departure and, 258

Iraq War stories and, 250–51

launch of, 217–20, 226–27, 255–56

9/11 stories and, 240–41, 245–46, 250

quality control of, 226

set of, 219–20

"*60 Minutes* Classic" segment of, 219, 255

success and popularity of, 226–27

60 Minutes Overtime, 201, 306–8

60 Minutes Wednesday, 263–64

smart gun story, *378*

Snowden, Edward, 365

"Som I Serem," 333

Sommer, Nathalie, 315

South Africa, *117, 305*

South Boston Social Club, 75

Soviet Union, 34–37, *157*

Afghanistan war of, 79, 186–87

Chernobyl story and, 34–35

collapse of, 81

and end of Cold War, 42

Krasnoyarsk-26 story and, 226

secret nuclear tests of, *92*

Vietnam War and, 144

see also Russia

Space Exploration Technologies Corporation (SpaceX), 345–46

"Spark, The," 315

Special Forces, US, *252*

Spider-Man, 11

Spitzer, Kirk, 272

Springsteen Bruce, *107*

Srebrenica story, 227–29

Stahl, Lesley, 7, 58–60, *59,* 310–13

Abramoff interview and, 323–24, *323*

Alvarez interview and, 88–89

Arafat profile and, *91*

Big Tobacco stories and, 97–99

Blanchett profile and, *347*

Boehner profile and, *319*

Bono interview and, *11*

Bosnia story and, *103*

Brin interview and, 278–79

Caine interview and, *378*

Carter interview and, *319*

China one-birth policy story and, *281*

Clarke interview and, 249–50, *250*

and clashes between *60 Minutes* and *60 Minutes II,* 231–32

comparisons between Vieira and, 59–60

comparisons between Wallace and, 324

Crawford interview and, 97–99

Dole interview and, *119*

Ginsburg interview and, 313, *313*

global warming story, *277*

Trump, Donald, Jr., *375*
Trump, Donald, 275, 345
  interviews with, profiles of, and
    stories on, *11,* 13, 362–63, *364,*
    371–72, *372,* 374–79, *375*
  Pence interview and, 371–72
  presidential campaigns of, 77, 363,
    364, 371, 374–75, 379
  Putin interview and, 363
Trump, Eric, *375*
Trump, Ivanka, *375*
Trump, Melania, *375*
Trump, Tiffany, *375*
Trump Tower, 363, *364,* 371, 374, *375*
tsunami story, 9–10, *11,* 276–77, *277*
Tunisia, *91,* 315
Turkalo, Andrea, 305–6
Turner, Ted, 206–7
Turner, Tina, 116, 124, *124*
Turner Joy, USS, 143–45
TV Guide, 58, 226
"$12 Billion Clean Up, The," 90
Tygart, Travis, 335–38

Ukraine, 34–35
Umm Qasr, 251, *251*
Unabomber (Ted Kaczynski), 121–24,
  122, 234
"Under Fire," 272–73
Unforgettable, 311
United Kingdom, 126
  Iran nuclear weapons accord and,
    366
  Iraq War story and, 248
  war between Argentina and, 238
  World War II orphans story and,
    229–31
United Nations, *99*
  Iraq stories and, 248–49, 261
  Srebrenica story and, 227–28
US Airways, 302
USA Today, 280
U.S. News & World Report, 45
U2, *11*

Vaccaro, Kara, 306
Vanderbilt, Gloria, *203*
Variety, 135
Vatican, Vatican City, 224–25, *366,* 367
Vieira, Meredith, 47–51, *48*
  babies of, 48–51, 60
  comparisons between Stahl and, 59–60
  firing of, 50–51, 58
  West 57th and, 47
Vietnamese boat people, 197, *197*
Vietnam War, 27, 79–81, 137, 307
  bombing North Vietnam in, 144–45
  Bush National Guard record story
    and, 263–65
  Cam Ne incident and, 142
  comparisons between Iraq War and,
    273
  end of, 197
  Fulbright interview and, 146
  and Gulf of Tonkin incident, 143–47
  McMaster on, 275
  peace talks on, 197
  Safer's reporting and, 142, 144–47,
    145
  Westmoreland's libel suit and, 79, 208
Vogue, 73
Voice, The, 17, 380
Vokey, April, 350, *350*

"Waiting to Explode," 114
Wallace, Chris, 26, 117
Wallace, George, 136
Wallace, Mary, 208
Wallace, Mike, 17, *20,* 23, *48,* 60–61,
    116–24, 136–40, *143, 160, 174*
  aging of, 280, 324
  Agnew interview and, 139–40
  Arafat interview and, *170,* 179
  assisted suicide story and, 221–23, *222*
  attempted suicide of, 208
  Big Tobacco story and, 95, 97, *97,*
    100–106, 118
  birthday lunch of, 218
  Bosnia story and, *103*

Canseco interview and, 335
Carson interview and, 183–85, *184*
and claims of unfairness and shoddy
  journalism, 196
comparisons between Cooper and, 326
comparisons between Hewitt and,
  7 7, 143
comparisons between Kroft and, 126
comparisons between Reasoner and,
  136
comparisons between Rose and, 326
comparisons between Safer and,
  158–59
comparisons between Stahl and, 324
competitiveness of, 26
Corcoran State Correctional
  Institution report and, 92–93
Day story and, 26
death of, 324–25, *325*
and departure of Howard, 264
Duvalier interview and, 156, *156*
Ehrlichman interview and, 148–50,
  149
Farrakhan interview and, 109–11, *110*
feared by interviewees, 122, 124
Fratianno interview and, 189–90, *189*
on good interviews, 118
Haldeman interview and, 152–54
and Hawn and Russell interview, *266*
Hewitt's relationship with, 5, 93–94,
  103, 117, 255–58
Hill interview and, 161–64, *161*
hiring Rather and, 155, 159–60
Horowitz interview and, *171*
Howard's relationship with, 116–17
Hussein interview and, 40
Jewell story and, 119–21
Jiang interview and, *11,* 234–36
Johnson interview and, 147
Karadzic interview and, *99*
Kennedy assassination and, 161–63
Khomeini interview and, 177–79, *178*
King family interview and, 137–39,
  138

ABOUT THE AUTHOR

JEFF FAGER is in his fourteenth season as the executive producer of *60 Minutes*, America's most-watched and honored news program. The former *60 Minutes* producer was chosen to lead the broadcast in 2004 and promptly refocused it on more timely and relevant stories as he guided it into the digital age. He was tasked in 2011 to continue that mission on a broader scale as the News division's first chairman, where he successfully revitalized its news platforms, including the remarkable turnaround of *CBS This Morning*. Jeff has covered the news around the world at each level of his distinguished career. As producer and then senior producer of the *CBS Evening News*, he reported on the presidential campaign of 1984; the collapse of the Soviet Union and the fall of communism in Eastern Europe; the Reagan-Gorbachev summits; the bombing of Libya in 1986; the death of the Japanese emperor; conflicts in Syria, Lebanon, and Jordan; the Palestinian Intifada in 1988; the Iraq-Iran War; the Persian Gulf War; the assassination of Yitzhak Rabin; and the War in Bosnia. Named the newscast's executive producer in 1996, he renewed its emphasis on hard news and added more than a million new viewers. Fager was born in Wellesley, Massachusetts. He graduated from Colgate University in 1977 with a BA in English.